Friendship
Processes

**SAGE SERIES ON
CLOSE RELATIONSHIPS**

Series Editors
Clyde Hendrick, Ph.D., and
Susan S. Hendrick, Ph.D.

In this series...

Friendship Processes

Beverley Fehr

SS
CR *Sage Series on Close Relationships*

 SAGE Publications
International Educational and Professional Publisher
Thousand Oaks   London   New Delhi

For information address:

SAGE Publications, Inc.
2455 Teller Road
Thousand Oaks, California 91320
E-mail: order@sagepub.com

SAGE Publications Ltd.
6 Bonhill Street
London EC2A 4PU
United Kingdom

SAGE Publications India Pvt. Ltd.
M-32 Market
Greater Kailash I
New Delhi 110 048 India

Printed in the United States of America

Library of Congress Cataloging-in-Publication Data

Fehr, Beverley Anne, 1958–
    Friendship processes / by Beverley Fehr.
        p. cm. — (Sage series on close relationships)
    Includes bibliographical references and index.
    ISBN 0-8039-4560-4. — ISBN 0-8039-4561-2 (pbk.)
    1. Friendship. 2. Intimacy (Psychology). 3. Man-woman
relationships. I. Title. II. Series.
    BF575.F66F435 1995
    158'.25—dc20   95-32479

This book is printed on acid-free paper.

99 10 9 8 7 6 5 4 3

Production Editor: Tricia K. Bennett   Typesetter: Christina M. Hill

Contents

❧

Series Editors' Introduction

When we first began our work on love attitudes more than a decade ago, we did not know what to call our research area. In some ways it represented an extension of earlier work in interpersonal attraction. Most of our scholarly models were psychologists (although sociologists had long been deeply involved in the areas of courtship and marriage), yet we sometimes felt as if our work had no professional "home." That has all changed. Our research not only has a home but also has an extended family, and the family is composed of relationship researchers. During the past decade, the discipline of close relationships (also called personal relationships and intimate relationships) has emerged, developed, and flourished.

Two aspects of close relationships research should be noted. The first is its rapid growth, resulting in numerous books, journals,

handbooks, book series, and professional organizations. As fast as
the field grows, the demand for even more research and knowledge seems to be ever increasing. Questions about close, personal
relationships still far exceed answers. The second noteworthy
aspect of the new discipline of close relationships is its interdisciplinary nature. The field owes its vitality to scholars from communications, family studies and human development, psychology
(clinical, counseling, developmental, social), and sociology as well
as other disciplines such as nursing and social work. It is this
interdisciplinary wellspring that gives close relationships research
its diversity and richness, qualities that we hope to achieve in the
current series.

The **Sage Series on Close Relationships** is designed to acquaint
diverse readers with the most up-to-date information about various topics in close relationships theory and research. Each volume
in the series covers a particular topic or theme in one area of close
relationships. Each book reviews the particular topic area, de-
scribes contemporary research in the area (including the authors'
own work, where appropriate), and offers some suggestions for
interesting research questions and/or real-world applications related to the topic. The volumes are designed to be appropriate for
students and professionals in communication, family studies, psychology, sociology, and social work, among others. A basic assumption of the series is that the broad panorama of close
relationships can best be portrayed by authors from multiple
disciplines, so that the series cannot be "captured" by any single
disciplinary bias.

The current volume, *Friendship Processes* by Beverley Fehr, is a
comprehensive examination of one important kind of close relationship. Friendship is a universal feature of the human condition,
today and in Aristotle's time, as Fehr aptly demonstrates with
several quotations from the master philosopher.

We believe that this book will be the definitive study of friendship processes for many years to come. It is broad in its coverage,
including an extensive reference section. The book is process oriented in the developmental sense of elaborating the life cycle of
friendship, from its first origins to its endings. Within each stage
of the cycle, there is careful attention to individual and interaction

processes that occur. The volume is also research based. Each phase of the friendship process is documented by empirical research, including a review of the classical studies as well as the most up-to-date empirical reports. The result is an excellent conceptual scheme, a developmental approach to processes, supported by a detailed examination of the latest research on friendship.

This volume illustrates well the fact that as a field of study, close relationships is maturing rapidly. A decade ago this volume would not have been possible, because not enough systematic research was available. Today, as we can testify, this book could easily have been much longer. This excellent book will be of interest to students as well as professionals. Indeed, we learned a great deal from it ourselves.

CLYDE HENDRICK
SUSAN S. HENDRICK
SERIES EDITORS

Preface

This book is about friendship. Its purpose is to illuminate friendship processes—how we make friends, how we become close, how we maintain friends, and how friendships deteriorate and dissolve. Thus, the book is loosely organized in terms of the life cycle of friendship. The first two chapters provide a foundation for the rest of the volume. Chapter 1 sets the stage by highlighting the importance of friendship in our lives. In addition, the chapter delves into the meaning of friendship for scientific experts as well as for ordinary people—young and old. In Chapter 2, the major theories of friendship, dating back to Newcomb's formulations in the 1950s, are presented. Chapter 3 focuses on the process of getting friendships started. Given that we meet many people in our lives, what leads us to like some individuals more than others? What are the factors that facilitate or impede the initiation of friendships? After contact is established, what variables are important in propelling the relationship forward? Chapter 4 continues this analysis by asking: once tentative steps toward friendship formation have been taken, how do people become close? Thus, in these chapters, the process by which friendships develop and are transformed into intimate, important relationships is explored. In Chapter 5, the focus is gender issues in friendship. The nature and experience of women's and men's friendships is the subject of analysis. Controversial issues such as whether women's friendships are more intimate than men's are discussed. The purpose of Chapter 6 is to discover how people maintain their friendship relationships. Issues involved in keeping up one's friendships are examined. Finally, Chapter 7 deals with the undeniable reality that some friendships are unsatisfying and eventually end. Thus, this chapter focuses on the deterioration and dissolution of friendships. But endings often bring new beginnings. By returning to the early chapters in the book, it is hoped that readers can face the prospect of developing new friendships equipped with pertinent, valuable knowledge about the formation and continuation of this intriguing personal relationship.

✖ Acknowledgments

There are many people whose help and support sustained me throughout the process of writing this book. I am grateful to Clyde and Susan Hendrick for their patience and encouragement, as well as their prompt, useful feedback on drafts of the manuscript. Dan Perlman's valuable input helped get this project off the ground during a summer I spent at the University of British Columbia. My understanding of friendship has been enriched through our ongoing discussions. Sue Sprecher contributed substantially through her detailed comments on the entire manuscript sent via E-mail along with large doses of emotional support. Thank you also to Harry Reis for his insightful comments on Chapter 5 and to my colleagues Mark Baldwin and Pat Keelan for their willing assistance and feedback. The encouragement and interest shown by other colleagues and friends in the Psychology Department of the

University of Winnipeg also is greatly appreciated. The research assistants who worked with me at various stages of the project deserve many thanks: Mary Kronenwald, Lisa Sinclair, Lisa Pippus, and Vicki Enns. I am indebted to Mavis Close and Connie Lambert for the competent secretarial assistance they provided.

On a personal note, I wish to thank my husband, Marvin, for the practical (particularly the homemade pies) and emotional support he provided. I believe that he is even happier than I am that this project has come to a close. Thank you also to my sister, Lois, for her unfailing enthusiasm and confidence that I could and would complete this project. A benefit of writing a book on friendship is that one is constantly reminded of treasured friends. I am especially grateful to Lorrie, Ann, Carla, Gerry, and Delores for their friendship and support. Finally, a special thank you to my cherished, longtime friend, Lydia, who exemplifies the qualities of a true friend.

This project was supported by the Social Sciences and Humanities Research Council of Canada. My summer at the University of British Columbia was made possible through a University of Winnipeg Summer Research Furlough Grant.

BEVERLEY FEHR

1

The Meaning of Friendship

A friend may well be reckoned the masterpiece of nature.
—Ralph Waldo Emerson (1868)

Friendships are clearly a core aspect of our lives. Yet the scientific study of this important relationship is relatively recent. In this book, research on friendship is presented, integrated, and discussed in order to paint a portrait of what is currently known about this fascinating relationship. The focus will be on friendship *processes*—the "how" of friendship. I will draw on extant research to answer questions such as: How do friendships form? How do they become close? How are they maintained? and finally, How do friendships end? Most of the research on these issues has been conducted with college students. However, research on children's and adolescents' friendships will be incorporated where possible. (Friendships of the elderly will receive less attention, given that this literature is presented elsewhere; Blieszner & Adams, 1992.)

This first chapter explores the basic nature of friendships. The chapter begins by demonstrating the importance of friendship in our lives. Then, the meaning of the term *friendship* is elucidated by examining both social scientists' and laypeople's conceptions. The chapter ends with a consideration of questions such as "How does friendship compare to other close relationships?" and "Are there different types of friendship?"

& The Place of Friendship in Our Lives

Think momentarily about how much time you spend with your friends, how you feel toward them, what you get from them, and what you give up to keep them. Think about social isolation and being without friends: how do you feel when you are alone? A few years ago, Reed Larson and his associates (see Larson & Bradney, 1988) had 271 individuals carry electronic pagers with them wherever they went for a week. The recruits for this research included 75 teenagers and 104 adults from Chicago plus 92 retired Canadians from the Kitchener-Waterloo area in Ontario. Once during every 2 hours of their waking day, Larson paged these individuals and asked them to indicate what they were doing and who, if anyone, was with them. Approximately 65% of the times when contacted, these people were in the presence of others. Time with friends per se fluctuated from nearly 30% among teenagers to 4% for adults aged 40 to 65 to approximately 8% for older Canadians.

Each time the participants were paged, they completed a short questionnaire on their mood. Analysis of these data revealed a striking tendency for the presence of friends to be associated with pleasure. Participants of all ages reported higher levels of enjoyment and excitement when they were with friends than when they were alone or with family. The married adults were even happier being with friends than they were being alone with their spouse. These adults' happiest times, however, were when they and their spouse were together with friends. Combining these results with data gathered on the participants' thoughts, Larson and Bradney (1988) concluded:

> With friends our attention becomes focused, distractions lessen, awareness of time disappears: We emerge into a world in which the intimacy and joy shared with others is the fundamental reality, and for a time the world becomes a different place. (p. 124)

It has become commonplace for social scientists to document the benefits of personal relationships, as well as to at least briefly note their costs (e.g., betrayal, annoyances, demands). Epidemiological studies (see, e.g., Atkins, Kaplan, & Toshima, 1991; Fehr & Perlman, 1985) have shown that socially integrated individuals have lower age-adjusted death rates than socially isolated individuals. That is, socially integrated individuals—as assessed via marital status, organizational memberships, or friendships—ultimately live longer.

Typically, the benefits and costs of social bonds are discussed in a general sense, without distinguishing too carefully among types of relationships. One might assume that people's most important social bonds are with family and kin. Research certainly supports the view that parents, spouses, and other relatives are crucial components in our social networks (see, e.g., Fehr & Perlman, 1985). Yet the significance of friendships should not be minimized. When Berscheid, Snyder, and Omoto (1989) asked nearly 250 unmarried undergraduates at the University of Minnesota to identify their "closest, deepest, most involved, and most intimate relationship," 47% named a romantic relationship and 36% named a friend. Family relationships came in a distant third, mentioned by only 14% of the respondents. Although family relationships figure more prominently in the lives of older adults, friendships still remain important. For example, in a large study of northern Californians, Fischer (1982a) found that respondents considered 58% of the people in their social networks to be friends. Of this 58%, 23% were exclusively friends ("just friends"), whereas 35% had some additional relationship to the respondent such as coworker, neighbor, or kin. Fischer asked these adults questions about the activities they did and the help they received from various network members. Even using the restrictive category of "just friends," friends constituted a larger proportion of the people with whom respondents engaged in companionship activities than did

Table 1.1 Friends and Kin as Sources of Support

	Source of Support (in %)	
Type of Exchange	Just Friends	Kin
Companionship		
Socialize	42	26
Discuss hobby	34	16
Counseling		
Discuss personal matters	22	49
Seek advice	18	56
Practical assistance		
Check on house	17	26
Household assistance	26	49
Borrow money	17	65

SOURCE: Adapted from Fischer (1982a, p. 386) with permission of the University of Chicago Press. Copyright © 1982 by The University of Chicago.
NOTE: Spouses are included in the kin category. Just friends consists only of people exclusively identified as friends; it does not include people with whom the respondent had both a friendship and some other form of relationship.

kin (see Table 1.1). "Just friends" also constituted a substantial portion of the people from whom respondents received various forms of help.

Research on everyday concepts also points to the significance of friendship. In particular, studies of conceptions of love show that when laypeople are asked to list types of love, friendship is listed most frequently (Fehr & Russell, 1991). Friendship love also is seen as capturing the meaning of love—more so than most other kinds of love, including romantic love (see Fehr, 1988, 1993, 1994).

In yet another research tradition, Klinger (1977) asked college students: "What is it that makes your life meaningful?" Nearly everyone named friends. Indeed, friends were mentioned as a source of meaning in life more frequently than were family, religious faith, or occupational success. In the same vein, there is research showing that friends are a common source of happiness in people's lives, independent of marriage and family (Argyle, 1987). Moreover, friends are regarded as the primary source of joy. These disparate areas of investigation converge on a common theme, namely, that friendships can be as important, if not more important, than other types of relationships.

Why are friendships valued so highly? Weiss (1969, 1974) has delineated several provisions of personal relationships. He maintains that different relationships meet different needs in our lives. Friendship relationships meet our need for social integration. A close friendship also may meet our need for attachment, although Weiss believed that this need was typically fulfilled in a marital relationship. Three functions of friendship were identified by Solano (1986). First, as was apparent in Fischer's (1982a) results shown in Table 1.1, friends meet our *material* needs. Friends provide various kinds of help and support. Second, friends meet our *cognitive* needs. Friends provide stimulation in the form of shared experiences, activities, and the lively exchange of gossip and ideas. Friends also provide a frame of reference through which we can interpret the world and find meaning in our experiences. Finally, friends meet our *social-emotional* needs through the provision of love and esteem. Given these benefits of friendship, it is little wonder that Aristotle proclaimed: "Without friends no one would choose to live" (trans. 1931, Book VIII, 1).

❧ Friendship: What Is It?

Everyone knows what friendship is—until asked to define it. Then, it seems, no one knows. There are virtually as many definitions of friendship as there are social scientists studying the topic. This diversity raises a disturbing question: Is it possible to meaningfully study a concept for which there is no agreed-on definition? The answer depends largely on one's theoretical position concerning the nature of concepts. According to the classical view, knowledgeable people should be able to reach a consensus on definitions. Once the set of necessary and sufficient criterial features is determined, categorization decisions are based on whether the instance in question possesses the defining features. Thus, from this perspective, it should be relatively easy to decide whether or not a particular relationship is a friendship—one simply examines whether it possesses each of the defining attributes of friendship. The problem is that so far social scientists have not been able to agree on a precise set of defining features. As Allan (1989) has observed, it is difficult, if not impossible, to generate the defining features of friendship because

> "friend" is not just a categorical label, like "colleague" or "cousin," indicating the social position of each individual relative to the other. Rather it is a relational term which signifies something about the quality and character of the relationship involved. (p. 16)

More contemporary psychological analysis suggests a less absolute view of definitions (see Mervis & Rosch, 1981, for a review). According to the prototype view, many natural language concepts have evaded classical definition because they do not possess a clear-cut set of features. Instead, such concepts are better described as fuzzy sets—a list of attributes that are typical of the concept, but are not always or necessarily present. Decisions about whether a particular relationship is a friendship are made by comparing the match between that relationship and the prototype—the mental representation of this fuzzy set of features. Although people's prototypes are likely to bear important similarities, universal agreement on exact definitions is not expected. Several writers have suggested that friendship may be best conceptualized as a prototype concept (e.g., Bradac, 1983; Wilmot & Shellen, 1990). Adopting this more relaxed standard of what constitutes a definition, a good deal can be said about the way laypeople and social scientists conceptualize friendship.

Defining Friendship: The Experts

Hinde (1979) defines an interpersonal relationship as "a series of interactions between two individuals known to each other" (p. 15). He, as well as many other social scientists, views relationships as comprising behavioral, cognitive, and affective (or emotional) components. By conceptualizing relationships as a *series* of interactions, Hinde implies that relationships involve a longer time period than a single encounter and that each interaction

Table 1.2 Definitions of Friendship

Friends are people who spontaneously seek the company of one another;
furthermore, they seek proximity in the absence of strong social pressures to do
so. (Hartup, 1975, p. 11)

Friendship: voluntary interdependence between two persons over time, that is
intended to facilitate social-emotional goals of the participants, and may involve
varying types and degrees of companionship, intimacy, affection, and mutual
assistance. (Hays, 1988, p. 395)

A friend is someone who likes and wishes to do well for someone else and who
believes that these feelings and good intentions are reciprocated by the other
party. (Reisman, 1979, pp. 93-94)

Friendship is defined as a relationship involving voluntary or unconstrained
interaction in which the participants respond to one another personally, that is,
as unique individuals rather than as packages of discrete attributes or mere role
occupants. (Wright, 1984, p. 119)

Friendship: It is an intimate, personal, caring relationship with attributes such as
reciprocal tenderness and warmth of feeling; reciprocal desire to keep the
friendship; honesty and sincerity; trust; intimacy and openness of self; loyalty;
and durability of the relationship over time. (Donelson & Gullahorn, 1977, p. 156)

episode is influenced by other interactions in the relationship.
A complementary conceptualization is offered by Berscheid and
Peplau (1983), who maintain that "two people are in a relationship
with one another if they have impact on each other, if they are
'interdependent' in the sense that a change in one person causes a
change in the other and vice versa" (p. 12).

Moving away from these generic conceptions of relationships,
social scientists also have offered specific definitions of friendship.
The sampling of definitions shown in Table 1.2 portrays friendship
as a voluntary, personal relationship, typically providing intimacy
and assistance, in which the two parties like one another and seek
each other's company. Similarly, Rawlins (1992) conceptualizes
friendship as voluntary, personal, implying affective ties (e.g.,
love, caring), and characterized by equality (see also Allan, 1989)
and mutual involvement.

Davis and Todd (1985) identified such attributes of friendship
as affection, confiding, receiving assistance, reliable alliance

(trust), and shared activity—themes also emphasized in the definitions of friendship. However, they focused on three additional properties: authenticity, self-respect, and conflict. Authenticity complements Wright's definition of friendship (see Table 1.2), indicating that friends respond to one another as unique and irreplaceable. Conflict acknowledges that friendships involve tensions and require maintenance efforts to preserve.

As is customary, these definitions concentrate on what friendship is. Such definitions can be augmented by specifying what friendship is *not*. Reisman (1979), for example, claims that friends do not assume one will be the superior of the other. Furthermore, friends are typically not blood relations, nor sexual partners. Of course, as implied by the high number of Fischer's respondents who saw friends as filling other roles as well, some people consider spouses or relatives to be friends. In this book, the emphasis will be on relationships that are exclusively friendships. However, the fact that some experts include romantic partners and family members among friends whereas others do not again highlights the fuzzy nature of this concept.

Defining Friendship:
Ordinary People's Conceptions

Fischer (1982b) observed that people use the term *friend* "loosely and often" (p. 298). What do people have in mind when they use this word? As will be seen, the answers vary, depending on the age and, to a lesser extent, the gender of the person who is asked.

Children

The fact that even young children possess knowledge of the concept attests to the importance of friendship. In fact, children's conceptions of friendship have received considerable attention (see, e.g., Berndt, 1986, 1988; Dickens & Perlman, 1981; Furman, 1982; Rubin, 1980; Selman, 1980; Serafica, 1982). When preschool children are asked "What is a friend?" three themes are apparent in their responses: play (someone who plays with you), prosocial behavior (someone who shares toys with you), and the absence of aggression (someone who doesn't hit you). Young children also frequently report that a friend is someone you like (see reviews by Berndt, 1988; Furman, 1982; Tesch, 1983). When asked why a particular individual is their friend, it is not uncommon for children to refer to the person's physical characteristics (e.g., she has red hair) or possessions (e.g., he has a nice bike).

As children get older, they are less likely to emphasize physical attributes or property. For example, when Furman and Bierman (1983) asked "What is a friend?" 6- and 7-year-olds mentioned concrete, observable features such as physical characteristics and common activities less frequently than did 4- and 5-year-olds. The older children also were more likely to list *relational* features such as affection and support (helping, sharing). Furthermore, on a forced-choice rating task, the 6- and 7-year-olds assigned higher ratings to features such as affection and support than to common activities. In contrast, the 4- and 5-year-olds regarded these features as equally important. These results are indicative of greater differentiation in the older children's concept of friendship.

There is also evidence that the way children think about the concept of friendship becomes more abstract with age (see, e.g., La Gaipa, 1987). Furman and Bierman (1984) asked children in Grades 2, 4, and 6 questions such as "What is a friend?" and "What should you do to be a friend?" Responses were categorized according to five features of friendship gleaned from the literature: support (e.g., sharing/helping), association (e.g., propinquity), intimacy, similarity (e.g., common activities), and affection. Remarkably, all five features of friendship were represented even in the youngest children's responses. However, they tended to produce only concrete behavioral exemplars of each. The older children provided both concrete and abstract responses, suggesting a more fully developed concept of friendship.

Finally, in an ambitious study, Bigelow and La Gaipa (1975) asked nearly 500 children in Grades 1 to 8 what they expected from their same-sex best friends. Most of the 21 dimensions identified in these accounts were listed more frequently with age (e.g., common activities, helping, similarity, intimacy, loyalty, commitment).

In addition, the older the students were, the greater number of friendship dimensions they generated, again, suggesting greater elaboration of the concept.

In summary, very young children possess a concept of friendship in which the typical features are concrete, observable characteristics. As children develop, their capacity for abstract thought is reflected in their conception of friendship. It is not clear from the research presented whether the concrete features then coexist with the abstract features, are sloughed off and replaced with abstract features, or are retained but assigned a more peripheral status. Nevertheless, one can conclude that there is evidence of both quantitative and qualitative development of children's conception of friendship.

Adolescents

According to Berndt (1988), the themes of play, prosocial behavior, and the absence of aggression that are identifiable in children's descriptions of friendship also extend to adolescence. What changes is the terminology. Thus, play becomes "hanging around"; prosocial behavior takes the form of "helping" rather than "sharing toys," and so on. Liking continues to be regarded an important aspect of friendship, although in adolescence this feature is more likely to be assumed, rather than explicitly mentioned. During this phase of the life span, the concept becomes defined in terms of its relational features. For example, Tedesco and Gaier (1988) found that among students in Grades 7, 9, and 12, the significance of interpersonal features of friendship increased with age, whereas the importance placed on features such as the friend's physical appearance, material possessions, and achievements decreased. These findings are bolstered by the results of longitudinal research. Bukowski, Newcomb, and Hoza (1987) assessed conceptions of friendship among a group of Grade 6 students (M = 11 years). One year later, features of friendship such as commonality (e.g., doing things together) were emphasized less, whereas relational features, such as support and loyalty, assumed greater importance.

During adolescence, two relational features of friendship become central: *loyalty* (reflected in a friend's willingness to "stick up for you" and not "talk about you behind your back") and *intimacy*, defined as sharing one's innermost thoughts and feelings (e.g., Berndt, 1986, 1988; Bigelow & La Gaipa, 1980; Furman, 1982; Kon & Losenkov, 1978; Tesch, 1983). In fact, Berndt (1988) suggests that intimacy is the prototypical feature of adolescent friendships. The importance of loyalty and intimacy is underscored in Bigelow and La Gaipa's (1980) research. When 13- and 16-year-olds described a best friend, they were much more likely to mention intimacy, authenticity, and especially loyalty, than were 9-year-olds. The only difference between the 13- and 16-year-olds was that the latter group mentioned intimacy more frequently. The three groups did not differ in their emphasis on common activities, helping, and similarity as features of friendship. With regard to gender differences, among the 13-year-olds, 23% of girls and only 9% of boys listed intimacy. This feature assumed greater importance for both girls (60%) and boys (40%) by the age of 16, although the gender difference persisted. When describing their best friend, the older girls also were more likely to mention loyalty and commitment, particularly in the form of confidentiality of intimate self-disclosure.

Other research also has found that sex differences begin to surface in adolescence, with girls placing a greater emphasis on intimacy as exemplified by self-disclosure and confiding (e.g., Berndt, 1982, 1986; Bukowski et al., 1987; Furman, 1982; Kon & Losenkov, 1978; Tedesco & Gaier, 1988). These findings foreshadow the kinds of sex differences that have become standard in the adult friendship literature (see Chapter 5).

Thus, in adolescence, conceptions of friendship expand to include relational features such as loyalty and intimacy. Moreover, these characteristics become central to the meaning of the concept. It appears that once these features emerge, the concept solidifies with few age-related changes thereafter. For example, when La Gaipa (1979) asked more than 4,000 adolescents (ages 12 to 17 years) and young adults (ages 18 to 20 years) to rate their friendships in terms of loyalty, intimacy, authenticity, and so on, the responses of the two groups were very similar. Thus, the meaning of friendship appears to coagulate quite early in adolescence with few qualitative changes occurring thereafter. As will be seen, this conclusion is reinforced in the literature on adults' conceptions of friendship.

Adults

In the literature on adulthood, the question "What is a friend?" has been posed in a variety of ways. Some researchers have focused on a close friend, others on a best, same-sex friend, and still others on an ideal friend. Tesch and Martin (1983) asked university students and alumni (ages 19 to 29): "What does friendship mean to you?" and "What do you value in your friendships?" Responses were coded using 23 dimensions, based on a modification of a coding system developed by Weiss and Lowenthal (1975). The largest proportion of responses (33%) was classified as reciprocity (in the form of dependability, caring, commitment, and trust). Compatibility, openness, acceptance, and similarity were next most frequent (at least 10% of responses), followed by dimensions such as role model, uniqueness, and time. There were few age, gender, or marital status differences in these conceptions.

Sapadin (1988) asked 156 professionals living in New York, Boston, and Los Angeles to complete the sentence "A friend is someone . . ." The most frequent responses were the following:

with whom you are intimate
you can trust
you can depend on
with whom you share things
who accepts you
with whom you have a caring relationship
with whom you are close
you enjoy

There were no gender differences in these responses.

In Britain, Crawford (1977) conducted a study of middle-aged adults' conceptions of friendship. Participants' responses fell into seven major categories, resembling those that emerged in

Sapadin's study. Specifically, when asked to complete the sentence "A close friend is someone . . . ," the answers, in order of frequency, were the following:

I can trust
I can call on for help
I can go out with
I see often
who comes into my home
I've known for a long time
whose company I enjoy

Trust was interpreted as keeping confidences and engaging in intimate self-disclosure. Women generated such responses more frequently than men, who were more likely to nominate the socializing categories (enjoying the friend's company, going out with the friend). Features such as trust, intimacy, sociability, and enjoyment of one another's company also have been emphasized in other research on adults' conceptions of friendship (e.g., Bell, 1981b; Fischer, 1982b; Hays, 1988).

Some researchers have conducted finer-grained analyses by comparing conceptions of different types of friendship. For example, La Gaipa (1977) asked university students in Canada and the United States to rate the applicability of six factors (authenticity, similarity, positive regard, strength of character, helping, and self-disclosure) to different kinds of friendship, ranging from social acquaintance to best friend. Generally, scores on these factors increased with the level of friendship. However, there also was some specific patterning of the data. For example, self-disclosure failed to discriminate between the less intimate types of friendship. However, close friends received higher ratings on this factor (and on the helping factor) than good friends; best friends scored even higher than close friends. Authenticity received high ratings for all levels of friendship.

As mentioned earlier, some researchers have examined adults' conceptions of an ideal friendship. Basu and Mukhopadhyay (1986) explored conceptions of the ideal male and female friend held by young adults in India. Both women and men believed that

the ideal male friend would possess the qualities of understanding, honesty, loyalty, cooperation, reliability, and so on. Characteristics such as noninterfering, prudent, and having similar
interests were seen as less important. Women and men differed,
however, in their conceptions of the ideal female friend. For men,
the ideal female friend was someone who possessed virtually the
same qualities that were valued highly in a male friend. In contrast, women desired characteristics such as good-tempered, sac-
rificing, witty, and loyal in an ideal female friend. (Research
conducted in the United States has found just the opposite pattern,
with women rating the ideal male and female friend more similarly than men; Banikiotes, Neimeyer, & Lepkowsky, 1981.)

Weiss and Lowenthal (1975) asked high school students, newly-
weds, middle-aged adults, and preretirement adults to describe
their actual friendships as well as an ideal close friend. The responses were grouped into six broad categories. For actual friends,
the most important category was similarity, particularly in terms
of shared experiences, followed by reciprocity, a category that
emphasized helping and support. The remaining categories, in
order, were compatibility, structural dimensions (e.g., proximity,
duration of friendship), role model, and a miscellaneous category.
The major difference between real and ideal friends was a reversal
of the first two dimensions. Thus, reciprocity was considered the
most crucial in an ideal friendship, followed by similarity. Perceptions of real and ideal friends were similar for the remaining
dimensions, with the exception that structural dimensions were
unimportant in descriptions of ideal friends. The main gender
difference was that women placed greater emphasis on reciprocity
(sharing, helping), whereas men valued similarity, especially in
the form of common activities.

This study is also important because age differences were examined. Weiss and Lowenthal (1975) discovered that "perceptions of
the qualities of friends and friendship are surprisingly similar
across the four life stages" (p. 58). The few differences that were
found reflected the kinds of life issues faced at that stage. For
example, ratings of actual and ideal friends were most discrepant
among high school students, and became less so with age, suggesting greater selectivity in friendship choices with increased matur-

ity. The authors concluded that the basic functions of friendship are established at a relatively early age and continue throughout life.

Weiss and Lowenthal's (1975) conclusion is supported in other research. Goldman, Cooper, Ahern, and Corsini (1981), for example, compared ratings of close friends in six age groups: 12 to 14 years, 15 to 17 years, 20s, 30s, 45 to 60 years, and 65 years and older. Four dimensions of friendship were rated as important by all groups: common interests, friend as giver, intimacy, and activities. The authors noted that these dimensions resemble the similarity and reciprocity dimensions that Weiss and Lowenthal found were characteristic of friendship at all ages. Dimensions such as appearance, common background, and proximity were considered unimportant at each age. Age differences reflected salient concerns for that phase of the life span. For example, dimensions such as humorous and entertaining, and ego reinforcement (bolstering self-esteem) received the highest ratings in the youngest two groups. Family commonalities were regarded as important by every group except the youngest two. Goldman et al. concurred with Weiss and Lowenthal's conclusion that the basic meaning of friendship is established at an early age and remains constant throughout the life span. However, there also was some variation, depending on current life issues.

A study along the same lines focused on conceptions of friendship among women ranging from 14 to 16 years to 60 years and older (Candy, Troll, & Levy, 1981). Ratings of best friends were compared along three dimensions (based in part on Weiss and Lowenthal). Intimacy-assistance was valued at all ages, power (egocentric, nonreciprocal friendship) decreased with age, and status fluctuated, depending on the life concerns faced by each group. These authors also concluded that their results were consistent with those of Weiss and Lowenthal. Finally, variations in men's friendships over time were explored by Wall, Pickert, and Paradise (1984). Two groups of men (ages 25 to 34 and 35 to 50) were asked about their conception of close friendships. Again, there were few age differences. Any variations were related to life issues, in this case marital status. For example, married men valued interpersonal or relational qualities (e.g., trusting, helpful), whereas single men also emphasized individual traits (e.g., sense of humor, intelligence).

To summarize, when asked about friendship, ordinary people list features such as intimacy, loyalty, honesty, trust, enjoyment in one another's company, and so on. These features also were prominent in many of the definitions offered by the experts. Although most social scientists would prefer a definition that applies to any form of friendship in any culture at any time, conceptions of friendship are undoubtedly influenced by characteristics such as age (and to a lesser extent, gender and stage of life). The changes in the ways that children view friendship vividly demonstrate this point. Early on, children see friends as people who play with you or do nice things for you. With age, they begin to regard friendship as involving relational features such as intimacy, loyalty, and trust.

Friendship in Comparison
With Other Close Relationships

Besides description, another way of understanding the nature of a relationship is through comparison. In comparing friendships with other relationships, some researchers have searched for the general dimensions underlying interpersonal relationships, whereas others have concentrated on comparing types of relationships. A study by Wish, Deutsch, and Kaplan (1976) illustrates the first tradition. They asked college students to rate 45 different relationships (e.g., master-servant, close friends, you and your father) on numerous bipolar adjectives. Analyses of the data uncovered four underlying dimensions: friendly/cooperative versus hostile/competitive, equal versus unequal, intense versus superficial, and socioemotional/informal versus task-oriented/formal. Close friendships were seen as friendly, equal, intense, and socioemotional. The relationship between a prisoner and a guard was virtually diametrically opposed to this pattern.

The second approach to comparative analysis, examining similarities and differences between various kinds of relationships, is more common. Several researchers have compared American adolescents' friendships with their dating, parental, and familial relationships (e.g., Blyth & Foster-Clark, 1987; Csikszentmihalyi & Larson, 1984; Raffaelli & Duckett, 1989; Thorbecke & Grotevant, 1982). Generally, comparisons are made in terms of intimacy, frequency and nature of conversations, affect experienced, and so on. In the former Soviet Union, Kon and Losenkov (1978) compared adolescents' closest friendship with their relationship with their father, mother, siblings, and favorite teacher. These researchers found that "the friend occupies the central privileged place" (p. 148) when these relationships were rated in terms of understanding, confiding (sharing innermost thoughts), and so on. Parents were valued for their help with practical problems. In France, Werebe (1987) focused on friendships and dating relationships of adolescents. She found that friends discussed a greater number of topics than dating partners, except for the relationship itself (a topic that daters talked about). Exchanges with friends were regarded as more intimate, unless sexual intercourse had occurred in the dating relationship. Participants also reported greater attachment to friends than dating partners.

Adults' relationships with friends, lovers, and family members also have been compared in terms of relationship attributes such as trust, respect, caring, intimacy, and exclusivity (see, e.g., Wilmot & Shellen, 1990), as well as communication or language patterns (e.g., Bradac, 1983; Duck, Rutt, Hurst, & Strejc, 1991). In one study, more than 200 adults reported on a friendship and a heterosexual love relationship, using Wright's (1985) Acquaintance Description Form. Participants depicted their friendships as less regulated by social norms and easier to dissolve than romantic relationships. Friends also were seen as less likely to commit free time to one another. Romantic relationships were regarded as higher in exclusiveness—the extent to which partners expected sole or preferential access to various mutually involving activities. In addition, romantic relationships involved more overt expression of positive emotions and affection (Wright, 1985).

Davis and Todd (1982) also delineated similarities and differences between friendship and romantic love relationships. They found that features such as trust, enjoyment, and acceptance were attributed to both kinds of relationships. However, romantic relationships were characterized by two additional clusters of features: passion (e.g., fascination, exclusiveness, sexual desire) and support (willingness to give one's utmost). Finally, Rands and Levinger (1979) compared perceptions of four relationship types (casual acquaintances, good friends, close relationship, married) in terms of two basic dimensions: behavioral interdependence (e.g., helping, advice) and affective interdependence (e.g., showing affection, physical and sexual contact). Casual acquaintances were rated lowest on the first dimension and married people the highest, with good friends and close relationships in between. A similar pattern was found for the second dimension, although ratings varied somewhat depending on the gender of the dyad (e.g., heterosexual pairs received higher ratings on affective interdependence than same-sex pairs). The results of these studies suggest that friendship overlaps with, but also is distinct from, other kinds of relationships.

Types of Friendship

Just as the larger world of personal relationships can be divided into friendship versus other kinds of relationships, so too can friendships be partitioned into subcategories. Indeed, there is a long history of attempts to create taxonomies of friendship, dating back to Aristotle, who delineated three kinds of friendship (trans. 1984, Book VIII, 3). In friendships based on *utility*, we are attracted to the other person because of what they can do for us. In friendships based on *pleasure*, we are attracted to the other person because we enjoy their company. In friendships based on *goodness*, we are attracted to the other person because of their virtuous character. Empirical support for this typology has been reported (Murstein & Spitz, 1973-1974).

Friendships frequently are categorized along demographic lines. For example, there are same- and opposite-sex friendships (see Chapter 5), men's friendships (Miller, 1983), women's friendships (O'Connor, 1992), children's friendships (Rubin, 1980), and older adults' friendships (Blieszner & Adams, 1992). O'Connor identified four distinct types of friendship among married women: confidant, nurturant, purely companionable, and latent (felt to be close despite infrequent contact). Adams (1985-1986) developed a typology of older women's friendships based on combinations of emotional and physical closeness/distance.

Friendships also can be categorized according to the social context in which they are maintained. Thus, sociologists have examined priests' friendships, the friendships of military personnel, and friendships maintained across long distances. One illustration of this tradition is Rosecrance's (1986) ethnography of "racetrack buddies" in which the social relationships among racehorse bettors at an off-track betting site were examined. Rosecrance found that these relationships were largely compartmentalized—the bettors rarely socialized outside the betting parlor. Yet at the betting site, they had their own special jargon; they helped each other deal with the negative consequences of losing streaks and the dizzying highs of big scores. The bettors also had certain interpersonal obligations such as lending each other money and sharing information related to racing. Although these friendships rarely reached deep levels of intimacy, they satisfied the participants. As one of the regulars, a dentist, told Rosecrance, "My dental colleagues bore me. They are so dull and uninteresting. I'd rather spend my time with the guys at the book" (p. 452). These relationships resemble descriptions of "mates" in Britain and Australia (e.g., Allan, 1989; Morse & Marks, 1985).

Finally, it is also common to classify friendships according to the level of closeness or intimacy in the relationship (see Chapter 4). La Gaipa's (1977) research in which conceptions of different kinds of friendship were compared has already been cited. Similarly, in Wright's (1985) study, individuals reported on their relationship with five levels of friends (e.g., acquaintance, good friend, best friend). Generally, the more intimate the relationship, the more clearly it manifested the various attributes of friendship. For example, consistent with Wright's ideas on the key attributes of friendships, more intimate friends were more likely to voluntarily commit time to one another. Intimate friends also were more likely to react to one another as "unique, genuine and irreplaceable in the relationship" (p. 45).

Thus, friendships can be classified in a variety of ways. The two most common ways are along demographic lines (e.g., age, gender) and in terms of the level of intimacy or closeness. The nature of this construct also can be illuminated through comparisons with other types of relationships.

✸ Summary

This chapter provides a backdrop within which the contemporary study of friendship processes can be better appreciated. It has dealt with the place of friendship in our lives and the meanings ascribed to this term by both laypeople and social scientists. These conceptions emphasize that friendship is a voluntary, personal relationship typically providing intimacy and assistance. In addition, the two parties like each other and seek each other's company. Both in the scholarly literature and in the views of laypersons, several additional attributes frequently are associated with friendship. Characteristics such as trust, loyalty, and self-disclosure emerge and solidify in adolescence and remain important throughout adulthood.

The nature of friendship was further elucidated by situating this relationship in the context of other close relationships and discussing the differentiation of this concept into types. In the multidimensional space underlying different types of relationships, close friendships were seen as cooperative and egalitarian. Research in which friendships were compared with other relationships showed that confiding and self-disclosure occur in many relationships, but are particularly characteristic of friendships. Familial relationships assume greater importance for concrete assistance, whereas romantic relationships are more likely than friendships to involve exclusivity and passion. Friendships have been divided into types on many bases, including demographic attributes, the social context in which the relationship occurs, and the closeness of the bond. The complexities of this fascinating concept will be further unraveled in the remaining chapters.

2

✿

Theories of Friendship

We feel friendly to those who have treated us well, either ourselves or those we care for; . . . And also to those who we think
wish to treat us well. And also to our friends' friends, and to those
who like, or are liked by, those whom we like ourselves. And also
to those who are enemies to those whose enemies we are, and
dislike, or are disliked by, those whom we dislike.
—Aristotle (trans. 1984, Book II, 4)

W hy do we choose some people as friends but not others?
Why are we happier in some friendships than others? Why
do some friendships end, whereas others flourish and grow? Various social scientists have developed theories of friendship to answer these kinds of "why" questions. The quotation from Aristotle
anticipates at least two of the major theoretical positions on this
issue (reinforcement and cognitive consistency). It is actually more
accurate to speak of theories of *attraction*, or theories of *relationships*, given that theories of friendship per se have not been devel-

oped. Thus, the focus in this chapter is on the theories of attraction or relationships that can, or have been, applied to friendship. Specifically, the theories identified by Perlman and Fehr (1986) as important in understanding friendship will be discussed: reinforcement, exchange and equity, cognitive consistency, and developmental. It should be noted at the outset that each of these is an umbrella term subsuming a number of specific theories. For each category, only the key theorists will be presented. In addition, representative research conducted to test predictions generated by each of the major theories will be described.

❧ Reinforcement Theories

Reinforcement theories grew out of the behaviorist tradition in psychology. The application of reinforcement principles to the study of attraction was spearheaded by Byrne and Clore (1970; Clore & Byrne, 1974) and Lott and Lott (1960, 1974). Both pairs of theorists adopted a central tenet of operant conditioning and predicted that we are attracted to people who provide us with rewards. (Aristotle captured the essence of these theories when he stated that "we feel friendly to those who have treated us well.") These theorists also imported principles of classical conditioning and further predicted that we like people who are merely associated with our experience of receiving rewards. In other words, if another person happens to be present when something good happens to us, we are likely to be attracted to him or her.

Byrne and Clore's Reinforcement-Affect Model

Byrne and Clore were aware that a complex phenomenon such as interpersonal attraction could not be explained by a single, simple reinforcement principle such as "We like people who reward us and dislike people who punish us." People's behavior toward one another is not uniformly positive or negative. Sometimes people are nice; sometimes they are nasty. Clore and Byrne (1974) therefore devised an attraction formula to take the variability of human behavior into account: "Attraction toward a person is a positive linear function of the sum of the weighted positive reinforcements (Number × Magnitude) associated with him, divided by the total number of weighted positive and negative reinforcements associated with him" (p. 152).

The influence of classical conditioning principles also is evident in this model. Byrne and Clore conceptualized reinforcement as an unconditioned stimulus producing an unconditioned response, namely, positive feelings (hence the label reinforcement-*affect* for their model). They postulated that any individual who is associated with the unconditioned stimulus will evoke the unconditioned response.

Research. Byrne (1971) developed a paradigm that became the dominant methodology for studying attraction in the 1970s. He set out with the assumption that we find it reinforcing to learn that others agree with us. Conversely, he assumed that it is punishing to interact with someone who holds attitudes that are very different from our own. Thus, it was predicted that when we first meet someone, we will like that person more if we believe his or her attitudes are similar to ours. To test this hypothesis, Byrne had participants complete an attitude questionnaire. Next, they were presented with another copy of the questionnaire, ostensibly filled out by another person. This hypothetical stranger's questionnaire actually was constructed by the experimenter to appear either similar or dissimilar to the participant's responses. The amount of attraction that participants reported feeling toward the stranger was a direct linear function of the proportion of similar attitudes. In other words, the greater the proportion of attitudes the stranger appeared to have in common with the participant, the more she or he was liked; the greater the proportion of dissimilar attitudes, the more he or she was disliked.

Lott and Lott's Classical Conditioning Approach

Lott and Lott (1960, 1974) also maintained that we like people who reward us. They further suggested that we will be attracted to someone if we are rewarded in the presence of that person. According to their formulation, attraction will be experienced even if the other person was not involved in giving the reward. In other words, the presence of the other person could be a chance occurrence, and yet we would still find ourselves liking him or her.

There are four main propositions underlying this theory of attraction (Lott & Lott, 1960). The first is that a person can be regarded as discriminable stimulus, to whom responses can be learned. Second, people respond positively when they receive rewards. Third, the pleasure that is experienced in response to a reward will become conditioned to all discriminable stimuli that were present at the time of the reward. Finally, an individual who was a discriminable stimulus when a reward was given can subsequently evoke the conditioned response (i.e., pleasure).

There are a number of additional postulates in Lott and Lott's formulation. For example, they predicted a positive association between frequency of reward and degree of liking; the more we are rewarded in the presence of another person, the more we will like him or her. They also posited that the more we value a particular reward, the greater our attraction to the person who is present when we receive it.

Research. Lott and Lott (1961) conducted a study with children to test the prediction that we are attracted to people who are present when we receive a reward. The children were divided into 3-person groups and played a game. Some received a reward (candy) while playing the game; others did not. Later, to assess attraction, the children were asked to name the two classmates they would most want to take along on a family vacation. Consistent with predictions, children who had been rewarded while playing the game were more likely to name fellow group members than children who had not received a reward. Lott and Lott concluded that the pleasure of receiving the reward had become conditioned to the other group members, thereby increasing attraction to them.

⠶ Social Exchange and Equity Theories

Like reinforcement theories, social exchange and equity theories emphasize the role of rewards in attraction. However, these theories go beyond reinforcement models in a number of ways. For example, they seek to explain behavior in ongoing relationships, rather than focusing only on initial attraction. Another difference is that these theories invoke a number of constructs, in addition to rewards, to account for satisfaction and commitment in relationships. One such theory that has had a major impact in social psychology is Thibaut and Kelley's (1959; Kelley & Thibaut, 1978) interdependence theory. This theory will be described first, along with an extension of the theory that has since been developed by Rusbult (1980a, 1980b). Finally, another very influential theory, equity theory, will be described.

Thibaut and Kelley's Interdependence Theory

A basic premise of exchange theories, including interdependence theory, is that for people to be satisfied in a relationship, the rewards must outweigh the costs. Thibaut and Kelley (1959) posited that relationship partners compare the outcomes in a current relationship with the outcomes they have experienced in the past, and with the outcomes they anticipate receiving in available alternative relationships. These standards of comparison are referred to as the *comparison level* and the *comparison level for alternatives*. The comparison level is the yardstick we use to evaluate how satisfying we find a relationship. According to the theory, the process of assessing satisfaction involves comparisons with the outcomes other people are receiving in their relationships, as well as comparisons with our own past relationships. Based on these comparisons, we develop a sense of the level of rewards and costs that we deserve in a relationship. If the outcomes in a current relationship meet this standard, the theory predicts that we will be satisfied with the relationship. If outcomes fall below the comparison level, we will be dissatisfied.

The standard that is used to evaluate whether to remain in a relationship is the comparison level for alternatives, defined as the lowest level of outcomes we will accept in light of available alternatives. The alternatives that people usually think about are potential relationships with available, attractive others. However, being alone also could be a more desirable option than remaining in a relationship. If we perceive that we can obtain better outcomes in a different relationship or by being alone, we are likely to leave the current relationship. On the other hand, if we believe that it is unlikely that we would fare better elsewhere, we are likely to stay. Thus, the comparison level for alternatives determines the level of commitment to a relationship.

In differentiating between these two standards, Thibaut and Kelley drew an important distinction between satisfaction and commitment to relationships. They acknowledged that usually people who are satisfied remain in relationships, and people who are unhappy end them. However, sometimes people stay in unhappy relationships. Why would someone remain in a relationship when in exchange theory terms, his or her outcomes fall below his or her comparison level? An interdependence theorist would answer that this person does not perceive that other alternatives to the current relationship are available. The theory can also explain situations in which someone's outcomes exceed his or her comparison level, and yet the person abandons this happy relationship. Such cases exist when an individual perceives that an especially attractive alternative relationship is available to him or her. Thus, the person anticipates an even higher level of outcomes in the alternative relationship.

If this theory is applied to friendships, it suggests that we develop a standard, the comparison level, for what we feel we deserve in a friendship. The theory would predict that we should feel satisfied with friendships that exceed this standard, and dissatisfied with friendships that fail to meet it. Furthermore, our level of commitment to a friendship should be determined by the availability of alternatives. If a number of attractive people are clamoring to be friends with us, we might abandon an existing friendship, even if we were relatively happy with it. Alternatively, we might remain in an unhappy friendship because we perceive that better alternatives are not available.

Kelley and Thibaut (1978) generally have tested the predictions of their theory using complicated outcome matrices. (The Prisoner's Dilemma is probably the best example.) Rusbult's research, in which these constructs have been assessed in ongoing friendships, is more relevant to this chapter.

Rusbult's Investment Model

Rusbult's (1980a, 1980b) investment model is an extension of Thibaut and Kelley's theory. Her focus has been on the prediction of commitment in relationships such as friendship. According to the model, commitment is predicted by three variables: satisfaction, comparison level for alternatives, and investment. Like Thibaut and Kelley, she maintains that outcomes (rewards minus costs) determine satisfaction. Satisfaction, in turn, is regarded as one of the determinants of commitment. She also retained another tenet of interdependence theory, namely, that the availability of alternatives predicts the level of commitment to a relationship. However, Rusbult argues that the degree of commitment also depends on how much one has invested in the relationship. Investments are defined as resources such as time, emotional energy, or even shared possessions that would be lost if the relationship ended. Thus, investments increase commitment to a relationship by making it more costly to end it—if one terminates the relationship, one loses the resources that have been invested in it. According to this model, then, commitment will be highest if satisfaction is high, if one perceives few alternatives to the current relationship, and if one has invested heavily in it.

Research. To test the investment model, Rusbult (1980b) asked university students to assess the level of rewards in a current friendship (e.g., quality of time together, sense of humor) as well as the costs incurred (e.g., friend's annoying habits, conflict). They also estimated the availability of alternative friendships and the degree of investment in the friendship (e.g., amount of time spent with friend, shared memories, emotional investments). Finally, participants rated how satisfied they were with the friendship and how committed they felt to it. As expected, satisfaction was predicted by calculating rewards minus costs. The more the rewards exceeded the costs of the friendship (i.e., the higher the outcomes), the greater the satisfaction. Importantly, commitment was predicted by a combination of variables: high satisfaction, low availability of alternatives, and high investment. Thus, Rusbult's model suggests that we are satisfied with a friendship to the extent that the benefits we receive outweigh the costs. Furthermore, we are likely to remain in the relationship if we are satisfied with it, if we believe no one else wants to be our friend, and if we have put a lot into the friendship.

Hatfield's Equity Theory

Like social exchange theories, a basic assumption of equity theory (Hatfield & Traupmann, 1981; Hatfield, Traupmann, Sprecher, Utne, & Hay, 1985; Hatfield, Utne, & Traupmann, 1979; Walster [Hatfield], Walster, & Berscheid, 1978) is that we try to maximize our outcomes in relationships. Equity theorists also posit that we evaluate our outcomes via comparison processes. However, at this point the theories diverge. Social exchange theorists argue that we compare the rewards and costs in our current relationship with those that we believe we could obtain in an alternative relationship. Equity theorists maintain that we compare our outcomes with those of our relationship partner. This is a key difference between the two theories, and it is elucidated when one examines predictions concerning relationship satisfaction. Social exchange theorists predict that as long as the rewards outweigh the costs in a relationship, we will be satisfied. Equity theorists, who believe that fairness is a central issue in relationships, predict that we will be satisfied with a relationship only if we perceive that our outcomes are comparable to those of our partner. Imagine a friendship between two people, Chris and Pat. When asked to assess the rewards and costs in her friendship with Pat, Chris reports that the level of rewards she receives is higher than the level of costs. Is Chris happy with the friendship? Social exchange theorists would answer yes. Equity theorists would want to pose another question before providing an answer. Specifically, they would want to ask Chris how her outcomes (i.e., ratio of rewards to costs) compare to Pat's. Does Chris think that she is getting a better deal, that Pat is getting a better deal, or that their outcomes are roughly equal? If Chris replied that her and Pat's ratio of inputs and outcomes (rewards and costs) was equivalent, an equity theorist then would confidently answer that Chris is satisfied with the friendship.

This difference between the theories is most apparent in the situation where Chris feels that her rewards far exceed her costs and that her reward/cost ratio is much higher than Pat's. Social exchange theories (and perhaps common sense) would predict that Chris would feel especially happy, given the high level of rewards relative to costs. Equity theorists would predict the opposite—that Chris would feel unhappy because she was getting a much better deal that Pat. According to the theory, when we are overbenefited, we experience guilt. If we feel underbenefited (i.e., believe that the other person's reward/cost ratio is more favorable than our own), we will feel anger. Thus, Hatfield and her colleagues maintain that people feel satisfied only in equitable relationships—relationships in which they believe that their outcomes are comparable to the outcomes of their partner. Inequitable relationships (both over- and underbenefited, but especially underbenefited) result in distress.

It is further postulated that when people are in inequitable relationships, they try to alleviate the resultant distress by attempting to restore equity. The theorists delineate a number of ways this is accomplished. The most obvious route is to change the ratio of benefits and costs. We can stop putting as much into the relationship if we feel underbenefited, for example, or attempt to increase the rewards. Alternatively, we can focus on our partner and take steps to either decrease his or her rewards, or try to convince our partner to increase his or her inputs. Thus, there are four possible avenues of change: altering our own level of inputs, changing our outcomes, or altering our partner's inputs or outcomes. Obviously, it is not always easy to change what we put in, or get out of, relationships. It is often even more difficult to change our partner's inputs and outcomes. For this reason, Hatfield posited that when it is not possible to restore *actual equity*, we will restore *psychological equity* instead. Put simply, we try to convince ourselves that the situation really is fair. This can be achieved by interpreting each person's input/outcome ratio differently, so that the relationship now appears equitable after all. If actual or psychological equity restoration attempts fail, the remaining and final option is to *terminate the relationship*.

Before leaving this theory, it is important to point out that equity theory deals with people's *perceptions* of fairness in relationships, regardless of whether these perceptions reflect reality. A social psychologist friend reports that after delivering a lecture on equity theory, a student came forward and exclaimed that he now knew why he was so unhappy with his girlfriend. He had made a list of his inputs/outcomes and of her inputs/outcomes and suddenly it was glaringly obvious that she was getting a much better deal! This student failed to realize this was only his perception—chances are his girlfriend would have provided quite a different assessment of their input/outcome ratios. However, from the perspective of equity theory, whether he was correct in his assessment is not particularly relevant. What is important is that he perceived the relationship as inequitable. As we will see, it is precisely these kinds of perceptions that determine how satisfied people are in a relationship and whether or not they remain in it.

Research. The research conducted by Hatfield and her colleagues has mainly focused on dating and marital relationships. For example, Walster [Hatfield], Walster, and Traupmann (1978) asked dating couples to assess their input/outcome ratios by answering questions such as, "Considering what you put into your dating relationship, compared to what you get out of it . . . and what your dating partner puts in compared to what she or he gets out of it, how well does your dating relationship stack up?" Based on their responses, participants were classified as overbenefited, underbenefited, or in an equitable relationship. The authors predicted that individuals in equitable relationships would be happy and content, whereas underbenefited individuals would feel angry and overbenefited individuals would feel guilty. Furthermore, they expected more stability in equitable than inequitable relationships. The results supported these predictions. Greatly underbenefited individuals felt angry, whereas greatly overbenefited individuals felt guilty. Those who were in equitable relationships (or only slightly under- or overbenefited) were most content and happy. When the researchers contacted the participants a few months later, those in equitable relationships were likely to still be dating, whereas those in inequitable relationships were more likely to have broken up.

In a study of the development of friendship, Berg (1984) adapted this methodology and asked college roommates who was benefiting more from their living arrangement. Perceptions of equity were positively correlated with satisfaction with the living arrangement but did not predict whether the roommates wanted to continue living together.

✍ Cognitive Consistency Theories

The basic assumption underlying cognitive consistency (or balance) theories is that we have a need for consistency or balance in our lives. Usually, balance is conceptualized in terms of attitudes (positive or negative) between people or objects in a triadic relation. The idea of balance is captured in Aristotle's observation that we feel friendly "to our friends' friends, and to those who like, or are liked by, those whom we like ourselves. And also to those who are enemies to those whose enemies we are, and dislike, or are disliked by, those whom we dislike."

Cognitive consistency theorists differ somewhat in what they consider to be a balanced relationship. However, they agree on a fundamental premise, namely, that human beings are motivated to maintain balance or consistency, because balanced relations are stable and unbalanced relations are not. Two classic theories will be presented here: Heider's and Newcomb's. The latter will be discussed more fully given that it relates more directly to interpersonal attraction. It is also for this reason that only Newcomb's research will be presented.

Before proceeding, it should be pointed out that, as with equity theory, these theories are concerned with the *perception* of imbalance, because it is this perception that motivates individuals to try to restore balance. Thus, in the same way that the perception of inequity initiates attempts at equity restoration, the perception of imbalance triggers restoration efforts.

Heider's Theory of Cognitive Organization

Heider (1958) was concerned with the relations between a perceiver (*P*), another person (*O*), and an object (*X*). His system is often portrayed as an upside down triangle, with *P* and *O* near the top and *X* in the middle below. Lines are drawn between *P*, *O*, and *X* to represent the relations between them. Positive relations are marked with a plus (+) sign and negative relations with a minus (–) sign. In mathematical language, the triad is balanced if the algebraic product of the three signs is positive and unbalanced if the product is negative. In other words, a balanced state exists if all possible relations are positive, or if two are negative and one is positive. So, for example, if *P* likes *O*, and *O* likes *X*, then *P* should have a positive attitude toward *X*. In other words, if you like me and I like my cat, then, according to Heider, you should have a positive attitude toward my cat. On the other hand, if *P* dislikes *O*, and *O* dislikes *X*, then *P* should like *X* in order to achieve balance. Thus, if you don't like me, and I don't like dogs, the situation would be balanced if you decided you liked dogs. If both *P* and *O* like *X*, or if both *P* and *O* dislike *X*, then balance is achieved by a positive relation between *P* and *O*. Therefore, if you and I discover we both like monkeys, then we should also like each other. The situation also is balanced if we both dislike monkeys (or other things—apparently, English clergyman Sydney Smith exclaimed, "Madam, I have been looking for a person who disliked gravy all my life; let us swear eternal friendship!"). Thus, Heider assumes that attitudes toward people and toward objects operate in similar ways.

This is a point of departure for Heider and Newcomb, who will be considered next. For Heider, minus signs are equivalent, regardless of whether they occur between the two persons or between a person and an object. Thus, in his theory, interpersonal disliking and negative attitudes have comparable effects.

Newcomb's Balance Theory

Unlike Heider, Newcomb (1961, 1971) believed that our attitudes toward people are qualitatively different from our attitudes toward objects. According to Newcomb, Person A's attitude toward Person B will be affected by Person A's beliefs about how he or she is regarded by B. Obviously, this is not an issue when discussing Person A's attitude toward an object (X). In fact, Newcomb preferred to use the term *attraction* when discussing the relation between Persons A and B, and the term *attitude* when discussing Person A's or B's relation to X. Newcomb further differed from Heider in that he was concerned not only with the direction of the relation (+ or –) but also with the *intensity* of attitudes and attraction.

In formulating his theory, Newcomb focused mainly on the attitudes of Persons A and B toward physical and social objects. He maintained that a balanced state exists if two people like each other and hold similar attitudes toward an object. If two people like each other but hold dissimilar attitudes toward an object, the triad is unbalanced. In this case, attempts to restore balance would be undertaken. One or both people would change their feelings toward each other, or change their attitude toward the object.

Because Newcomb distinguished between attitudes toward people (attraction) and attitudes toward objects, his theory made differential predictions for disliking a person versus having a negative attitude toward an object. For instance, he postulated that if Person A and Person B dislike one another and have dissimilar attitudes, the situation is neither balanced nor imbalanced. Instead, it is an in-between state that Newcomb referred to as "nonbalanced." In his view, for balance to exist in a situation with two minus signs, the negative relations must be between Person A and X and between Person B and X, not between Persons A and B.

Newcomb's theory also dealt with other issues, including the effects of the *degree* of imbalance or strain in the system, the probability of communication about the imbalance, and strategies for reducing imbalance. For example, he posited that the amount of strain or pressure to restore balance will vary as a function of the discrepancy between Person A's and Person B's attitudes toward the object (X) and the importance of X; the more important the object, and the greater the discrepancy between both people's attitudes, the greater the strain. Newcomb further postulated that the greater the degree of imbalance in the system, the greater the likelihood that Person A will communicate with Person B about their attitudes toward X. Finally, Newcomb (1959) delineated seven ways in which balance could be restored:

> (a) by reduction in the strength of attraction; (b) by reduction of object-relevance; (c) by reduction of perceived ("other's") object-relevance; (d) by reduction of importance of the object of communication; (e) by reduction of perceived ("other's") object of communication; (f) by changes in cathexis or in cognitive restructuring of own attitudes, such that there is increased similarity with the other's perceived attitudes; and (g) by changes in perceived attitudes (cathectic or cognitive) of the other such that there is increased similarity with own attitudes. (p. 403)

These strategies are reminiscent of the strategies for reducing inequity (see section on equity theory), in that some appear to be ways of restoring actual balance, whereas others would seem to restore psychological balance.

Research. In his classic study, Newcomb (1961) invited students who were new to the University of Michigan to live in a shared house. At the beginning of the study, they completed an extensive battery of personality tests, attitude questionnaires, and so on. At various intervals throughout the year, the students were asked to indicate which of the other students in the house they preferred as friends. They also were asked to report on the attitudes and friendship choices of their housemates. Consistent with his theory, Newcomb found that the students were most attracted to housemates with whom they had similar attitudes (values) and who liked the same people they did. As will be seen in the next two chapters, these sorts of findings continue to permeate the friendship literature.

❧ Developmental Theories

Developmental theories are concerned with changes in relationships over time. Thus, these theories have the potential to answer questions such as: Do the determinants of attraction or liking change over the course of a friendship? Several stage theories of relationships have been developed (e.g., Kerckhoff & Davis, 1962; Lewis, 1972; Murstein, 1971). However, these theories deal primarily with courtship and mate selection and therefore will not be discussed here.

Altman and Taylor's (1973) social penetration theory is applicable to a wide range of relationships, although it is primarily a theory of self-disclosure in developing relationships, rather than a general theory of interpersonal attraction. Thus, only a short synopsis will be provided. According to Altman and Taylor, relationship development is characterized by an increase in both the depth and breadth of intimate self-disclosure. Based on the pattern of self-disclosure, they identified four stages of relationship development: orientation, exploratory affective exchange, affective exchange, and stable exchange. They postulated that in the early stages of a relationship, we disclose information about ourselves in only a few, superficial areas. As the relationship progresses, we become more intimate and personal in our disclosures. This increase in depth is accompanied by a corresponding increase in breadth of disclosure. Thus, by the later stages of relationship development, we will have revealed our innermost thoughts and feelings across a wide range of topics. Altman and Taylor's theory continues to be influential and important. The emphasis on self-disclosure processes makes the theory particularly relevant when discussing the formation of relationships. Thus, this model will surface again in subsequent chapters.

Probably the most relevant developmental theory for purposes of this chapter is that offered by Levinger. Originally, Levinger and Snoek (1972) published a four-stage formulation beginning with *zero contact* and ending with *mutuality*. This model will be presented, followed by Levinger's (1980, 1983) subsequent theorizing in which a five-stage model (ABCDE; Acquaintanceship to Endings) was advanced.

Levinger and Snoek's Levels of Pair Relatedness

According to Levinger and Snoek (1972), there are four levels of pair relatedness: zero contact, unilateral awareness, surface contact, and mutuality. At Level 0, zero contact, the two people are not even aware of one another. The three remaining levels, where the partners are in contact with one another, are distinguished from one another along seven dimensions, such as the basis of the attraction, the knowledge the partners have of each other, the nature of the communication between them, the importance placed on maintaining the relationship, and so on.

At Level 1, unilateral awareness, only one person is aware of the other. Thus, there is no interaction, no shared knowledge, and relationship maintenance is not an issue. At this stage, attraction is based on external attributes such as physical appearance and one-sided forecasts of the outcomes that might be obtained if a relationship were formed. If this preliminary assessment is positive, efforts may be taken to ensure contact.

Level 2, surface contact, is characterized by the superficial exchange of information between the partners. Interaction follows socially prescribed rules. Knowledge is limited to the impressions formed from one another's public self-presentation. Maintenance continues to be a relatively unimportant issue, given that the relationship is peripheral in the partners' lives. Nevertheless, at this stage, each person uses what little information is available to begin assessing the outcomes (rewards and costs) of the nascent relationship. If the result is positive, the relationship may progress to the next and final stage.

Level 3, mutuality, represents the gradual intersection of the partners' lives. The pair relies less on cultural norms and, instead, develops their own, unique style of interaction. Mutual knowledge increases as each person discloses more personal and intimate information about him- or herself. Both partners are invested in maintaining and nurturing the relationship. Levinger (1974) conceptualizes this stage as a continuum: "Its baseline is a Level 2 surface contact; its ultimate realization is the total interpenetration of two human beings, as defined by their joint attitudes, joint behavior, and joint property" (p. 101).

Levinger's ABCDE Model

More recently, Levinger has extended the pair-relatedness model to account for the deterioration and dissolution of relationships. In his ABCDE model (Levinger, 1980, 1983), A refers to Acquaintanceship, B to Buildup, C to Continuation, D to Deterioration, and E to Ending. Thus, the earlier model focused on the development of attraction, whereas the later model emphasizes the dynamics and dissolution of established, close relationships. Moreover, in these later formulations, Levinger was concerned not only with the processes of development at each stage but also with the *transitions* between stages. The conceptualization of the early stages (A to C) is quite similar to that of Levels 1 to 3, respectively, in Levinger and Snoek's model. Therefore, mainly the deterioration and ending stages will be described.

According to Levinger, a number of factors can contribute to the deterioration of a relationship. For example, the frequency, duration, or diversity of interactions may change in ways that are harmful for the relationship. Changes in the valence of affect (from positive to negative) or in the intensity of affect also may play a role. Negative changes can occur in many other domains, including open, honest communication, trust, and communality of outcomes and future plans, to name a few. In Levinger's view, the causes of deterioration may rest with personal characteristics of an individual partner or characteristics of the relationship, or may stem from external pressures.

Just because a relationship reaches the deterioration stage does not mean that it inevitably will proceed toward the next stage, Ending. Levinger maintains that deteriorated relationships can continue indefinitely. Whether or not the relationship eventually ends depends on factors such as the availability of attractive, alternative relationships. In his writings on marital dissolution (e.g., Levinger, 1979), he also suggested that barriers develop around relationships, thereby making it difficult to end them. As will be seen in Chapter 7, the barriers to ending friendships are not nearly so strong as the barriers to ending relationships such as marriage. Thus, one might expect that deteriorated friendships would be more likely than other kinds of relationships to move to the Ending stage.

Research. There is a paucity of empirical research on Levinger's model, despite the fact that it has been well received. Levinger

(1980) described an unpublished study conducted with DeLamarter, which explored behavioral manifestations of pair relatedness. They presented pairs of strangers and established couples with a large sheet of paper and asked them to paint a picture. It was expected that the greater mutuality of the couples would be reflected in the construction of a joint picture, with both partners freely painting on each other's half of the sheet. In contrast, they anticipated that strangers would each paint a separate picture on their own side of the paper. The results were not entirely consistent with this hypothesis. However, there were various indications of mutuality that had not been predicted. For example, the couples were much more likely to touch one another, borrow paints without asking, and trade places at the table than were the strangers.

✒ Comparison of the Theories

In an earlier exposition on theories of friendship (Perlman & Fehr, 1986), eight dimensions on which the theories could be compared were identified. Table 2.1 summarizes the key constructs of each theory and highlights similarities and differences between them. In constructing the table, it became apparent that the various reinforcement theories were similar enough that they could be treated as a unit. The same was true for the cognitive consistency theories. However, within the social exchange camp, equity theory differed sufficiently from the others (Thibaut and Kelley; Rusbult) to warrant its own entry. Levinger borrowed concepts from Thibaut and Kelley, such as availability of alternatives, in discussing the later stages of his ABCDE model, which accounts for some of the overlap between these two theories in the table.

The dimensions used to compare and contrast the theories are largely self-explanatory, although it may be useful to clarify the *breadth* dimension. This dimension classifies the theories based on whether they account primarily for initial attraction or go beyond attraction to account for the dynamics of ongoing, established relationships. On this basis, reinforcement theories were classified

Table 2.1 Five Approaches to Attraction: A Comparative Analysis

Dimension	Reinforcement	Interdependence	Equity	Cognitive	Developmental
Central concepts	Reward	Behavioral seqences, rewards, costs, CL, CL$_{Alt}$	Fairness of input/outcome ratios	Balance among attitudes	Stages, positive and negative forces, barriers, behavioral outcomes
View of human nature	People can be molded via reinforcement	People seek to maximize outcomes	People are concerned with fairness	People are intellectual, seek consistency	Needs change; emphasis on maximizing outcomes
Determinants of attraction, historical vs. contemporary	Emphasis on current levels of reinforcement, histories, and past pairings of CS with UCS	Emphasis on contemporary forces; some concern with past investments	Contemporary	Contemporary, but established cognitive structures can influence information processing	Contemporary, yet implies change in attraction is based on progression through earlier stages
Emphasis on internal processes vs. external forces	Largely external (rewards), but internal factors can influence what is rewarding	Both: depends on rewards received plus comparison processes	Both: depends on rewards received plus judgment of their fairness	Internal	Emphasis first on perceptual processes and then on behavioral outcomes

(continued)

Table 2.1 (Continued)

Dimension	Reinforcement	Interdependence	Equity	Cognitive	Developmental
Concern with stages	Very little	Some	Some	Very little	Considerable
Breadth of relationship phenomena considered	Narrow	Broad (satisfaction, love, commitment, power, etc.)	Moderate	Narrow (liking and attitudes)	Moderate
Concern with constellation of relationships	Very little	Concern with alternatives available	Focus mostly on dyad	Third persons treated like attitude object	Concern with alternatives available
Treatment of decline: implicitly the reverse of attraction or object of specific consideration	Implicitly the reverse of attraction	Specific consideration	Implicitly the reverse of attraction	Decline ignored; disliking considered a special case	Specific consideration

SOURCE: Perlman and Fehr (1986, pp. 28-29). Reprinted with permission from Springer-Verlag Publishers.
NOTE: CL = comparison level, Alt = alternative, CS = conditioned stimulus, UCS = unconditioned stimulus.

as narrow, even though the concept of reinforcement itself has been widely applied in psychology.

In addition, the *concern with stages* dimension requires a comment. When Berscheid (1977) published her review of theories of attraction, she observed that "relationship development has been relatively ignored by general social psychological theories of attraction" (p. 203). Since then, Levinger and others have taken noteworthy steps to ameliorate this deficit. Although Levinger's model still awaits extensive empirical validation, it is one of the few comprehensive developmental models that can be applied to friendship as well as other kinds of relationships.

Finally, it should be pointed out that each of the theories has not been without its critics. The purpose of this chapter has been to present the various theoretical perspectives that have been, or can be, brought to bear on the study of friendship. Thus, a critical evaluation of each theory is beyond the scope of this chapter but can be found in Perlman and Fehr (1986).

✒ Summary

This chapter presented four major classes of theories that were developed to explain relationships in general, but are applicable specifically to friendships. Reinforcement theorists maintain that we like people who reward us, as well as people whom we associate with the receipt of rewards. Social exchange and equity theories also emphasize the importance of rewards. In exchange theories, it is predicted that rewards determine the level of satisfaction in a relationship. Additional constructs such as availability of alternatives and investments are imported to account for the level of commitment. In explaining relationship satisfaction and commitment (stability), equity theories emphasize the importance of perceptions of one's partner's level of rewards relative to one's own. Cognitive consistency theories regard the need for balance as a fundamental human motivation and therefore postulate that we will be attracted to people whose attitudes are consistent with ours. Finally, developmental theories seek to explain the unfolding of relationships by charting a sequence of stages. Generally, such theories begin with the stage at which partners are strangers to one another and end with either the establishment of a mutual intimate relationship or the dissolution of the relationship. Thus, these theories are useful when considering issues such as why we are drawn to some people but not to others, the course of friendship relationships, and what determines whether we are satisfied with, and committed to, a friendship.

3

✢

Friendship Formation

You can make more friends in two months by becoming interested in other people than you can in two years by trying to get
other people interested in you.

—Dale Carnegie (1936, p. 58)

This chapter focuses on the process of friendship formation.
The basic question to be answered is: How do friendships get
started? Showing an interest in other people is certainly part of
friendship formation as Dale Carnegie says, but other factors are
important as well. Specifically, for a friendship to begin, four kinds
of factors must converge: environmental (being in the same place
at the same time), individual, situational, and dyadic. Each set of
factors will be discussed in turn, along with relevant supporting
research. Then, research that has examined these sets of factors in
conjunction will be presented.

❧ Environmental Factors

A first step in the formation of most friendships is that two individuals are brought into contact with one another through physical proximity or *propinquity*. In other words, people who inhabit the same physical environment are more likely to become friends than those who do not. The effects of propinquity on friendship formation have been shown for the location of one's residence, as well as the environment in which one spends one's day (e.g., workplace, university). Factors such as the population density of one's environment and the kind of social network in which one is embedded also can influence friendship development.

Residential Proximity

Decades ago, Festinger, Schachter, and Back (1950) discovered that propinquity leads to liking. They asked residents of a married students' apartment complex to name the three people in the housing complex with whom they socialized most. Two thirds of the people named lived in the same building, and two thirds of those people lived on the same floor. The person who was most frequently named was the person next door, followed by the person who lived two doors down, and so on. Festinger et al. also discovered that people who lived on different floors were much less likely to become friends than those who lived on the same floor—even when the distance between them was the same. Presumably, it took more effort to walk up or down the stairs to a different floor than to simply walk down the hallway on one's own floor. To take such effects into account, Festinger et al. coined the term *functional distance*, by which they meant that the probability of two people interacting is a function of both the design of the environment as well as the actual physical distance.

This study was replicated by Ebbesen, Kjos, and Konecni (1976) with residents of a condominium complex in southern California. These researchers, too, found that people were more likely to be friends (and incidentally, enemies) with those who lived closest to them. Moreover, they discovered that friendship *quality* was related to proximity—the friends who lived closest were more likely to be considered best friends than those who lived farther away. Similarly, when Nahemow and Lawton (1975) conducted a study of 270 adults living in a public housing project, they found that 88% of people's best friends in the complex lived in the same building; nearly half lived on the same floor. Proximity was an especially important variable in friendship formation between dissimilar people. The authors reported that "friendships between people of different ages and races existed almost exclusively among those who lived very close to one another. These people resided on the same floor 70% of the time" (p. 210).

A number of studies have shown that university students often become friends based on dormitory room proximity (e.g., Caplow & Forman, 1950; Menne & Sinnett, 1971). Holahan and Wilcox (1978) found that students living in high-rise mega-dormitories reported greater dissatisfaction with opportunities for friendship formation than students living in smaller, low-rise dormitories. In high-rise dormitories, those who lived on lower floors (to which there was easier access) reported a greater number of dormitory-based friendships than those living on the middle or upper floors (Holahan, Wilcox, Burnam, & Culler, 1978). Finally, in a longitudinal study of friendship formation among new university students, Hays (1985) found that the physical distance between the participants' residences (ranging from dormitory roommates to living across town) was inversely related to friendship development. In fact, Griffin and Sparks (1990) found that at least among men, having been roommates in college predicted friendship closeness 4 years later, when they were no longer attending college.

Thus, proximity is one of the standard predictors of friendship formation. Obviously, to become friends with someone, you have to come in contact with him or her—or do you? Recent developments in computer-mediated communication (electronic mail, computer networks) are opening up whole new worlds of friendship possibilities. (See Wilkins, 1991, for examples of friendships that were formed through computer communication, without any face-to-face contact.) As Lea and Spears (1995) comment:

One of the effects of the connectivity afforded by computer networks is that it vastly increases the "field of availables" for forming relationships far beyond the limits set by physical proximity—or even the extended horizons offered by other communication media. (p. 206)

Thus, the historical emphasis on proximity as a prerequisite for the development of friendship ultimately may be revised in light of new technology.

The Workplace and Other
Settings for Becoming Acquainted

The workplace is an important locus of friendship formation. When nearly 1,000 men living in the Detroit area in 1965-1966 were asked the source of their closest friendships, it was found that the largest percentage of their friendships were made at work (26%), followed by the neighborhood (23%). Other categories included childhood and juvenile friends (20%), kinship (7%), and voluntary organizations (7%) (Fischer et al., 1977; Fischer & Phillips, 1982). The workplace and the neighborhood were especially important sources for forming new friendships: 79% of these men's most recent friendship ties (less than 3 years) were formed there, compared to 35% of their oldest ties (more than 13 years). Similarly, in a survey of adults' friendships (outside of their households), Shulman (1975) found that friends were typically recruited from work, school, and through other friends and kin (see also Roberto & Scott, 1987).

Rather than ask about friendships, Sykes (1983) observed the interaction patterns of units of naval apprentice trainees who lived together over a 2-week period. The best predictor of who was chosen as a conversation partner (during unstructured, free time) was past membership in the same recruit company. Thus, these men preferred to interact with someone who was familiar to them from a previous setting, even though pretest measures showed they had not been close friends earlier in their shared environment. The second best predictor of social interaction was current proximity: those whose bunks were close to one another and who sat near one another in their classroom were more likely to spend time talking to each other.

The latter finding was also uncovered in a study of state police trainees by Segal (1974). The trainees were assigned alphabetically by surnames to dorm rooms and classroom seats. Friendships were most likely to form between those whose surnames began with the same, or a nearby, letter of the alphabet.

The role of the workplace in the formation of women's friendships has received less attention. It has been suggested that for women who remain at home, the neighborhood may serve a role analogous to the workplace for men (O'Connor, 1992). Indeed, some studies have found evidence of neighborhood-based friendships among women (e.g., Jerrome, 1984), although others have not (Oliker, 1989). For women with family responsibilities, the demands of combining domestic work with paid work tend to inhibit the development of work-based friendships (e.g., Allan, 1989; Wellman, 1985). For example, women may use their lunch hour to buy groceries or run household errands rather than dine with coworkers. Leslie and Grady (1985) found for divorced mothers, however, that the workplace was second only to kin as a source of relationships.

What is it about the workplace that is conducive to friendship formation? Fine (1986) pointed out that in addition to opportunities for contact (i.e., proximity), certain features of the work environment can facilitate the formation of friendships. In his research on restaurants as work settings, Fine found that many tasks required (or at least allowed for) friendly, cooperative behaviors between the workers. Thus, to the extent that the work/school environment fosters interaction, noncompetitiveness, and interdependence between people, friendships will be more likely to form (see also Farrell, 1985-1986). Consistent with this notion, Parker (1964) found that women and men in service occupations (e.g., child care and social services workers, teachers) were more likely to have friends in the same line of work than were business people. Those whose jobs encroached on their free time (e.g., who worked long hours, did job-related entertaining in their homes) were more likely to have close friends from work than those who worked a strict "9 to 5" day. In addition, attitude toward one's job affected friendship patterns—people who enjoyed their jobs were more likely to have close friends from work.

The Effect of Urban
Versus Rural Settings

Some environments are more conducive to friendship formation than others. For example, a commonly held stereotype is that large city dwellers are unfriendly compared to residents of small towns. Thus, one might expect that it would be more difficult to form friendships in urban centers. Indeed, in a study of graduate students who moved to a large city or a smaller town, Franck (1980) found that it took longer to make friends in the city. Within 2 months of their arrival, those in the city group had an average of 3.51 friends; those in the town group had 6.32. City dwellers also reported that they found their new environment a difficult one for making friends. However, when the students were interviewed 7 or 8 months later, both groups named approximately the same number of friends ($M = 5.34$ for the city group; 5.12 for the town group). Fischer (1982a) found that adults living in urban areas had more friends than those in rural areas.

Van Vliet (1981) compared the friendships of teenagers living in urban Toronto with those who lived in much less densely populated suburbs. Suburban adolescents were more likely to complain about a lack of neighborhood friends and, in fact, had fewer neighborhood-based friendships than those who lived in the heart of the city. The results of these studies are consistent with the suggestion that cities ultimately may be conducive to friendship formation because they offer more potential partners and more occasions for informal interaction (see Creekmore, 1985). Thus, cities may provide more opportunities for making friends than smaller centers, although it may take longer for friendship ties to form.

The Role of Social
Networks in Friendship Formation

When people are asked the sources of their friendships, "other friends and relatives" are mentioned frequently. These sources of friendships have been studied by Parks and Eggert (1991), who maintain that an important variable in predicting friendship formation is *communication network proximity*. In their words, "I am more likely to meet the friends of those who are already my friends than to meet the friends of those who are not already my friends" (p. 6). These researchers predicted that pairs of friends would already have been connected through network proximity before actually meeting one another. Imagine you were a participant in their study: Think of a same-sex friend, and list the four family members/relatives and eight nonkin (friends) to whom your friend is closest. Then, check off how many of the 12 people on your list you had met prior to meeting your friend. Parks and Eggert found that about two thirds of the university and high school students in their study had met at least one person in their friend's network prior to meeting their friend. Nearly half (47.3%) had prior contact with 1 to 3 members, 13.2% had contact with 4 to 6 members, and 5.8% had met more than 6 of their friends' closest associates before they ever were introduced to their friend. Furthermore, it was discovered that the communicative distance between people in the network determined who became friends with whom. That is, as the number of people one had to go through to reach the other increased, the probability that the two people would actually meet declined. In the same vein, Salzinger (1982) found that people who are in a network that does not have many connections to other networks have fewer friends.

These studies are important in showing that our current friends are a source of new friendships for us. These introductions may be unintentional (e.g., you happen to run into your friend having coffee with his or her friend) or intentional (e.g., you've heard your friend talking about this person and ask to be introduced; your friend believes that you and this person would like each other so the three of you get together).

Social networks also influence friendship formation through network members' reactions to our friendship choices. Parks and Eggert (1991) described a study in which high school students were asked to what extent their own and their friend's network of family and friends supported the friendship. As expected, friendship development was positively correlated with the perceived level of support from these networks. Presumably, such effects are not limited to adolescents' friendships. As Allan (1989) points out, in adulthood, a spouse, for example, may discourage or even attempt to terminate a particular friendship; "In such ways, patterns of existing ties can push the individual toward some relationships . . . while more or less subtly discouraging participation in others" (p. 44). Thus, not only are social networks a source of potential friends, but the reactions from network members may influence the extent to which we cultivate a certain friendship.

ᴥ Individual Factors

The kinds of structural, or external, factors that were just discussed are instrumental in bringing two people into contact with one another. However, obviously we do not pursue a friendship with every person we meet. What factors determine which acquaintanceships we will develop and which we will let atrophy? One answer might be that we survey our pool of potential friends and decide who seems most likable. Not so, according to Rodin (1982). In her view, we first examine the pool of available people and decide whom we do *not* want as a friend. In other words, we begin by "writing off" people and then we decide whom we would like to include in our friendship network. Each of these processes will be discussed in turn.

Deciding Whom We Don't Want as a Friend: Exclusion Criteria

Rodin (1982) maintained that exclusion judgments precede inclusion judgments; we decide whom we don't want to be friends with before we decide whom we do want as a friend. She discussed two kinds of exclusion criteria: dislike and disregard.

Dislike Criteria

Think about someone you like a lot. List one or two qualities that you like best about that person. Then ask yourself, "Is there anyone I *do not* like who possesses those same qualities?" For most people, the answer is yes. Let's say you listed "great sense of humor" as a favorite quality of the person you like. Chances are that there are also people you dislike who have a good sense of humor. Now, think about someone you dislike very much. List one or two things you dislike most about that person. Then ask yourself, "Is there anyone I like who has these qualities?" The answer is usually no. As Rodin (1982) points out, "We never like people who meet our dislike criteria regardless of what likable qualities they may also possess" (p. 32). Thus, judgments of liking and disliking are asymmetrical. We may attribute likable qualities to disliked people, but we do not attribute disliked qualities to people we like. In Rodin's view, the characteristics that cause us to dislike or reject others play a key role in the early stages of relationship formation. Once someone meets our dislike criteria, we immediately discard that person from our pool of possible friends.

Disregard Criteria

There is a second kind of exclusion judgment, namely, the use of disregard criteria. In this case, we eliminate people from our pool of potential friends not because we dislike them, but rather because they seem unsuitable candidates for friendship. We may disregard people because of their race, educational background, physical attractiveness, age, the way they dress, and so on. The purpose of disregard criteria, according to Rodin (1982), is that they "enable us to operate on actuarial or 'best-guess' strategies so that our energy and attention are not expended fruitlessly on people we are unlikely to like" (p. 37). People do not want to spend time cultivating a relationship with someone who strikes them as an unlikely friendship choice.

Thus, if Rodin is correct, when forming friendships, we begin by eliminating people whom we dislike or judge as unsuitable. So far, these ideas have not been subjected to extensive empirical testing. However, when Gouldner and Strong (1987) conducted friendship interviews with 75 middle-aged women, they found evidence of the use of dislike and disregard criteria to narrow down the set of possible friends. For example, potential friends were disregarded on the basis of dissimilarity of race, education, mode of dress, and especially, age.

Deciding Whom We Do Want
as a Friend: Inclusion Criteria

Once we have whittled down the set of eligibles, what determines whether or not we will form a friendship with a given
person? One answer is that it depends on the characteristics of the
other person—if he or she possesses qualities or attributes that we
desire in a friend, we will be more inclined to pursue a relationship
with him or her. Another answer is that it depends on the situation
(e.g., whether both people have room in their lives for another
friendship). Yet another answer is that it depends on how well we
interact with the other person. The situational and dyadic factors
that contribute to friendship formation will be discussed later. In
this next section, the focus will be on characteristics of other
people that make it more or less likely that we will want to pursue
a friendship with them. These include physical attractiveness,
social skills, responsiveness, shyness, and similarity.

Physical Attractiveness

One might think that physical attractiveness would play a role
only in the formation of romantic relationships. However, research
shows that physical appearance also affects the development of
same- and other-sex friendships (see Patzer, 1985). The importance
of physical attractiveness in nonromantic attraction has been
widely demonstrated—in studies using photographs of attractive
and unattractive persons as well as in laboratory and real-life
(nonlaboratory) studies of face-to-face interaction (e.g., Friedman,
Riggio, & Casella, 1988). These effects obtain even for children's
friendships. For example, Kleck, Richardson, and Ronald (1974)
found that the friendship choices of children after 2 weeks of
intense social interaction were strongly and positively related to
physical attractiveness.

Why are we drawn to physically attractive people? One reason
is that we assume that physically attractive people are more likely
than unattractive people to be similar to us in terms of personality
and attitudes (e.g., Patzer, 1985). It also may be more enjoyable to
interact with good-looking people. As Brehm (1985) suggests,

"Perhaps people's initial positive responses to physically attractive others enable them to develop more self-confidence about social interactions and greater social skills" (p. 68). There is some evidence that physically attractive people are more skillful in communicating with others, although the findings are not unequivocal (e.g., Riggio, 1986). Moreover, it is not clear whether physically attractive people necessarily have better social skills, or whether attractiveness and social skills are separate paths to social success. Reis et al. (1982) found that for men, both were true. Men who were good looking also reported having good social skills (i.e., confident in their social abilities, assertive, not afraid of rejection). However, physical attractiveness alone was also related to social success. For women, physical attractiveness and social skills each independently predicted positive social experiences. Contrary to the findings for men, physical attractiveness was not associated with social skills—in fact, the most attractive women tended to report low social skills. Thus, for women, it appears that there are two separate routes to social success: good looks or good social skills. For men, the two are likely to go hand-in-hand. The role of social skills in friendship formation is explored further in the next section.

Social Skills

According to Cook (1977), making friends is a skilled performance much like playing tennis or driving a car. Some people have difficulty developing relationships because they lack social skills such as responding appropriately to what the other person says, showing appropriate sequencing of gaze or posture, or following appropriate conversational turn-taking norms. Failure to perform such behaviors can undermine the formation of a friendship. For example, Argyle, Lefebvre, and Cook (1974) found that abnormal gaze—looking at an interaction partner too much or too little— was associated with decreased liking.

Social skills are important even in the formation of children's friendships. For example, in a study by Gottman, Gonso, and Rasmussen (1975), there was some evidence that children in Grades 3 and 4 who had good social skills had more friends and interacted more positively with peers than children with poor social skills. When Asher, Renshaw, and Geraci (1980) presented popular and unpopular children with hypothetical social situations, the responses of popular children were judged as more socially competent (e.g., more effective and relationship enhancing).

Similar findings have been reported in the adult literature. For example, in Riggio's (1986) research, socially skilled university students reported a greater number of close friends and daily school acquaintances than less skilled students. In a subsequent laboratory study, students had a brief conversation with two confederates. The better a student's social skills, the more the confederates liked him or her. In the same vein, Friedman et al. (1988) found that during a first encounter, individuals' social skills, especially nonverbal expressiveness, were positively correlated with how much their interaction partner liked them.

A longitudinal investigation of the role of social skills in adult friendship formation was undertaken by Shaver, Furman, and Buhrmester (1985). Their measure of social skills contained three components: initiation (e.g., introducing yourself), negative assertion (e.g., asking someone to change an annoying mannerism), and self-disclosure (revealing personal information). This scale was administered to a large group of students shortly before they entered the university and several times throughout their first year. Social skills turned out to be the most important determinant of satisfaction with relationships at the point of greatest disruption in the students' social networks—in the autumn. This was a time when the students had just separated from their old friends and had not yet established new, close friendships. Later on, when their networks were more stable, social skills were not as important in predicting satisfaction. When analyses were conducted separately for each component, initiation skills were found to be the most important in the fall (when students had just begun attending the university). Self-disclosure was moderately important throughout the year but especially in the summer when most relationships were fairly close. Negative assertion was unimportant at all times.

Thus, we are likely to form friendships with people who have good social skills. Shaver et al.'s finding that the correlation between social skills (especially initiation skills) and relationship satisfaction was strongest at the beginning of the academic year confirms the view that social skills are especially important during the early stages of relationships (e.g., Cook, 1977; Spitzberg & Cupach, 1989). Consistent with this notion, Buhrmester, Furman, Wittenberg, and Reis (1988) found that when interacting with a same-sex *acquaintance*, satisfaction with the encounter was most highly correlated with individuals' skill at initiating interactions. However, when interacting with a same-sex *friend*, satisfaction was strongly associated with the provision of support, self-disclosure, and management of conflict, and least correlated with initiation competence. The authors comment that "initiation competence may be important in beginning relationships, but may lessen in impact once a relationship is well-established; instead competence in providing warmth and support becomes important" (p. 1006).

Responsiveness

We also are attracted to potential friends who are responsive to us. In the first of two studies by Davis and Perkowitz (1979), participants exchanged information with a confederate who either did (responsiveness condition) or did not answer most of the questions the participant asked. In the second study, the confederate gave a reply that was related (responsiveness condition) or unrelated to the topic the participant had chosen. In both studies, the responsive confederate was perceived much more positively than the unresponsive one. Participants believed the responsive confederate liked them more and was more interested in them, and saw the confederate as the kind of person with whom they could become close friends. Other research also has shown that when someone behaves in responsive ways (e.g., showing interest and concern), their interaction partner likes them more (Berg & Archer, 1980; Godfrey, Jones, & Lord, 1986).

According to Miller, Berg, and Archer (1983), some people are characteristically more responsive than others. They developed a scale to measure individual differences in responsiveness, called the Opener Scale, which assesses the ability to elicit self-disclosure from others. Miller et al. found that women who scored high on the Opener Scale were able to elicit more self-disclosure from a typically low-disclosing person than were women who scored low. In another study, they found that high "openers" who lived in a sorority house were disclosed to more by other women in the house than low openers. In explaining these results, Berg (1987) remarked that "presumably, the responsive actions of these high 'openers' conveyed to the other that she was liked, that the opener was interested in and concerned with her, and so encouraged the other to disclose more" (p. 104). Thus, Carnegie's (1936) observation that "you can make more friends in two months by becoming interested in other people than you can in two years by trying to get other people interested in you" (p. 58) may be sage advice!

Shyness

Those who suffer from shyness may be especially likely to show social skills deficits and a lack of responsiveness. Studies on the interactions of shy and nonshy university students have found that shy people tend to initiate fewer conversations (see Jones & Carpenter, 1986). When they do interact with others, they are slower to reply to the other person's comments, they smile less, make less eye contact, and are generally less responsive than are nonshy people. These kinds of behaviors have the unfortunate consequence of leading their interaction partner to infer that they do not wish to interact. It is perhaps not surprising, therefore, that shy people tend to report fewer friends than those who are not shy.

Several other important findings have emerged from Jones and Carpenter's program of research, such as that shy people report greater loneliness (see also Cheek & Busch, 1981), less intimacy, and less closeness in their relationships than do nonshy people. In one study, Jones and Carpenter assessed the social relationships of students in their first week of classes and again 2 months later. Shyness was correlated with having fewer friends in general, having made fewer new friends at the university, being less involved in campus activities, and so on.

When shy people do form friendships, they are likely to last longer than those of nonshy people. However, shy people tend not to be very satisfied with their friendships and unfortunately, as Jones and Carpenter discovered, their friends tend to perceive them rather negatively (e.g., not warm, likable, or fun to be with). According to this research, then, we will be more interested in cultivating a friendship with a nonshy rather than a shy person.

Similarity

Long ago, Aristotle observed that "those, then, are friends to whom the same things are good and evil; and those who are, moreover, friendly or unfriendly to the same people" (trans. 1984, Book II, 4). By now, there is a very large body of research that supports Aristotle's astute observation: We tend to form friendships (and other relationships) with people who are similar to us. In fact, this "rule of homogamy" has been described as "one of the most basic principles that has come from the study of interpersonal attraction" (Brehm, 1985, p. 70). Similarity effects have been found for demographic characteristics (e.g., age, physical health, education, religion, family background; see Brehm, 1985, for a review), social status (Sinha & Kumar, 1984; Verbrugge, 1977), attitudes (e.g., Byrne, 1971, chap. 2), and so on. Friends are even likely to be similar in terms of physical attractiveness (Cash & Derlega, 1978). As Woolsey and McBain (1987) point out, similarity is a necessary starting point for a friendship. However, it is also the basis on which friendships become close. Thus, this literature will be discussed in greater detail in the next chapter on achieving closeness in friendships.

In summary, we are most likely to pursue a friendship with someone who is good looking, socially skilled, responsive, not shy, and similar to us in a variety of ways. However, even if a person possesses all of the attributes we desire in a friend, this does not ensure that a friendship necessarily will develop. First, a variety of situational factors come into play (e.g., how often you will cross paths with the person; whether both of you are available for a friendship). Second, even if the situation is "right" for a friendship to develop, this does not guarantee that you will become good friends with that person once you actually start spending time together. In the next section, the situational factors that influence friendship formation are considered, followed by an examination of the kind of dyadic interaction most conducive to friendship development.

❧ Situational Factors

A number of situational factors influence whether or not a friendship is likely to develop. Initially, factors such as how often we are likely to see the person and whether we are dependent on the person for something we want are important. Another consideration is whether we are able to accommodate another relationship, given our other commitments.

Probability of Future Interaction

Sometimes when we interact with someone, we are aware that this is probably the only time we will see him or her (e.g., striking up a conversation with someone on an airline flight). Other times, we anticipate ongoing interactions (e.g., meeting a new roommate). Do people respond differently to others depending on whether or not future interaction is expected? To answer this question, Darley and Berscheid (1967) presented female participants with ambiguous information about two other female students. Participants were led to believe that they would be having an intimate conversation with one of the women. Greater liking was reported for the woman with whom participants expected to interact.

Similarly, Tyler and Sears (1977) conducted two experiments in which they manipulated whether or not participants expected ongoing interactions with another person. Likable or pleasant individuals were evaluated positively regardless of whether future interaction was expected. However, individuals who were not likable were rated more positively by participants who expected continuing interactions, compared to participants who did not. Subsequent research has shown that this effect is stronger for some people than for others (Lassiter & Briggs, 1990). However, in general, if we anticipate ongoing interactions with someone, we tend to augment the positive and diminish the negative so that future encounters with this person will be as pleasant and harmonious as possible (Knight & Vallacher, 1981; Miller & Marks, 1982).

Frequency of Exposure

The research just presented showed that we evaluate people more positively if we expect to interact with them on an ongoing basis. Does it matter how often we actually do interact with them? The answer is yes. In fact, simply *seeing* someone on a frequent basis causes us to regard them more positively. Zajonc (1968) relays a story of a student who attended university classes covered in a large black bag. First, the other students reacted with hostility, then with curiosity, and eventually they became friends with "it"! Since the publication of Zajonc's (1968) pioneering studies demonstrating this *mere exposure* effect, hundreds of experiments have shown that the more we are exposed to other people (or even photographs of them), the greater our attraction to them, even if no interaction actually takes place (see Bornstein, 1989, for a review). There are some limits to this phenomenon, however. For example, if we initially dislike someone, repeated exposure to that person may actually lead to less, rather than more, liking (Perlman & Oskamp, 1971).

A study by Moreland and Zajonc (1982) points to a reason why repeated exposure leads to liking. They obtained the usual finding that as frequency of exposure to a photograph of a person increased, so did ratings of liking for the person. Interestingly, this increased attraction, in turn, led to an increase in perceived similarity. In other words, as individuals became more familiar with the person, they were more likely to assume that she or he was similar to them. As mentioned earlier, similarity is a major determinant of attraction—we like people who are (or whom we believe are) like us.

Outcome Dependency

We also are more attracted to someone on whom we are dependent for various outcomes (Berscheid & Graziano, 1979). The term *outcome dependency* refers to situations where another person is in a position to provide us with rewards or punishment. Berscheid, Graziano, Monson, and Dermer's (1976) classic study was conducted with potential dating partners, although their results seem applicable to friendships as well. These researchers controlled students' dating lives for 5 weeks. The participants (students) first watched a videotape of three people having a discussion. Some students were told which of the three people would be their dating partner for a 5-week period. Others were told they would date the person only once. Still others were told they would not be dating anyone shown on the videotape. Presumably, outcome dependency would be highest for the first group of students (in the sense that their designated dating partner could make their dating life enjoyable or miserable for 5 weeks) and lowest for the group who did not expect to date any of the three people. In fact, ratings of attraction and liking for potential dating partners increased as outcome dependency increased. In other words, the most positive ratings were given when the dating partner had the greatest capacity to affect the participant's life (i.e., dating for 5 weeks). Thus, if we are in a situation where we are dependent on someone, we tend to like that person more than someone who does not have the power to reward (or punish) us.

Availability

We have seen that if we expect to have continuing interaction with someone, come into frequent contact with him or her, and if we are dependent on the person for something we want, we probably will like the person. However, this still does not ensure that a friendship will be formed. Another situational factor comes into play as a necessary precondition for friendship, namely, that you and the other person must both be *available* for this kind of relationship.

According to Berg and Clark (1986), judgments of availability involve assessments of accessibility and assessments of both people's prior commitments and alternatives. Accessibility refers to the likelihood that you and the other person will have opportunities for frequent interaction and to engage in the kinds of activities that friends do. In addition, each person's prior commitments and alternatives influence how available he or she is for a new friendship. For example, one or both of you may have too many friends already or be involved in a time-consuming job or course of studies. If either of you is in an exclusive romantic relationship, it may be more difficult for a friendship to develop, especially a cross-sex friendship (see Chapter 5).

Gouldner and Strong (1987; see also Allan, 1989) noted the practical limitations on the number of friends the middle-aged women they interviewed felt they could form. An individual's "friendship budget" depended on how many friends she wanted, as well as how many new friendships she thought could be maintained given existing friendships and the demands of job and family. It was a consideration of these kinds of constraints on friendship formation that prompted Brenton's (1974) rather macabre observation that "the graveyard of social relationships is littered with the bones of friendships that might have been" (p. 119).

✇ Dyadic Factors

Imagine that you have moved to a new city to attend a university. You and the 30 other new students are at an orientation session and are all enrolled in several mandatory first-year courses. Because most of the other students are also new to this city, almost everyone is available for a friendship. As you look around, you notice that many of the students are attractive and seem warm and friendly. You know that you will be spending time with them, and yet by the end of your first year, you probably will not have formed friendships with each one. There will be certain people, but not others, with whom you will hit it off. In this section, the nature of dyadic interaction most conducive to the formation of friendships is explored. First, as you might expect, we are more likely to be attracted to someone if we believe that he or she likes us. Whether or not this initial liking leads to a friendship depends, to a large extent, on what you and the other person reveal to one another.

Reciprocity of Liking

The 19th-century English writer Charles Lamb declared, "How I like to be liked, and what I do to be liked!" Social psychological research conducted in the 20th century suggests that Lamb was not unique. In a classic experiment, Backman and Secord (1959) had groups of same-sex strangers engage in weekly discussions over a 6-week period. Prior to the first discussion, each person was told which group members the researchers expected would like him or her, based on personality information gathered earlier. (The experimenters actually randomly selected the names.) Participants showed the greatest liking for the group members whom they believed liked them. However, this effect held only for ratings made after the first, not subsequent, group discussions.

Backman and Secord's findings have been replicated many times, and the conditions under which reciprocity does not lead to liking have been identified (see Berscheid & Walster [Hatfield], 1978). Overall, it appears that we are attracted to people who like us, at least where our initial judgments of attraction or liking are concerned. Moreover, research by Curtis and Miller (1986) shows that if we believe someone likes us, we actually interact with them in ways that makes our belief come true. In their study, participants were told that they were either liked or disliked by their interaction partner. Those who believed they were liked self-disclosed more intimately, were more pleasant, and engaged in fewer distancing behaviors. The effect of these behaviors was to produce liking. Thus, individuals who believed they were liked actually ended up being liked more by their partner than individuals who thought they were disliked.

Self-Disclosure

As mentioned in the last chapter, according to social penetration theory (Altman & Taylor, 1973), when we first meet someone, we begin by disclosing information at a superficial level. If we find that level of interaction enjoyable, we will increase the intimacy of our self-disclosures, both in terms of *breadth* (discussing a wider variety of topics) and *depth* (discussing more personal, less superficial topics). Altman and Taylor posited that if each interaction is rewarding (has a positive outcome), we will continue to increase both the breadth and depth of our disclosures until we are revealing virtually everything about ourselves on virtually every topic. If, however, the exchange of disclosures becomes uncomfortable or unpleasant, we will retreat to our earlier, more superficial and circumscribed mode of self-disclosure.

This model has generated a number of predictions. For example, it follows that we should be attracted to people who reveal personal information to us because intimate disclosure signals a desire to develop closeness. Indeed, many studies have shown that people who engage in intimate self-disclosure are liked more than those who disclose nonintimately (see Collins & Miller, 1994, for a review). However, there are limits to this effect. For example, if someone we have just met discloses highly intimate information to us, we might feel uncomfortable and not be attracted to the person. Several studies have found that disclosures that are too intimate may, in fact, result in disliking for the discloser and a failure to reciprocate with equally intimate self-disclosure (Archer & Berg, 1978; Cozby, 1972; Rubin, 1975). A related point is that the timing of self-disclosure affects relationship development. According to the model, self-disclosure begins at a superficial level, and then progresses to more intimate topics. Thus, revealing too much too soon should have negative effects. Consistent with this hypothesis, there is evidence that a person is better liked when he or she discloses intimate information late, rather than early, in a conversation (Archer & Burelson, 1980; Wortman, Adesman, Herman, & Greenberg, 1976).

Finally, at the early stages of a relationship, when people have just met, it is important for disclosure to be reciprocal. In other words, if I reveal something personal about myself, then you should reciprocate and reveal something personal about yourself. Berg and Archer (1980) found evidence of greater liking when self-disclosure was reciprocated during a first encounter. Research by Davis (1976) suggests that reciprocity of disclosure during an initial encounter is not exactly mutual, however. In this study, the most disclosing partner of a same-sex pair set the tone, and the other person reciprocated. High disclosers did not match their partner's nonintimate disclosures. Finally, a positive relation between disclosure reciprocity and liking has been found for children as young as in Grade 6 (but not in Grades 2 or 4; Rotenberg & Mann, 1986). Given these findings, it is not surprising that people perceive greater reciprocity of disclosure during an interaction than actually was the case (Sprecher & Duck, 1994).

Reciprocity is important for the development of trust in a relationship (Altman, 1973). However, later on, once trust has been established, it should not be necessary for each partner to always reciprocate in kind. This idea was tested by Derlega, Wilson, and Chaikin (1976). Participants received notes, varying in the intimacy of disclosure, from a friend or stranger. Consistent with predictions, with a stranger, participants tended to reciprocate with disclosures of the same level of intimacy. With a friend, they maintained the same low to moderate level of intimacy, regardless of the intimacy of their friend's disclosure. These studies suggest that to get a relationship off the ground, reciprocity of disclosure is important. However, once a friendship is established, it is not necessary that intimate self-disclosures be reciprocated immediately.

Most of the studies reported so far have involved interactions between strangers in a laboratory setting or, as is frequently the case, with a fictional stranger (e.g., studies where participants pass and receive notes without any face-to-face interaction). Do people report following the same kind of sequencing of disclosure and self-revelation when initiating actual friendships? Apparently they do. Miell and Duck (1986) asked 37 new university students how they would gather information about a potential friend, decide whether or not to pursue a friendship, and restrict or intensify the rate of friendship development. Based on the students' responses, they were able to identify a "new partner script," which entailed two main processes: gathering information and delaying tactics. Gathering information included strategies such as asking questions, being responsive, reciprocating self-disclosures, and observing the person's behavior in various situations. Delaying tactics served to prevent the pitfalls associated with revealing too much about oneself too soon. These strategies included being polite and reserved, discussing only a limited range of topics, and not seeing the person too often. Both processes were operative when interacting with a potential friend. For example, if, based on the information gathered, a decision was made to pursue a friendship, then delaying tactics were reversed (i.e., participants reported that they discussed a wider range of topics, disclosed more intimately, and saw the other person frequently). The information-gathering process also continued, aimed at increasing both the depth and breadth of interaction.

❧ Convergence of Environmental, Individual, Situational, and Dyadic Factors

This chapter was introduced with the statement that for a friendship to begin, four kinds of factors must coalesce: environmental, individual, situational, and dyadic. So far, each of these factors has been discussed independently. The purpose of this section is to demonstrate the convergence of these factors in studies of friendship formation. Not all studies have included all of these classes of variables. However, when one considers studies on friendship formation in conjunction with one another, there is considerable evidence that environmental (e.g., proximity), individual (e.g., physical attractiveness), situational (e.g., availability), and dyadic (e.g., self-disclosure) factors all play a role in the process of making friends. This conclusion holds whether one examines prospective accounts, retrospective accounts, or studies of actual friendship formation.

Prospective Accounts

In Miell and Duck's (1986) study, new students on campus were asked what criteria they would use in deciding whether or not to develop a friendship with someone. Students reported that they would be more likely to pursue a friendship with someone who was available to be a friend, similar to them, easy to talk to, trustworthy, and easygoing.

Retrospective Accounts

Other researchers have asked people to focus on a current friendship and reflect on how it developed. Knapp and Harwood

(1977), for example, presented 500 men and women with 39 variables extracted from the friendship formation literature and asked them to rate the importance of each in the formation of an intimate same-sex friendship. These variables formed six clusters: proximity (of homes, ease of getting together, having the same friends), superficial similarity (e.g., physical attractiveness, age, education), personableness (e.g., being considerate, courteous, understanding), attitudinal similarity (including similar personalities), intimate accessibility (e.g., willingness to spend time together, expectation of being liked), and reciprocal candor (feeling free to talk about anything, honesty). The last three clusters were regarded as the most critical in friendship formation.

In a study along the same lines, 100 adults in a weekend adult-education seminar were asked to describe an experience of " 'falling in friendship'—some experience in which you went from not knowing or caring much about a person to a very strong positive feeling towards the person" (Aron, Dutton, Aron, & Iverson, 1989, p. 248). These accounts were coded for the presence of 11 variables drawn from the attraction literature. Reciprocal liking, desirable characteristics (e.g., physical attractiveness), similarity, and propinquity (proximity) were mentioned most often (by 42% to 46% of respondents). Similar findings were obtained when university students provided "falling in friendship" accounts.

Studies of Actual Friendship Formation

There are basically two types of studies on actual friendship formation: observational and self-report. The development of children's friendships is often investigated via observational methods. In contrast, research with adults usually relies on the participants' ability to provide verbal or written assessments of their relationship with a new friend.

Friendship Formation in Children

Gottman (1983) audiotaped the conversations of pairs of unacquainted children (ages 3 to 9) during three play sessions in one child's home. Later, the mothers answered a questionnaire about the children's relationship. The best predictor of progression to friendship was the proportion of agreement expressed by the guest child. A second group of children was audiotaped while playing with a best friend and with a stranger. Proportion of agreement also distinguished friends from strangers (with higher levels of agreement among friends). Based on the content of the tapes, Gottman identified seven conversation processes as potential predictors of friendship formation: communication clarity and connectedness, information exchange, exploration of similarities and differences, establishment of common-ground play activities, resolution of conflict, positive reciprocity, and self-disclosure. All of these conversational processes were found to predict friendship formation, although some were more important at certain stages of friendship than others. For example, in the first meeting it was important to interact with one another in a low-conflict and connected fashion in order to exchange information and establish common-ground activity.

Parker (1986) designed an experimental study to investigate the role of Gottman's conversational processes in friendship formation. Children (ages 4 and 5) interacted with a talking doll. The doll's voice was produced by a confederate who acted either skilled or unskilled in these processes (e.g., reciprocating vs. not reciprocating the child's self-disclosure). Children who interacted with a doll who was skilled in these conversational processes were more likely to hit it off with the doll (e.g., they chose to play with the doll again later, reported to their parents that they liked the doll). Parker concluded that these conversational processes played a causal role in friendship formation.

Friendship Formation in College Students

A number of studies have charted the course of friendship development between previously unacquainted roommates in dormitory residences. Dyadic-level factors tend to be emphasized in this research. Berg (1984), for example, studied the relationships of same-sex roommates 2 weeks after classes began and again 6 months later. Satisfaction with the living arrangement and liking for the roommate were positively correlated with self-disclosure, equity, and general rewards, and negatively correlated with dissimilarity and availability of alternatives. The latter three variables were the strongest predictors of satisfaction and liking at both times.

Hays (1985; see also Hays, 1984) also focused on dyadic variables, although other kinds of factors received some consideration. In this research, university students completed a questionnaire on multiple occasions during their first year on campus. An environmental factor, residential proximity, was positively correlated with friendship development; an individual-level variable, shyness, showed a weak, negative relation. There was some evidence that the situational factor of availability influenced the development of friendship. For example, interaction with friends decreased over the semester, as academic demands presumably increased. Also, improvements in the convenience of getting together (due to schedule changes) were positively correlated with friendship development. At the dyadic level, the relationships were rated in terms of the degree of intimacy in four global categories: companionship (e.g., sharing an activity or experience), consideration (helping, providing goods, services, or support), communication (self-disclosure, exchanging ideas and opinions), and affection (expressing one's feelings toward the other). Consistent with social penetration theory, the friendships that had become the closest were characterized by increases in breadth (i.e., the number of items in each category that were endorsed) and depth (higher intimacy ratings) over the course of the year.

The results of these studies, taken together, suggest that friendship formation involves a convergence of environmental, individual, situational, and dyadic factors. This research underscores the complexity and multifaceted nature of the process of developing a friendship.

➤ Summary

A necessary first step for the development of most friendships is that two people's paths must cross. This is more likely to occur if the two people live near one another (e.g., same neighborhood, same building, same floor, same room) than if they do not. Living in a city or, more important, sharing the same work or school environment also increases the likelihood of contact. People who know people also are more likely to become friends. The probability that two individuals will meet increases to the extent that their social networks overlap.

Once two people meet, whether or not they decide to pursue a friendship depends on several additional factors. At the individual level, each scrutinizes the other for evidence of disliked qualities or other characteristics that may make him or her unsuitable as a friend. If these exclusion tests are passed, then inclusion tests will follow. It is likely that a friendship will be sought if each perceives the other as attractive, socially skilled, responsive, not shy, and if the two people are similar in a variety of ways.

If both exclusion and inclusion tests are passed, one might think that a friendship would be inevitable. However, situational factors influence whether or not a friendship actually is formed. Research on these factors suggests that two people are more likely to develop a friendship if they anticipate ongoing interactions, if they are dependent on one another, if they see one another frequently, and if each person's "friendship dance card" still has some room on it.

Finally, the likelihood of friendship formation depends on dyadic variables such as whether the two people like one another and whether there is an appropriate sequencing of the depth and breadth of self-disclosure. Given the myriad factors that must coalesce, it seems remarkable that people are able to form friendships at all!

4

Achieving Closeness

You can probably remember times in your life when you were a
stranger to everyone around you; perhaps as a "new kid" in
school, your first meeting when you joined a club, or your first
day on a new job. You longed to get over the stranger stage so
you could be included in the apparently effortless and friendly
interaction around you. And gradually it happened, the new-
ness wore off, you became more familiar with the others and felt
included in their activities and conversations. By some unspo-
ken mutual agreement, you grew particularly close to a few of
them, and you became friends.

—Wilmot and Shellen (1990, p. 414)

Some relationships develop from acquaintanceships to casual
friendships; some casual friendships develop into close friendships or even best friendships. One way of trying to understand
the process of becoming close to another person is to compare
these various kinds of relationships. If we find, for example, that
people rarely talk about personal information at the acquaintance

stage but disclose more at the casual friendship stage and even more at the best friend stage, then we might surmise that one way in which closeness is achieved is through increasing levels of intimate self-disclosure. Of course, one must be careful in drawing such conclusions on the basis of cross-sectional studies. It is also necessary to conduct longitudinal research to determine whether the same people disclose more as they progress from acquaintanceship through to close friendship. In this chapter, findings from both cross-sectional and longitudinal studies are relied on to identify the factors associated with achieving closeness in friendships.

The characteristics of relationships with strangers versus friends are compared first, followed by acquaintances versus friends, through to comparisons of close friends versus best friends. By far the greatest number of studies has compared acquaintances with friends. Differences between these types of relationships usually are explored in three domains: interaction patterns, self-disclosure, and similarity.

❧ Strangers Versus Friends

Interaction Differences

Differences in interactions between friends and strangers (i.e., people who were unacquainted prior to the interaction) have been observed from infancy onward. Table 4.1 summarizes the findings from a number of studies. The results of these studies show that, in general, friends are more intensely engaged with one another. This includes both verbal and nonverbal interaction. For example, most studies report that friends spend more time talking to one another than do strangers. Duck et al.'s (1991) studies show that communication between friends also is regarded as higher in quality. Furthermore, when friends interact with one another, there is greater proximity, touching, and body contact.

In some of the studies presented in Table 4.1, friends also looked at one another more, whereas in other studies they did not differ from strangers in this regard. Presumably, looking can take on

Table 4.1 Interaction Differences: Friends Versus Strangers

Study	Participants	Friends	Strangers	No Difference
Lewis, Young, Brooks, and Michalson (1975, Study 2)	Infants	• More imitation • More gesturing (boys) • Greater proximity, touch, body contact • More positive social activities when playing with toys (e.g., sharing)	• More gesturing (girls) • More negative affect	• Vocalizations • Looking time • Negative proximity (hitting, pushing) • Positive affect • Negative activities when playing with toys (e.g., taking)
Gottman (1983)	Children (ages 2-6) (Study 1)	• Greater agreement expressed		
	Children (ages 3-9) (Study 2)	• Greater disagreement expressed		
Jormakka (1976)	Children (ages 5 and 6)	• Greater exploration of environment • More representational play • More laughing • More talking • More negative reactions such as criticism and blame	• More tense • More "sizing up" other child • More looking at other • Greater gaze avoidance • More stationary • More automanipulation • More personal questions when talking occurred (girls)	

			Conflict
Foot, Chapman, and Smith (1977)	Children (ages 7 and 8) (Study 1)	• More touching • More smiling and laughing • More looking • More talking • Greater mutuality of above behaviors	
	Children (ages 7 and 8) (Study 2)	• More smiling and laughing • More looking • More talking • Greater mutuality of above behaviors	
Duck, Rutt, Hurst, and Strejc (1991)	University students (Study 1)	• Higher communication quality • Higher value of interaction for the future of the relationship • Greater mutual control	• Greater change brought about by the interaction • Greater variability in ratings of the interaction
	University students (Study 2)	• Higher communication quality • Higher value of interaction	Control of interaction • Greater change • More conflict • Greater variability in ratings

different meanings, depending on the context. For example, Jormakka (1976) reported that when children were placed in a novel situation with another child, they looked at the child more if she or he was a stranger as opposed to a friend. In this situation, looking seemed to take the form of scrutinizing the other. At the same time, the children resisted scrutiny by avoiding the other child's gaze. In contrast, in a study such as Foot, Chapman, and Smith's (1977), where children were watching cartoons, the greater looking on the part of friends seemed to indicate greater social responsiveness. This interpretation is underscored by the finding that looking was mutually reciprocal between friends.

The interactions of friends are also characterized by positive behavioral expressions such as smiling and laughing. This result does not imply that affect is uniformly positive, however. Gottman (1983) found that children who were friends both agreed and disagreed with one another (although degree of agreement was a stronger predictor of friendship formation). Similarly, Jormakka (1976) reported that the greater amount of talking among friends also included a higher incidence of negative reactions such as criticism and blame. Thus, one might conclude that friendships are affectively richer than relationships between strangers, encompassing both positive and negative feelings.

❧ Acquaintances Versus Friends

Interaction Differences

Studies that have examined interaction differences between acquaintances and friends are summarized in Table 4.2. In the first set of studies, acquaintances and friends were compared along several global dimensions (e.g., positive or negative behavior). The next set focuses on interaction differences in the context of task performance. The final studies deal with prosocial interactions, particularly patterns of sharing between friends versus acquaintances.

Before summarizing the findings, the variety of methodologies and participant groups used in these studies deserves mention.

Table 4.2 Interaction Differences: Friends Versus Acquaintances

Study	Participants	Friends	Acquaintances	No Difference
Hindy (1980)	Children (Grades 1-8)	• Greater perceived cohesiveness, especially among girls	Perceived as less likely to withstand threats to the relationship	
Rotenberg (1986)	Children (Grade 4)	• More frequent secrets • Greater trust • Higher proportion of secrets kept • Higher proportion of promises kept		Number of promises made

Berndt and Perry (1986)	Children (Grades 2, 4, 6, 8)	• More positive comments about other
		• Higher ratings of supportiveness in interactions for:
		  play/association
		  prosocial behavior (e.g., sharing)
		  intimacy (e.g., talking about problems)
		  loyalty
		  attachment
		  self-esteem enhancement
		  absence of conflicts
			More negative comments about other	

(continued)

Table 4.2 (Continued)

Study	Participants	Friends	Acquaintances	No Difference
Lederberg, Rosenblatt, Vandell, and Chapin (1987)	Hearing and deaf children (ages 3-5)	• Greater reciprocity (among hearing children) of: language behavior play initiation positive behavior	• More negative behaviors • Greater reciprocity of negative behaviors	• Language behavior • Success at initiating play • Positive behavior
Howes (1983)	Infants, toddlers, preschoolers Emotionally disturbed toddlers and preschoolers	• Greater success at initiating interactions • Increased number of elaborated exchanges • More time in complementary and reciprocal play • More time in positive, affective exchanges • Increase in frequency of vocalizations		• Agonistic interactions • Frequency of object exchanges (e.g., toys)
Duck, Rutt, Hurst, and Strejc (1991)	University students (Study 1)	• Higher value of interaction for the future of the relationship	• Greater change brought about by the interaction • More conflict	• Communication quality • Mutual control • Variability in ratings of the interaction

Study	Sample	Findings	
	University students (Study 2)	• Greater change brought about by the interaction	• Value of interaction • Communication quality • Mutual control • Conflict • Variability of ratings
Newcomb and Brady (1982)	Boys (Grades 2 and 6)	• Superior task performance • Greater synchrony of task-related behaviors • More mutual crediting of discoveries • Greater mutuality of communicative exchanges • More talking • More smiling and laughing • More looking • More touching • Greater matching of other's affective expressions	
Sharabany and Hertz-Lazarowitz (1981)	Children (K, Grade 1)	• Superior task performance • Less exchange of supplies • Less looking • Less smiling • Less talking	

(continued)

Table 4.2 (Continued)

Study	Participants	Friends	Acquaintances	No Difference
Birch and Billman (1986)	Children (ages 3-5)	• Greater overall sharing (girls) • Greater sharing of preferred snacks • Greater sharing of non-preferred snacks (girls) • More successful at eliciting sharing from other • More attempts made to take food from other	• Greater "dumping" of nonpreferred snacks (boys)	• Overall sharing (boys) • Success of attempts to take food from other
Berndt (1981)	Children (K, Grades 2 and 4)	• Greater intention to share, help (girls) • Less sharing of crayons in a competitive situation (boys) • More likely to deny requests for crayons (boys)		• Intention to share, help (boys) • Personal and social norms (e.g., how much you *should* share with others) • Sharing crayons in a competitive situation (girls)
Jones (1985)	Children (K, Grades 2 and 4)	• More successful in appeals for a crayon • More expanded refusals when appeals denied • The relationship was the basis for sharing		• Number of appeals made for crayon

These approaches provide different, but complementary, perspectives on the interactions of friends and acquaintances. For example, in Hindy's (1980) study, children were presented with cartoon characters who were described either as acquaintances or best friends. The cartoons depicted various events that threatened the relationship between the two characters. Variables such as perceived cohesiveness were assessed by asking the children whether the cartoon characters would play together again tomorrow.

By far the most common methodology is to ask participants questions about the nature of their interactions with an acquaintance and/or friend. This technique was used by Berndt and Perry (1986), for example, who assessed children's perceptions of supportiveness in their interactions with friends versus acquaintances. Although such studies offer useful information, they do not tell us whether friends actually are more prosocial in their interactions with one another than acquaintances. However, observational research can answer this question. For instance, Birch and Billman (1986) assessed children's preferences for a variety of snacks, ranging from M&Ms® to raw broccoli. One week later, potential sharers received their most and least preferred snacks and were given an opportunity to share with a friend and an acquaintance. This methodology uncovered a number of interesting findings, such as that girls were more likely to share all snacks with friends. Boys shared preferred snacks with friends and were quite willing to share nonpreferred snacks by dumping them onto the plate of a protesting acquaintance!

The methodologies of assessing perceptions as well as actual interactions were successfully combined by Berndt (1981). This study is important because it revealed that children verbally subscribed to the prosocial norm of sharing in both kinds of relationships. For example, the children believed that they should let another child ride their bikes, regardless of whether he or she was a best friend or an acquaintance. However, when asked about behavioral intentions, girls expressed greater willingness to share with friends than acquaintances, whereas boys did not differentiate between the two kinds of relationships. In the observation phase, these attitudes were put to the test by promising the children a monetary reward, depending on how much they colored.

Sharing certain crayons that were in demand meant more rewards for the other and fewer for oneself. In this situation, girls shared equally with friends and acquaintances. However, boys became competitive with their friends and shared less with them than with acquaintances. These behaviors would not have been predicted based on the children's earlier self-reports.

Some studies have compared the interactions of friends and acquaintances while performing tasks. Newcomb and Brady (1982) attributed friends' superior performance on a problem-solving task to the greater responsiveness and mutual exchange that characterized their interactions. For example, friends shared more task-related information through discussion, attended to their partner's monologues, and issued and complied with a greater number of mutually oriented commands. Sharabany and Hertz-Lazarowitz (1981) gave children in Israel various supplies to produce a drawing. Contrary to expectations, friends exchanged fewer communicative behaviors such as looks, smiles, and talking. In fact, friends talked only half as much as nonfriends (acquaintances), and most of it was related to task performance. The authors suggest that friends were free to focus on the task at hand because of their history of common activities and established level of intimacy. Thus, their relationship facilitated working together effectively. In contrast, nonfriends had to invest time in social communication so that they could establish rapport and learn to coordinate their efforts.

The research by Duck et al. (1991) bears some similarities to the studies on actual interactions of acquaintances and friends. The primary difference is that the participants themselves, rather than observers, rated interactions along a number of dimensions immediately after they occured (see Table 4.2). In this research, interactions with acquaintances tended to differ only from interactions with a "best friend," not a "friend."

Finally, all of the studies described so far are cross-sectional studies in which groups of friends and acquaintances were compared. However, the most definitive answers to questions about the process of becoming close are provided by the labor-intensive methodology of tracking relationships as they develop from acquaintanceship to friendship. Two such studies are presented in

Table 4.2 (Howes, 1983; Lederberg, Rosenblatt, Vandell, & Chapin, 1987). These studies are especially ambitious because both also included groups of special-needs children as participants. For example, Howes (1983) examined friendship patterns among infants, toddlers, and preschoolers in community-based child care facilities and among toddlers and preschoolers in outpatient programs for emotionally disturbed children. At the beginning of the study, all of the children were unacquainted. They were observed on six occasions over a 1-year period and classified into one of three categories: nonfriends, sporadic friends, and maintained friends. Although the specific findings are presented in Table 4.2, overall, the interactions of friends were found to be more complex than those of nonfriends. In fact, the greatest increase in complexity of interaction was observed in maintained friendships. By the last testing session, among maintained friends, virtually all attempts to initiate interactions were successful. These children were able to smoothly develop a play sequence, whereas nonfriends were still spending time negotiating whether or not a play sequence would occur. Emotionally disturbed children formed fewer friendships than the other children, and all of these friendships were sporadic.

Summary

The results from research using these disparate methodologies and participant groups show a remarkable degree of convergence. First, an examination of Table 4.2 reveals that comparisons between acquaintances and friends appear similar to comparisons between strangers and friends (Table 4.1) in many ways. Friends are more fully and more happily engaged in their interactions with one another relative to acquaintances. Most studies reported greater looking, talking, smiling, and laughing among friendship pairs. The exception was Sharabany and Hertz-Lazarowitz's (1981) study in which social interaction was minimal when friends were concentrating on jointly performing a task.

Greater positivity was associated with friends than acquaintances. For example, Berndt and Perry (1986) found that children made more positive comments about their friends and more negative comments about their acquaintances. Howes (1983) reported that the incidence of positive, affective exchanges was higher among friends, and Lederberg et al. (1987) observed greater reciprocity of positive behaviors in friendships.

Although children are generally more prosocial in interactions with friends than acquaintances (see also Price & Ladd, 1986), Berndt's study suggests that at least among young boys, situational factors (i.e., inducing competition) may temporarily override these effects. This tendency has surfaced in other research with boys in Grades 3 to 5 (Berndt, Hawkins, & Hoyle, 1986; Staub & Noerenberg, 1981) but reverses by Grade 8 (Berndt et al., 1986). Thus, in middle childhood, prosocial behavior may wane somewhat in situations where a friend's gain can mean one's own loss. Overall, however, children—especially girls—intended to share, and actually did share, more with friends than acquaintances.

The studies of sharing also showed that friends usually were more successful at eliciting sharing from one another than were acquaintances (e.g., Birch & Billman, 1986; Jones, 1985). Moreover, in Jones's study, when appeals for a desired commodity were unsuccessful, friends still were treated more favorably in that they were granted a fuller explanation for the negative decision; acquaintances were more likely to receive a terse "no."

Finally, the studies reviewed show that friends are better able to coordinate and synchronize their efforts to achieve desired goals. For example, several studies found that friends were more successful in their attempts to initiate and sustain reciprocal play (e.g., Howes, 1983; Lederberg et al., 1987). In addition, the studies by Newcomb and Brady (1982) and Sharabany and Hertz-Lazarowitz (1981) demonstrated that friends show superior performance on task-related activities.

Self-Disclosure

In the previous two chapters, Altman and Taylor's social penetration model was mentioned. In short, as a relationship progresses, the breadth and the depth of self-disclosure increases. Knapp (e.g., 1978, 1984; Knapp, Ellis, & Williams, 1980) elaborated on this theory by delineating eight communication dimensions along which intimate and nonintimate relationships can be differentiated. These include depth and breadth of interaction, along with other interaction properties such as uniqueness, flexibility, spontaneity, smoothness, and so on. In a study by Knapp et al., more than 1,000 individuals, ranging in age from 12 to over 65, rated the extent to which these communication dimensions applied to various types of relationships. The ratings were factor analyzed, resulting in three factors labeled *personalized communication* (depth of self-disclosure, uniqueness, flexibility), *synchronized communication* (coordination and smoothness of communication, spontaneity), and *difficult communication* (barriers to communication, strained, awkward interactions). Acquaintance relationships were rated lower on the first two factors than friend or best friend relationships. The relationships received similar ratings on the difficult communication factor.

Most research on actual relationships has focused on the aspects of self-disclosure captured by Knapp et al.'s personalized communication factor. As will be seen, consistent with the perceptions of Knapp et al.'s participants, researchers typically find that friends disclose more personal, or intimate, information to each other than do acquaintances.

Content of Self-Disclosure

Differential disclosure to friends versus acquaintances is evident even among young children. For example, in a study by Rotenberg and Sliz (1988), children in kindergarten, Grade 2, and Grade 4 received a list of highly personal or nonpersonal topics and were asked to make a tape recording for two classmates—one who was a good friend and one who was not. Across grades, disclosure of high personal topics was greater to friends than to nonfriends (acquaintances). However, for low personal topics, approximately the same number of disclosures was made to each child. Thus, greater disclosure of highly personal information to friends was already apparent at kindergarten age. The different pattern of findings for high and low personal topics suggests that the transition from acquaintanceship to friendship is characterized by both qualitative and quantitative changes in self-disclosure.

The majority of studies on self-disclosure to acquaintances versus friends has been conducted with university students. Rubin and Shenker (1978) targeted pairs of dormitory roommates and hallmates (same floor, but not same room). Participants were given items varying in intimacy of self-disclosure and rated how much they had revealed to the other person. As predicted, there was greater disclosure among roommate than hallmate pairs, although generally disclosures tended to be fairly superficial (e.g., one's tastes). Analyses also were performed comparing dyads who did and did not consider themselves to be close friends. Again, the greatest amount of disclosure occurred for the less intimate topics of tastes and attitudes. However, within each domain, close friends disclosed more than nonclose friends. This difference was most pronounced for intimate topics: interpersonal (e.g., relationships) and sex. There also was an interaction with gender such that relation between intimacy of self-disclosure and closeness of friendship was stronger for women than for men. The authors posit a reciprocal causal relation between intimate self-disclosure and closeness: "People may be more likely to reveal intimate matters to their close friends than to less close friends, and they may come to be closer friends . . . as a result of intimate revelations" (Rubin & Shenker, 1978, p. 17).

Rubin and Shenker's findings again provide evidence that not only the quantity, but also the quality, of self-disclosure separates friends from acquaintances. A series of studies by Hornstein and Truesdell point to the same conclusion. In their first study (Hornstein & Truesdell, 1988), the telephone conversations of 10 female college students were recorded. The content of disclosures to strangers, acquaintances, and close friends was analyzed using a fourfold classification based on high or low descriptive intimacy (disclosing personal information about oneself) and high or low evaluative intimacy (disclosing personal, intense feelings and judgments). Friends scored higher than the other two groups in high descriptive/high evaluative intimacy. Conversely, the disclosures of strangers and acquaintances were more likely to be low on both dimensions. However, both friends and acquaintances were significantly more likely than strangers to engage in low descriptive/high evaluative disclosures. Thus, acquaintances resembled strangers in that they did not use descriptive disclosures but were similar to friends in that they used evaluative disclosures, at least when discussing nonpersonal topics.

In a subsequent study, pairs of female friends and acquaintances had three conversations at monthly intervals. Friends engaged in more high descriptive/high evaluative and high descriptive/low evaluative disclosure; acquaintances used significantly more low descriptive/high evaluative disclosures. Contrary to predictions, the conversations of the acquainted pairs did not become more intimate over time.

A study of self-disclosure in conversations between cross-sex friends and acquaintances was conducted by Won-Doornink (1985). Data were gathered in two countries—Korea, where cross-sex interaction between adults is discouraged, and the United States, where cross-sex interaction is accepted. In both countries, nonintimate self-disclosure was highest among early acquaintances. Intimate self-disclosure was most common for middle acquaintances (known for 3 months to a year), whereas best friends engaged in medium-intimate disclosures. Thus, a curvilinear relation was found between stage of the friendship and intimacy of self-disclosure, with the greatest intimacy at the middle stage.

Finally, the results of longitudinal research (Hays, 1984, 1985) tracing the development of friendships among first-year university students corroborate the findings from these studies. Hays found that for all pairs, there was more casual and superficial, than intimate, self-disclosure. Dyads who progressed from acquaintanceship to close friends exchanged more information in all categories than dyads who did not. However, this difference was most pronounced for intimate topics.

Structure of Self-Disclosure

So far, the focus has been on the *content* of self-disclosure between friends and acquaintances. Hornstein (1985) examined the *structure* of the telephone conversations recorded by Hornstein and Truesdell (1988). She found that friends used highly implicit opening sequences (e.g., "Hi, it's me"), whereas strangers used explicit opening sequences. Acquaintances showed an intermediate pattern—wanting to recognize, but not exaggerate, the familiarity that existed. Friends initiated many more topics (reflecting greater breadth of self-disclosure), asked more questions, and made more minimal responses (hmms, yeahs, etc.) than either strangers or acquaintances. Thus, friends engaged in more behaviors to continue and sustain the conversation.

For stranger and acquaintance conversations, the person who initiated the call also initiated its ending. This was less true for friends, who also took longer to terminate calls. Hornstein comments that the style of closing mirrored the purpose of the conversation. Strangers typically called to give or receive specific information, whereas friends generally called just to chat. Hence, it was less clear when the call actually should end—each had to be careful not to end the conversation before the other had sufficient opportunity to say all she wanted. Generally, acquaintances were more similar to strangers than friends, which again implies that "when a relationship becomes a friendship, it undergoes a qualitative and not simply a quantitative transformation from a nonintimate to an intimate relation" (Hornstein, 1985, p. 680).

Using Self-Disclosure to Differentiate
Acquaintances From Friends

The findings from the research discussed so far suggest that it should be possible to distinguish between friends and acquaintances based on the content of their disclosures. Planalp and Benson (1992) tested this hypothesis by asking students in a communication class to record a conversation with a friend or an acquaintance. Other students then listened to the tapes and tried to identify the kind of relationship. They were able to do so with remarkable accuracy—approximately 80% of the conversations were correctly classified. The most common basis on which the students discriminated between acquaintances and friends was the greater mutual knowledge exhibited by friends, including demographic information; knowledge of one another's schedules, plans, and activities; and shared knowledge of other people, places, and events. (The importance of this variable for differentiating between these relationships was underscored in a subsequent analysis of these tapes by Planalp, 1993.) The second most common basis for making discriminations was the intimacy of conversations—friends' conversations were more intimate, emotional, detailed, and involved greater self-disclosure on a greater number of topics (i.e., greater breadth). Acquaintances tended to exchange shallow, frequently demographic, information.

The conversations differed in a number of other ways. Friends were more likely to criticize and disagree with one another than were acquaintances. However, friends also seemed more involved, interested, and laughed more. When friends used pronouns such as "we," it was usually with reference to the other person; acquaintances used such pronouns to refer to someone other than their conversation partner. Planalp and Benson note that "in these ways, friends indicated that they considered themselves a social unit; acquaintances indicated they had unit relationships with other people" (p. 502). They concluded that their findings support Altman and Taylor's model as well as Knapp's extension of it.

Summary

The findings of the studies reviewed support Altman and Taylor's model; the self-disclosure of friends is characterized by greater breadth and depth than the self-disclosure of acquaintances. Knapp's prediction that this would take the form of increased personal, intimate communication also was confirmed. The greater intimacy of friends' disclosure should not be taken to mean that friends do nothing but disclose intimate, personal information. Studies by Hays (1984, 1985), Rubin and Shenker (1978), and others (e.g., Altman & Haythorn, 1965; Duck & Miell, 1986; Duck et al., 1991) have shown that both friends and acquaintances do the bulk of their disclosing in nonintimate areas. In fact, Rubin and Shenker found that friends disclosed even more than acquaintances in nonintimate areas, although other studies have reported either no difference or greater disclosure of nonintimate information among acquaintances (e.g., Hornstein & Truesdell, 1988; Rotenberg & Sliz, 1988; Won-Doornink, 1985). Although this issue remains unresolved, there is a clear bottom line regarding disclosure of personal, intimate self-disclosure: Friends do it more than acquaintances do it.

Fun and Relaxation

The importance of fun and relaxation as indicators of closeness in friendships has not received much attention. However, in Planalp and Benson's (1992) study, when students described the basis on which they discriminated between friends' and acquaintances' conversations, two unexpected dimensions emerged: Friends were more relaxed, casual, and friendly than acquaintances and were more likely to use informal language such as slang, joking, and teasing. Acquaintances tended to be more polite and formal. Knapp et al.'s (1980) synchronized communication factor included an item "Our conversations are spontaneous, informal and relaxed." Consistent with Planalp and Benson's findings, friends received higher ratings on this dimension than did acquaintances.

Brenton (1974) commented that relaxed, spontaneous behavior is a sign that a relationship has progressed from an acquaintanceship to a friendship. Similarly, Swain (1989) observed that the male university students he interviewed "used the degree of comfort and relaxation experienced with men friends as an indicator of closeness" (p. 75).

In a study of a female friendship group (dubbed the "Tremendous Ten"), Jerrome (1984) was struck by the amount of joking, laughing, and giggling that characterized their interactions. The opportunity to "let down your hair" with friends in the group was highly valued by these middle-aged and older women. Recently, Jones (1991) reported that the amount of fun and enjoyment experienced was one of the strongest predictors of friendship satisfaction for both women and men. She concluded that "regardless of sex, having fun with friends and revealing personal information and feelings to friends heightens the sense of satisfaction with friendships" (p. 180). Jones's findings are confirmed by longitudinal research. Hays and Oxley (1986) reported that among new students, the amount of fun and relaxation experienced was one of the strongest predictors of relationship intimacy and adaptation to university life. When pulled together, these scattered findings suggest that fun and relaxation are more characteristic of friend-ships than acquaintance relationships.

Similarity

Early research on the relation between similarity and attraction focused on attitude similarity (see Byrne, 1971, for a review). Byrne's program of research revealed that we are more attracted to a stranger whose attitudes are similar rather than dissimilar to our own (see Chapter 2). Although this work has not been without its critics (e.g., Kaplan & Anderson, 1973; Rosenbaum, 1986), Byrne's paradigm and findings continue to be influential. Since Byrne's pioneering work, research in this area has reached beyond the domain of attitudes to examine the relation between other kinds of similarity and attraction. In addition, the issue of whether different kinds of similarity characterize relationships at different stages has been raised. The causal relation between similarity and attraction has received some attention in later investigations.

What Kind of Similarity?

In extending Byrne's work on attitude similarity, researchers have focused on similarity in terms of personality, values, social skills, and personal constructs (the kinds of categories one uses to describe other people). Table 4.3 presents a sampling of research in each of these areas. Some researchers have followed the Byrne tradition and tested whether similarity in a particular domain is associated with greater attraction (or liking, or deciding to con-tinue a relationship). Others have compared whether friends are more similar than acquaintances (nonfriends) in a given domain.

As the table shows, there is little evidence of attraction or friend-ship on the basis of personality similarity. (This is also the case with dating and marital partners; see Brehm, 1985.) However, the personal construct studies show that people who view the world in the same way are more likely to be attracted to one another and form a friendship. There also is some evidence that those who have similar values show greater attraction and friendship. However, the strength of these effects seem to vary, depending on the stage

Table 4.3 Relation Between Similarity and Friendship

Type of Similarity	Study	Participants	Results
Personality	Curry and Kenny (1974)	8-person groups of college residents, initially unacquainted	No relationship between personality similarity and attraction over time
	Feinberg, Miller, and Ross (1981)	Best friend pairs (college students)	Participants perceived themselves as similar to friend in terms of locus of control, but no evidence of actual similarity
Personal constructs	Duck (1973b)	Reciprocated and nominal (non) friendship pairs (trainee teachers living in residence)	Personal constructs of reciprocated friend pairs were more similar than those of nominal pairs
			Perceived construct similarity was greater than actual similarity for reciprocated friend pairs
	Erwin (1985)	Reciprocated and nominal friendship pairs (children ages 7-10)	Personal constructs of reciprocated friend pairs were more similar than those of nominal pairs
	Neimeyer and Neimeyer (1981)	10-person groups of college students, initially unacquainted	Dyads high in functional similarity (i.e., who applied constructs in a similar way when rating other group members) were more attracted to one another than dyads low in functional similarity

	Neimeyer and Neimeyer (1983)	10-person groups of adults arrested for drunken driving, initially unacquainted	Dyads high in structural similarity (i.e., who showed similar differentiation/organization of personal constructs when rating group members) were more attracted to one another than medium- or low-similarity dyads (when tested after 18 weeks of interaction; these effects were not evident after 4 weeks)
Values	Hill and Stull (1981)	College roommate pairs	Female pairs who chose each other as roommates were more similar than those who were assigned to one another
			Among pairs who chose one another, value similarity assessed in the fall was correlated with liking in the fall and in the spring
			Roommates (chosen and assigned) high in value similarity were more likely to remain roommates
			None of these effects were significant for male pairs
	Curry and Kenny (1974)	8-person groups of college residents	Both actual and perceived value similarity were correlated with attraction over time

(continued)

Table 4.3 (Continued)

Type of Similarity	Study	Participants	Results
			Perceived value similarity had greatest effect on attraction early on; actual similarity assumed greater importance in later interactions
Cognitive complexity	Burleson, Kunkel, and Birch (1994, Study 1)	College students	Some evidence that participants were more attracted to a hypothetical target person who was similar versus dissimilar to them in cognitive complexity
Social skills	Burleson (1994)	Children (Grades 1 and 3)	Some evidence that children were more attracted to peers who were similar versus dissimilar to them in terms of social skills (especially skills reflecting emotional sensitivity and responsiveness)
Communication skills	Burleson, Samter, and Lucchetti (1992, Study 1)	Best friend pairs (college students)	Friends were more similar than nonfriends in terms of the importance assigned to various communication skills (e.g., comforting, conflict management, ego support)
	Study 2	Reciprocated and nominal friend pairs (undergraduate residents of fraternities and sororities)	Generally, degree of similarity in perceived importance of various communication skills did not vary as a function of length of relationship
Pattern of findings similar to Study 1 (although somewhat weaker)

of the relationship. This issue will be discussed in greater detail later. The program of research by Burleson and his colleagues provides some support for the hypothesis that people are more likely to be attracted to and form a friendship with someone who is similar to them in terms of social skills, communication skills, and so on.

Rather than focus on a particular domain, some researchers have assessed similarity in multiple areas in order to identify where similarity effects are strongest. A selection of these multiple measures studies is presented in Table 4.4. As the table shows, children, adolescents, and adults have friends who are similar to them in terms of demographic characteristics such as age. (Hill and Stull's 1981 study is an exception, but the age range in their sample of college roommates was very limited.) There also is evidence that friends are more similar than acquaintances in terms of education and academic standing. In an article on adolescents' friendships, Berndt (1982) underscored the importance of similarity in attitudes toward school. For example, if one person believes it is important to work on a homework assignment but the other insists they go to a shopping mall, it will be difficult to sustain the friendship. Among college students, Berg (1984) found that those who did not want to continue living with their roommates perceived greater dissimilarity in their orientation to university life (e.g., emphasis on studying vs. social activities) compared to those who wished to remain roommates. On a related note, the research presented in Table 4.4 shows that friends also are more likely to be similar than acquaintances in terms of activity preferences.

The findings for similarity in political views, religion, and economic status are somewhat mixed, perhaps in part because the studies that examined these issues used very different methodologies (e.g., attraction to a hypothetical person [Davis, 1981] vs. comparisons among one's three closest friends [Verbrugge, 1977]). In a study of women's friendships, Oliker (1989) reported that similar economic status and religion were less important than similar employment status and life stage (e.g., parenthood) because the latter "powerfully shape the experiences of personal life that women best friends talk about" (p. 89).

Table 4.4 Relation Between Similarity and Friendship: Multiple Measures

Study	Participants	Results
Johnson (1989)	Middle-class adults and two of their close friends, two acquaintances, and two non-friends	*Similarity* • Nonfriends were less similar than acquaintances and friends in terms of income, parental status, age • Nonfriends were more similar than acquaintances and friends in terms of leisure activities • Close friends were more similar than acquaintances in terms of education and hobbies • Close friends were less similar than acquaintances in terms of participation in sports, residential proximity, and income *Attraction* (when asked what attracted them to the other person) • "Similar values and interests" mentioned most frequently for all groups followed by "friendly and pleasant" but rate of endorsement highest for close friends • Friends mentioned physical appearance, residential proximity, and work together less often than acquaintances and nonfriends • Acquaintances mentioned residential proximity and work together more often than friends or nonfriends • Nonfriends mentioned physical appearance more often than acquaintances or friends
Lederberg, Rosenblatt, Vandell, and Chapin (1987)	Hearing and deaf children (ages 3-5)	Long-term friends were more similar in age than acquaintances Temporary and long-term friends were more similar in terms of ethnicity and gender than acquaintances

Kandel (1978a)	Reciprocated best friend pairs (ages 13–18)	Friends were most similar in terms of demographic variables (gender, race, age, grade in school) and drug use
		Lowest similarity between friends was found for psychological states (e.g., isolation), quality of relationship with parents, and attitudes (e.g., toward parents, occupational values)
		Among the set of attitudes, strongest similarity effects were found for attitudes toward drug use
Hill and Stull (1981)	Same-sex college roommates	Roommates who chose one another were more similar in terms of year in college than those who were assigned to one another
		Among male roommate pairs who chose one another, similarity in year of college was correlated with liking and staying together as roommates
		No significant effects for similarity of major area of study, religious background, age, race, father's education
Werner and Parmelee (1979)	Same-sex pairs of friends (college students)	Friends were more similar in terms of activity preferences than attitudes
		Friends believed their attitudes were more similar and their activity preferences less similar than they actually were
		Friends and strangers did not differ in terms of attitude similarity
		Friends were more similar than strangers in terms of activity preferences

(continued)

Table 4.4 (Continued)

Study	Participants	Results
Davis (1981)	College students	Participants were more attracted to a hypothetical person portrayed as similar to them in terms of "interests and hobbies" and "basic values (e.g., morals, religion)" than someone similar to them in terms of "political opinions" and "opinions about matters of fact"
Erwin (1985)	Reciprocated and nominal friendship pairs (children ages 7-10)	Reciprocated friend pairs (especially boys) were more similar in terms of attitudes regarding social activities, interests (e.g., reading comics), evaluations, etc. than nominal pairs
Verbrugge (1977)	1966 Detroit Area Survey Study Sample (adult men) 1971 Altneustadt Survey (West Germany) adult women and men	Of participants' three closest friends, greatest similarity was found in terms of age, marital status, sex, political preference (Altneustadt sample), religious preference, education, and residential mobility was found for first-named (best) friend, followed by second-, and then third-named friend Similarity in terms of occupation, employment status, and occupational prestige relatively equal across the three friends
Werebe (1987)	Adolescents (ages 15-19) from different types of public schools in France	When rating closest friendship: • Strongest similarity effects for age and academic's standing • Perceived similarity less strong for tastes • Very little similarity perceived in terms of personal attributes, especially those pertaining to social competence (e.g., shy) or ideas (e.g., politics, religion)
Griffin and Sparks (1990)	College student friendship pairs (not in their freshmen year)	Perceived similarity in status strongly predicted closeness 4 years later but only for male-male pairs Academic major similarity was weakly related to closeness 4 years later for same-sex pairs

Overall, there is substantial evidence that in many domains similarity is associated with attraction and the development of friendships. The most common explanation for similarity effects is that our views are validated by interacting with someone who shares them (see Berscheid & Walster [Hatfield], 1978; Byrne, 1971). Stated differently, we feel more confident that we are "right" in our thinking if we associate with someone who thinks just like us. Another possibility, the rewards-of-interaction explanation, is recently receiving some attention. In Berscheid and Walster's [Hatfield's] words:

> If a person feels as we do about things, we feel fairly confident that it would be rewarding to spend some time with that person; if a person despises everything we cherish, we might well be apprehensive about associating with the person. (p. 66)

Evidence that we are drawn to people who enjoy the same kinds of activities we do (e.g., Davis, 1981; Erwin, 1985; Werner & Parmelee, 1979; see Table 4.4) is consistent with this interpretation. In fact, Werner and Parmelee discovered that friends were more similar in terms of activity preferences than attitudes. In the same vein, Davis (1981) found that the similarity-attraction relation was stronger for interests and hobbies than political views. Her explanation was that similarity in interests and hobbies has greater implications for interaction. Similarly, Burleson maintains that interaction is more likely to be pleasurable if partners are similar in terms of social and communication skills (see Table 4.3).

Different Kinds of Similarity at Different Stages of Friendship?

Despite the research presented so far, to simply conclude that "friends are more similar than acquaintances" glosses over a number of complexities and nuances that must be considered to fully understand the role of similarity in achieving closeness. For instance, studies such as Johnson's (Table 4.4) reveal that certain *kinds* of similarity are more characteristic of friends (e.g., interests and values), whereas others typify acquaintances (e.g., residential proximity, working at the same place). If one assumes that every friendship starts out as an acquaintanceship, then it appears that even within the same relationship, the kinds of similarities that once were attractive may lose their appeal as other kinds of similarities assume greater importance.

Personal Construct Similarity. The notion that different kinds of similarity characterize relationships at different stages has been explored most fully in the domain of personal construct similarity. For example, Duck (1973a) theorized that acquaintances should be similar in terms of superficial, or observable, personality dimensions. As they develop a friendship, greater similarity should emerge at a deeper level, namely, similarity in personal constructs (i.e., the individual's personal hypotheses about the world). At this stage, similarity at superficial levels should no longer predict attraction. These hypotheses were tested with a sample of dormitory residents. The results supported predictions.

This research was extended in a longitudinal study by Duck and Craig (1978). They predicted that at the beginning of a relationship, friends would again show greater similarity in terms of superficial personality information. A few months later, the pair would have had the opportunity to learn about one another's values, and hence, value similarity would be evident. Finally, at the long-term friendship stage, friends should show greater similarity in personal constructs. Participants were dormitory residents who listed their friends and completed measures of personality, values, and personal constructs after 1, 4, and 8 months on campus. At Time 1, no significant differences were found on any measures, although it had been hypothesized that personality similarity in terms of accessible traits would characterize the friendship pairs. However, consistent with the other predictions, at Time 2, friendship pairs were more similar to one another in terms of values than nominal pairs but did not differ on the other two measures. At Time 3, friendship pairs were more similar than nominal pairs in terms of personal constructs, but not in terms of personality or values. Thus, again, established friends were similar in deeper, more meaningful ways.

Neimeyer and Neimeyer (1981, Study 1; see Table 4.3) extended Duck's work by predicting that in addition to construct similarity, friends would differ from acquaintances in terms of *functional* similarity—the extent to which people apply constructs similarly to aspects of their experience. In a second study, 10 male dormitory residents were asked to designate three friends and three nominal acquaintances from the dorm. Each individual rated the others using three classes of constructs: physical (e.g., tall vs. short), interactional (e.g., shy vs. outgoing), and psychological (e.g., sensitive vs. insensitive). Friends showed higher functional similarity than acquaintances for interactional and psychological, but not physical, constructs. Thus, not only is there greater similarity in deeper-level constructs as a friendship develops, but there also is greater similarity in the application of these constructs to known others.

Value Similarity. In the study by Duck and Craig (1978) described earlier, value similarity was found to differentiate reciprocal friendship pairs from nominal pairs at the 4-month mark. The role of value similarity in predicting attraction has been elaborated in subsequent research by Lea (1994; Lea & Duck, 1982). Lea and Duck (1982) focused on two aspects of value similarity. First, they reasoned that similarity in terms of values that are regarded as important would be more attractive than similarity in values about which one felt neutral or indifferent. Second, they proposed that similarity in values that are uncommon would lead to greater attraction than similarity of commonly held values. The former should nevertheless be revealed later in a relationship than the latter because revealing uncommon values carries with it a greater risk of rejection. It was predicted, therefore, that students would be more likely to regard a new acquaintance as a friend if he or she was similar in common values that were also important to the student. For longer-term relationships, it was expected that individuals would regard as friends those who were similar in uncommon values. Finally, in established friendships, it was thought that value similarity would no longer be salient, but instead would be replaced by other concerns (e.g., need complementarity).

Students in dormitory residences were asked to nominate their friends 1 to 2 months after initial acquaintanceship, after 4 to 6 months, and again after 1 year. Values were assessed at each time. Overall, friendship pairs tended to be more similar in terms of values than nominal pairs. However, the hypothesis that common value similarity would predict friendship early on (but not later) and that uncommon value similarity would predict friendship later (but not earlier) was not supported.

These predictions were tested again in a more comprehensive study by Lea (1994). He hypothesized that for friendships of only 1 month's duration, a positive relation should be found between similarity of commonly held values and variables such as liking and interdependence. However, similarity of common values was not expected to correlate with various measures of self-referent rewards (e.g., self-affirmation), given that they are not as relevant to the self as are uncommon values. At this early stage of friendship, it was anticipated that uncommon value similarity would not be revealed yet and therefore would be unrelated to all measures. For friendships of 4 months' duration, it was thought that uncommon values would have been communicated and would be associated with the receipt of self-referent rewards. Common values were expected to lose their predictive power at this stage. Finally, for year-long friendships, it was anticipated that neither kind of value similarity would be important. Individuals participated in this study with another person with whom they had a friendship duration of either 1 month, 4 months, or 1 year. The results confirmed predictions.

A follow-up study was conducted 3 months later with individuals who initially had been in 1-month friendships. This enabled Lea to determine if the cross-sectional findings when the 1- and 4-month friendships were compared in Study 1 would be replicated longitudinally. Consistent with the results of the first study, common similarity was no longer associated with attraction as it had been when these relationships were 1-month friendships. Instead, uncommon similarity now had emerged as important.

Similarity as the Result of Attraction. Two people may pursue a friendship because they are similar in certain ways. Once a relationship is formed, they may also become more similar to one another. Bell (1981b), for example, observed that "close friends may develop similar styles in voice and gesture, dress and manner" (p. 16). In a longitudinal study of more than 1,800 adolescents, Kandel (1978b) found that best friend pairs were similar at the outset. However, they also became more similar to one another over time. As Berndt (1982) explains, "Adolescents select friends who are similar to themselves on certain characteristics, but because friends differ on other characteristics there is still room for further similarity to develop through social influence" (p. 1455).

The research on personal construct similarity showed that as a friendship develops, there is greater similarity in the content of personal constructs (particularly psychological constructs), as well as greater similarity in the application of these constructs to other people. A by-product of this process may be that friends become more similar to one another in their self-conceptions. A study by Deutsch, Sullivan, Sage, and Basile (1991) is evocative in this regard. The assumption underlying their research was that people apply their own self-schema dimensions when describing or evaluating others. It was predicted that friends would eventually incorporate aspects of one another's self-schemas because each person would become familiar with the dimensions used by the other. This hypothesis was tested with 58 pairs of female roommates who were classified as friends, nonfriends, or ambiguous (pairs in which the roommates gave different classifications). Each roommate was asked to list 10 self-descriptive traits. Results indicated that the overlap in self-descriptive traits was significantly greater for friends than for nonfriends or ambiguous pairs. Roommates who were friends also reported greater liking, expected to become closer, and spent more time talking and being together than roommates who were nonfriends.

Presumably, it is through talking that friends are able to learn about the constructs that each applies. Consistent with this conjecture, in a regression analysis, time spent talking was a more important predictor of self-concept overlap than was liking. In fact, Deutsch and Mackesy (1985) found that when previously unacquainted pairs discussed another person, they subsequently demonstrated greater similarity in their self-schemas and greater use of one another's self-schema dimensions for describing both the target person and themselves. Deutsch et al. (1991) concluded that similarity in self-conceptions develops "because friends adopt new dimensions for describing themselves through exposure to each other's ways of construing the interpersonal world" (p. 410).

Summary

The statement that friends are more similar than acquaintances must be qualified in light of research showing that different kinds of similarity characterize each type of relationship. Friends are more similar in terms of deeper personal constructs, whereas acquaintances are more similar in terms of more superficial constructs. The situation is analogous for other kinds of similarity. For example, there is evidence that acquaintances are more likely to be similar in residential and other kinds of incidental proximity that keep them in contact with one another. For friends, similarity in these more circumstantial ways is less important. Friends and acquaintances also differ in the kind of value similarity that is most highly correlated with attraction. However, this effect holds only for friendships of relatively short duration. For example, Lea's results showed that within 1 year, value similarity ceased to be an important predictor of variables such as liking and interdependence.

The results of these studies suggest that similarity is not a static construct. Different kinds of similarity are important at different stages of relationships. Moreover, whereas people generally are more likely to become friends with those who are similar to them, this is a reciprocal process—people are also more likely to become similar to one another once they have initiated a friendship.

❧ Friends Versus Close Friends

Research by Roberto and Kimboko (1989) suggests that for laypeople, at least, friend and close friend relationships differ largely in terms of degree. They asked elderly adults ($M = 72$ years) for a definition of friend and to delineate the differences between friends and close friends. The major difference was that close friends were "more" of the attributes assigned to friends. For example, participants reported having a deeper, more intimate relationship with a close friend and had more contact with the person. Compared to "just a friend," a close friend also was more likely to be confided in and relied on. Men were not as likely to distinguish between the two types of relationship as were women.

In a study of university students' same-sex friendships (Barth & Kinder, 1988), close friends were rated highest on a measure of relational involvement, followed by good friends, and then casual friends. The same pattern was found for duration of the relationship and amount of time spent together (25.2 hours per week for close friends, 16.5 for good friends, and 10.3 for casual friends). Contrary to expectations, the groups did not differ significantly on a measure of depth of conversations.

The results from an extensive research program on the interactions of casual and close friends conducted by Hays (see Hays, 1988, for a review) suggest that there are both quantitative and qualitative differences between these relationship types. For example, in a longitudinal study, pairs who became close friends interacted more frequently than those who did not, although a high frequency of contact was not required for the friendship to be close. Close friends also were more likely to be regarded as a confidant and a source of emotional support (Hays, 1985).

In another study, Hays (1989) asked university students to complete questionnaires following their interactions with a close and a casual friend over a 1-week period. Close friends interacted more frequently and across a wider range of days, times, and locations than casual friends. For example, casual friends' interactions were more likely to take place on campus, were not deliberately initiated, and lasted only 10 minutes or less. Close friends were more likely to interact in their own homes and regarded these interactions as more exclusive. The students also assessed the benefits and costs of each interaction. Interactions with close friends provided more benefits such as emotional and informational support. However, there was no difference on less personal benefits such as having fun, task assistance, and intellectual stimulation. The two groups also did not differ in the amount of benefits offered, nor in perceived costs of the interaction (e.g., irritation, boredom). Nevertheless, interactions with close friends were rated as having a more positive effect on the total relationship than were interactions with casual friends.

Finally, a series of multiple regression analyses were conducted to determine the best predictors of relationship progress. The results suggested that with casual friends, participants were especially sensitive to the negative consequences of the interaction (i.e., costs), whereas with close friends, benefits had the biggest impact. For both groups, the amount of fun and relaxation experienced was most highly correlated with perceptions that the relationship was progressing (see the section "Fun and Relaxation").

⍟ Friends Versus Best Friends

When more than 200 children enrolled in elementary schools in Manhattan, Detroit, and Los Angeles were asked "What makes a best friend different from all other friends?" their answers reflected quantitative, not qualitative, distinctions (Brenton, 1974). Boys and girls responded that you can depend more on your best friend, you like to do more of the same things together, you play more, share more, and so on.

Studies conducted with adults also typically report differences of degree. For example, in Knapp et al.'s (1980) study discussed earlier, acquaintances received lower ratings on the personalized communication and synchronized communication factors than either friend or best friend. When the latter two types were compared, the ratings for best friends were higher than for friends, although the differences were not large. (The groups did not differ on the difficult communication factor.)

Friend and best friend also were categories in Duck et al.'s (1991) studies. In Study 1, friend and best friend interactions did not differ in terms of degree of change brought about by the interaction, value of the interaction for the future of the relationship, degree of mutual control, or amount of conflict. However, variability of ratings was greater for interactions with friends, whereas the quality of communication was rated higher with best friends. In the second study, only ratings of the value of communication differed significantly, with best friends again receiving higher ratings. A final, relevant study investigated the therapeutic value of women's friendships (Davidson & Packard, 1981). Women, ages 20 to 61, rated the extent to which a "best" and a "slight" friend had contributed to their personal growth through the provision of guidance, hope, understanding, self-disclosure, and so on. Best friends received significantly higher ratings, although it was concluded that both kinds of friendship had therapeutic effects. Taken together, the results of these studies suggest that the difference between friend and best friend is mostly quantitative.

⭒ Close Friends Versus Best Friends

Davis and Todd (1982) predicted that close and best friends would differ in intimacy (measured by confiding and understanding scales) and support, because "the ability to count on the other, no matter what, is for many people the definition of a best friendship" (p. 103). The results supported predictions. Best friends also received higher ratings on exclusiveness and enjoyment scales.

Other researchers have compared good and best friends. In Wright's (1982, 1985) research, ratings of best friends generally are higher on Acquaintance Description Form variables (e.g., voluntary interdependence, self-affirmation, stimulation value) than good friends, although not always significantly so. Differences are more likely to be obtained when women, rather than men, rate these types of friendship (e.g., Wright, 1982). Hardy, Doyle, and Markiewicz (1991) found that schoolchildren (Grades 3-6) in Montreal believed that good and best friends were comparable terms of companionship, but that best friendships were characterized by greater help, support, and closeness. Thus, again, it would appear that differences between these friendship types are largely a matter of degree.

❧ Other Friendship Typologies

Friendships have been categorized in many different ways. For example, in Howes's (1983) longitudinal study of young children's relationships, friendships were categorized as sporadic or maintained. Comparisons of these types showed that maintained friends were more successful at initiating interaction and spent more time in complementary and reciprocal play than sporadic friends. These groups did not differ on the other variables (e.g., elaborated exchanges, agonistic interaction). In Lederberg et al.'s (1987) study, children's friendships were classified as temporary versus long-term. Temporary friends spent a smaller proportion of play time together. In addition, long-term friends were more likely to engage in interactive, rather than parallel, play.

Unilateral Versus Reciprocal Friendships

By far the most common alternative to categorizing friendships on the basis of types (e.g., acquaintance, friend, best friend) is classification based on whether or not the relationship is reciprocated. For example, in Hallinan's sociometric research (e.g., Hallinan & Tuma, 1978) children indicate whether each classmate is a best friend, friend, or "know but isn't a friend" on multiple occasions and reciprocity of nominations is calculated. In Deutsch et al.'s study described earlier, roommates were classified as *ambiguous* if one member of the pair considered the relationship to be a friendship but the other did not. Other researchers speak of reciprocated versus unilateral (or nominal) friendships, or mutual versus nonmutual friendships. Regardless of the terminology, there is evidence that relationships in which only one person desires a friendship differ from relationships in which both people want to be friends. Unfortunately, the dependent variables differ greatly from one study to the next, making cross-study comparisons difficult. In addition, the way in which reciprocity is calculated can affect results (see Epstein, 1986). For example, it matters whether researchers ask about friends or best friends, given that fewer best friend choices can be reciprocated. Nevertheless, there are some conclusions that can be drawn. First, as shown earlier, reciprocated friendship pairs are more similar than unreciprocated pairs in terms of demographic characteristics, personal constructs, and the like (e.g., Duck, 1973b; Erwin, 1985; Kandel, 1978b; see Table 4.3). As Table 4.5 shows, reciprocated friend pairs also are more similar in terms of activities engaged in (e.g., Gershman & Hayes, 1983; Hayes et al., 1980). Hartup, Laursen, Stewart, and Eastenson (1988) found that in the reciprocated friendships of preschoolers, conflicts were less intense and resolved more constructively, although Hardy, Doyle, and Markiewicz (1991) found no difference in the amount of conflict reported in each kind of relationship. Studies of children's friendships show that children in reciprocated friendships report a higher incidence of prosocial behaviors such as playing together, helping, and supportiveness. Finally, reciprocated friendships are characterized by greater stability than unreciprocated friendships, both for preschoolers (Gershman & Hayes, 1983) and adolescents (Kandel, 1978b).

Overall, the pattern for reciprocated versus unreciprocated friendships is reminiscent of the findings presented on comparisons of acquaintances and friends. This suggests that if one person does not desire a friendship, the relationship may be relegated to an acquaintanceship status. Stated differently, it appears that a prerequisite for the formation of a close friendship is that both people must want it.

Friends Versus Friendly Relations

Kurth (1970) defines friendship as "an intimate interpersonal relationship involving each individual as a personal entity" whereas a friendly relation is an "outgrowth of a formal role relationship and a preliminary stage in the development of a friendship" (p. 136). Four dimensions differentiate the two kinds of relationship. First, voluntary interaction is more limited in friendly relations. Second, a sense of uniqueness characterizes friendship, whereas friendly relations are much more substitutable. Third, friendships are more intimate. Fourth, obligations are more limited in friendly relations than in friendships. "True" friends are expected to do almost anything for one another. This last dimension accounts for why people frequently prefer friendly

Table 4.5 Unilateral Versus Reciprocated Friendships

Study	Participants	Reciprocated Friends	Unreciprocated Friends	No Difference
Hardy, Doyle, and Markiewicz (1991)	Children (Grades 3–6)	Higher ratings on: • Play/companionship • Help/support • Closeness		Amount of conflict Security
Hayes, Gershman, and Bolin (1980)	Preschoolers	Reasons for liking other: • Common activities mentioned more frequently • Evaluation (e.g., "she's nice") mentioned more frequently • General playing mentioned more frequently (marginally significant)		8 reasons for liking (e.g., sharing, reciprocal liking, physical appearance, possessions)
Gershman and Hayes (1983)	Preschoolers	More likely to be maintained over time Reasons for liking other: • Common activities mentioned more frequently • General playing mentioned more frequently		A number of reasons for liking other (e.g., propinquity, reciprocity of liking, helping, sharing)

Study	Sample			
Staub and Noerenberg (1981)	Boys (Grades 3 and 4)	More likely to refuse friend's offer of candy if they believed friend earned it Less sharing of pencil (under certain conditions)	Retaliated against other's previous selfishness with candy	Sharing pencil (under certain conditions)
Hartup, Laursen, Stewart, and Eastenson (1988)	Children in nursery schools or day care centers (ages 3–5)	Lower intensity conflicts Termination of conflict through disengagement (e.g., distraction) Compromise solution to conflict more likely Continued socializing after conflict		Instigators of conflict Amount of conflict Duration of conflict Nature of conflict Presence of aggression during conflict Social context (e.g., proximity of teacher)
Sharabany, Gershon, and Hofman (1981)	Students in Grades 5, 7, 11 in Israel	Higher scores on the Sharabany Intimacy Scale		
Kandel (1978b)	Adolescents		More unstable	

relations to friendships. Kurth points out that although friendships provide many rewards, they also entail substantial costs. Friendly relations may not be as rewarding, but they can be pleasant, provide support in performance of our formal roles, and are not as costly.

The dimensions that distinguish friendships from friendly relations could again apply to acquaintanceships and friendships. The research presented earlier is consistent with these dimensions (e.g., greater intimacy in friendships), although the issue of obligations in these relationships has not received much empirical attention.

Communal Versus Exchange Relationships

According to Clark and Mills (1979; Mills & Clark, 1982), in communal relationships, concern about the other person's welfare is paramount. Benefits are given because they are needed, without an expectation of anything in return. In contrast, in exchange relationships, individuals keep track of the benefits they provide and expect repayment in kind. Clark and Mills classify friendships as communal relationships and relationships with acquaintances and strangers as exchange relationships. The hypothesis that friends exchange noncomparable benefits, the hallmark of a communal relationship, was tested by Clark (1981). Participants were presented with scenarios varying in the comparability of benefits exchanged. Imagine, for example, that Kate has run out of coffee and her roommate Rita gives her a small jar. Later, Kate buys Rita a small jar of coffee in return. Do Kate and Rita seem like friends? What if Kate repays Rita by giving her two felt-tip pens instead of coffee? Clark found that in the latter case—where noncomparable benefits were exchanged—participants inferred greater friendship. In a study along the same lines, Greenberg (1983) presented individuals with a scenario in which one person ordered a full meal in a restaurant, and the other ordered a snack. Those who were told that the bill was divided equally gave the relationship higher ratings on a scale from acquaintanceship to best friend than those who were told that each person paid for what he or she ordered. Finally, in a study of actual roommates, Murstein and

Azar (1986) found that an exchange .orientation was negatively related to friendship development, although the findings were rather weak.

➤ Summary

The process of achieving closeness in friendships is elucidated by examining the characteristics of relationships at various levels of intimacy. This chapter began by comparing the interactions of strangers and acquaintances versus friends. A review of this literature revealed that friends are more fully engaged in their interactions with one another than are strangers or acquaintances. Friends' interactions are characterized by greater physical proximity, affective expression, prosocial behavior, and the like. These differences also typify reciprocated, compared to unreciprocated, friendships.

Friends also differ from acquaintances in terms of the depth and breadth of self-disclosure. In particular, intimate self-disclosure appears to be a hallmark of friendship. Presumably, this accounts for the greater mutual knowledge that is evident in friends', as opposed to acquaintances', interactions. Parallels can be drawn between the self-disclosure findings and the research on similarity. At the early stages of a friendship, there is evidence of similarity in relatively superficial domains. As the relationship becomes closer, the partners show greater similarity in terms of deeper, more meaningful constructs.

Finally, once a relationship reaches the point where it is defined as a friendship rather than as a stranger or acquaintance relationship, subsequent changes in closeness appear to be largely quantitative, rather than qualitative. Thus, the progression from friend to close friend to best friend is characterized by increments in the qualities associated with friendship: intimacy, trust, support, loyalty, and so on.

In conclusion, the process of achieving closeness involves becoming more fully engaged, affective, and prosocial in one's interactions with another person. It also involves gradually revealing more intimate information about oneself in an increasing number of domains. People who are close also are similar to one another in important, psychological ways. In short, the process of becoming close can be described as an upward spiral in which the characteristics of friendship are instantiated to an increasingly greater degree.

5

❦

Gender Issues in Friendship

It seems that some winters ago, Mark and Bob were sitting around a gas station with not much to do. . . . If Mark and Bob had been women, they probably would have passed the time in some nonproductive manner, such as nurturing their friendship, exploring their innermost feelings or helping each other gain significant insights into the important relationships in their lives. But, fortunately for humanity, Mark and Bob are not women. Mark and Bob are guys and what they did is invent snowplow hockey.

—Dave Barry (1995, p. C4)[1]

U ntil this point, the processes of friendship initiation and achieving closeness have been described as though they were relatively uniform phenomena. Gender differences have been noted in places, but they have not been a major focus. The commonalities of the friendship experience are less evident, however, once friendships have achieved closeness. The literature on gender differences in friendship suggests that women and men may vary in the amount of time they spend with friends, the activities that they engage in, what they talk about with friends, and so on. Although an extensive analysis of age differences is beyond the scope of this chapter, developmental origins of these gender differences will be highlighted where possible. There also is a large body of research in which women's and men's friendships are compared in terms of intimacy, affection, supportiveness, satisfaction, and the like. In fact, currently, there is considerable controversy over whether women's or men's same-sex friendships are more intimate. This issue will be examined in some detail, followed by a discussion of the effect of gender role on friendships. The chapter ends with a consideration of issues in cross-sex friendships.

❧ Amount of Time Spent With Friends

Some studies report gender differences in the amount of time spent with friends, whereas others do not. For example, Crockett, Losoff, and Peterson (1984) found that among Grade 8 students, the majority interacted with their friends on a daily basis. Although the frequency of face-to-face contact was similar for boys and girls, 85% of girls reported having daily telephone conversations with their friends compared to 50% of boys. The amount of time spent with friends increased from Grades 6 to 8, although time spent chatting on the phone increased only for girls. A very similar pattern was observed in a study of daily interactions of students in Grades 5 to 9 (Raffaelli & Duckett, 1989).

The findings from research with college students are mixed. Some studies have not found gender differences in frequency of interaction with casual, good, and close friends (Barth & Kinder, 1988), a close same-sex friend (Johnson & Aries, 1983b), or best friend (Caldwell & Peplau, 1982; Omoto & Mooney, 1993, Study 2). Wheeler, Reis, and Bond (1989) did not find gender differences in the quantity of social interaction among students in the United States and in Hong Kong. However, in other studies, women report spending more time with best friends (e.g., Omoto & Mooney, 1993, Study 1). In Reis's (1988) research where individuals tracked their daily interactions, women engaged in a greater number of social interactions per day. However, when analyses were conducted only for best friend, same-sex interactions, there was no sex difference (M = 1.26 times per day).

In Booth's (1972) study of middle-aged adults, women interacted with friends more frequently than men did (although there was no gender difference among lower-class participants). In contrast, Aries and Johnson (1983) found that women and men (M = 50 years) did not differ in frequency of contact with a close, same-sex friend, although women were more likely to spend time interacting over the telephone. Overall, the evidence suggests that women and men are not vastly different in the amount of time spent with friends. When gender differences are found, they are in the direction of women spending more time with friends, particularly in the form of telephone conversations.

✖ Activities

There is a well-documented pattern of differences in women's and men's activities with friends. Simply put, "talk is the substance of women's friendship" (Johnson & Aries, 1983a, p. 354), whereas men prefer to engage in activities, typically attending or participating in sports events (e.g., Johnson & Aries, 1983a; Pulakos, 1989; Richey & Richey, 1980; Rubin, 1985, 1986; Williams, 1985; Winstead, 1986; Woolsey & McBain, 1987). When Caldwell and Peplau (1982) asked American university students whether they would rather engage in some activity or "just talk" with a same-sex friend, more than three times as many women as men chose "just talking," whereas nearly twice as many men as women chose an activity. These findings were replicated in New Zealand by Aukett, Ritchie, and Mill (1988). Based on interviews with 300 men and women, Rubin (1986) declared: "What [men] do may differ by age and class, but that they tend to *do* rather than *be* together is undeniable" (p. 166).

Pulakos (1989) reported that among college students, women talked and shopped with a close friend more frequently than did men. Presumably, talking can still occur while engaging in an activity such as shopping. Consistent with this observation, Johnson and Aries (1983a) found that even when the women in their middle-aged sample were performing an activity such as sewing or canning, talk remained central.

These gender differences in activity preferences also emerged in a study by Sapadin (1988), who asked professional women and men: "What do you like most about your friendships?" At first blush, it seemed surprising that for same-sex friendships, a significantly greater percentage of men than women endorsed "sharing/enjoying." However, for men, sharing revolved around activities, sports, and having fun with their friends, whereas women conceptualized sharing as dyadic, verbal interaction. Overall, the literature supports Sherrod's (1989) conclusion that "the typical woman tends to look for an intimate confidante, someone who shares the same feelings, while the typical man tends to seek a partner for activities, someone who shares his interests" (p. 167).

Before leaving this topic, it should be acknowledged that recently some writers have begun to challenge the standard depiction of women's friendships as "face to face" and men's friendships as "side by side" (Wright, 1982). Some have criticized the side-by-side portrayal of men's friendships, arguing that men talk more than we give them credit for (e.g., Walker, 1994). There also have been objections to the face-to-face description of women's friendships, arguing that women do more activities than is assumed (e.g., Walker, 1994). It is difficult to evaluate this research when the same methodology (i.e., interviews) produces strikingly opposite conclusions (e.g., Rubin, 1985, 1986, vs. Walker, 1994). Nor are empirical studies unanimous in their results. Wright himself has revised his much-cited depiction of women's and men's friendships in light of recent research in which women were both expressive and instrumental in their friendships, whereas men were instrumental but not expressive (Wright & Scanlon, 1991). In addition, a recent reanalysis of several data sets revealed that both women and men endorsed *talk* as the primary purpose for interacting with friends, followed by *task*, and then *relationship issues* (although the latter two were sometimes reversed for women; Duck & Wright, 1993). The authors acknowledge that these data do not address what was talked about or the meaning of the talks for each gender. They muse that "perhaps the 'friendship talk' of women centers on topics like how to get along with significant others whereas that of men centers on topics like where to get the best deal on aluminum siding" (p. 718). In summary, the depiction of men's friendships as activity based and women's as affectively based is still prominent in the literature. However, recently this portrayal is being questioned, if not attacked. As will be seen later, these differing perspectives have fueled, or at least added fire to, the debate over whose friendships are more intimate—women's or men's.

Developmental Origins

The tendency for boys to play in groups and for girls to interact in dyads is perhaps one of the most well-established findings in the children's friendship literature (e.g., Maccoby, 1990). The group structure of boys' friendships is conducive for playing team sports, whereas the dyadic structure of girls' friendships lends itself to intimate conversation. Thorne and Luria (1986) observed that girls in Grades 4 and 5 were much more likely to talk with one another than were boys. Best friends monitored one another's emotions, self-disclosed, and shared secrets. Girls also were apt to notice and comment on one another's appearance (haircuts, clothes). In contrast, boys were primarily interested in sports, using forbidden words, and testing limits.

These patterns also are evident in adolescence. For example, Csikszentmihalyi and Larson (1984) randomly paged 75 high school students over a 1-week period. They found that boys spent twice as much time per week (approximately 6 hours) on sports and games than girls did. In an ambitious application of this methodology, Raffaelli and Duckett (1989) paged more than 400 students in Grades 5 to 9, also for 1 week. In their analysis, they focused specifically on conversations. In each grade, girls spent significantly more time talking with friends than did boys. There was also an overall increase with age in the amount of time spent talking. In fact, for girls, time spent talking with friends doubled from Grade 5 to Grade 9. Thus, by Grade 9, girls spent an average of 9 hours per week "just talking" to friends. (This estimate is conservative because only occasions where talking was the primary activity were counted. Talking was also frequently reported while engaging in activities such as playing a game.) The amount of time spent talking also increased for boys (to nearly 4 hours per week by Grade 9). However, girls still spent more than twice as much time talking with friends than did boys.

Cultural Differences

Even though these gender differences are firmly entrenched in the Western world, they may not be universal. Unfortunately, cross-cultural comparisons of friendship are rare in the social science literature. An exception is a study by Berman, Murphy-Berman, and Pachauri (1988), who observed that in India, men are much more interdependent and emotionally expressive than in the United States. For example, in India it is not uncommon for men to show physical affection (e.g., holding hands). These researchers compared best, same-sex friendships in the two countries and found that gender differences were, in fact, more pronounced in the United States. For example, when asked about friendship activities, in India there were no gender differences in response to the item "private conversations," but in the United States, women endorsed this item more than men. Similar, although somewhat more complicated, findings were obtained for self-disclosure to one's best, same-sex friend. Berman et al. comment that in contrast to American men, men in India are not socialized to be "rugged individualists." They also speculate that Indian men may have more intimate friendships because unlike their American counterparts, they live in a gender-segregated society in which premarital relationships with women are not condoned.

Consistent with these results, in a study of daily interactions, Wheeler et al. (1989) found that female students in the United States reported higher levels of self-disclosure than male students. Among Chinese students in Hong Kong, there was no gender difference.

❧ Conversation Topics

What do women and men talk about when they are with their friends? Again, the gender differences are rather striking. Women are more likely to talk about their close relationships and other personal matters. For example, when Caldwell and Peplau (1982) asked individuals to list three topics they typically discussed with their best friend, personal topics such as feelings and problems were mentioned twice as often by women than men. Women also were significantly more likely to talk about other people. Men's conversations tended to revolve around sports, work, and vehicles, rather than personal issues or problems. These self-report differences were corroborated in a follow-up study where women and men role-played having a conversation.

Similar findings have been reported in other studies of college students (e.g., Bendtschneider & Duck, 1993; Pulakos, 1989; Williams, 1985). Johnson and Aries (1983b), for example, found that topics such as close relationships, personal problems, and secrets from the past were discussed more frequently and in greater depth with a same-sex close friend by women than men. The topic of sports was discussed frequently by a greater number of men than women (65% vs. 16%) and in greater depth. Men also were more likely to talk about hobbies and shared activities and to reminisce about activities done together in the past, although gender differences on these topics were not large.

Research with middle-aged and elderly adults shows the same pattern. In a study of a broad cross-section of American adults (ages 17 to 80), Haas and Sherman (1982) reported that men talked to their same-sex friends about women, the news, music and art, spectator sports, and participant sports. Women talked to same-sex friends about men, food, relationship problems, family, and fashion. Oliker (1989) found that women in their 20s to 50s talked to female friends about motherhood, personal problems, housework, and personal appearance. These themes are apparent in other research as well. For example, in Booth's (1972) study, confiding in friends about personal problems was more typical of middle-aged women than men. Johnson and Aries (1983a) reported that the mostly middle-aged women in their sample talked to friends about the significant relationships in their lives: children, husband, in-laws, coworkers, other friends, and so on. Finally, Lewittes (1989) observed that elderly women often discussed their families when talking with friends.

Gender differences were not particularly pronounced in a study of adults ($M = 50$ years) by Aries and Johnson (1983). They obtained the usual finding that women discuss personal problems and relationships more than men, and that men discuss sports more than women. However, more than 90% of both women and men talked about their daily activities, community/civic affairs, and family activities, although the frequency and depth of these discussions differed somewhat (e.g., women discussed family activities in greater depth with friends).

The conclusion that men discuss topics such as sports and vehicles whereas women prefer to talk about personal issues and relationships is consistent with commonsense notions of what women and men do with friends. While writing this chapter, I received a greeting card that pictures a Victorian-looking picnic scene. The two men in the scene, lounging on a picnic blanket, have walking sticks and are wearing formal jackets. They appear deeply engrossed in conversation—so deeply that they are oblivious to their female companions. One woman has removed her clothing and is lying on the blanket with one leg high in the air. The other has shed all but her bloomers and is performing handstands on the grass. The caption reads: "They tried everything to stop the men talking about sport."

The Benefits of Talk

Women treasure talk with friends. In Johnson and Aries's (1983a) study, women between the ages of 27 and 58 ($M = 39$ years) reported that having someone to talk to was the most important benefit of their relationship with a close friend. Similarly, in Lewittes's (1989) research on the friendships of older women, intimate self-disclosure was a highly valued aspect of close friendships. In fact, it was rated as more important than concrete help or shared activities.

One of the benefits of talking with friends is self-clarification (e.g., Becker, 1987; Johnson & Aries, 1983b). Rosenfeld and Kendrick (1984) reported that this was one of the primary motivations reported by their participants for engaging in self-disclosure. The authors explain that "friends appear to provide opportunity and support for a discloser's being open and honest without fear of ridicule, allowing for self-concept clarification" (p. 337). Self-clarification took a particular form among the elderly women in Lewittes's study. As they faced death, there was a need to review and reintegrate the past. However, family members often were uncomfortable with this process. Talk with friends, especially long-term friends dealing with the same issues, helped these women maintain a sense of continuity.

A related theme in these studies is that talk with friends is valued because friends listen in a noncritical way (e.g., Johnson & Aries, 1983a; Lewittes, 1989; Oliker, 1989). For example, in Lewittes's study, the statement "She listens without judging" received high ratings when referring to a close friendship; with relatives these women were more likely to feel judged or pressured to meet certain expectations.

Women also report enhanced feelings of self-worth as a result of talk with friends (e.g., Bell, 1981a; Oliker, 1989). In Johnson and Aries's study, friends were perceived as giving validity to aspects of one's self that could not be shared with others. In fact, half of the respondents reported that the kind of communication they shared with their close friends was not experienced with their husbands. (Oliker, 1989, also found that many women in her sample valued talk with friends more than talk with their husbands.) This kind of intimate, exclusive disclosure may account for the finding that women feel they know and are known better by their female, than their male, friends (e.g., Buhrke & Fuqua, 1987).

Finally, talk with friends also has interpersonal benefits. Each of Oliker's (1989) respondents claimed that talk with a female friend had been helpful in resolving disagreements with her husband. Jerrome (1984) reported similar findings when she interviewed women in England. Both authors maintain that these women supported one another's marriages and family relationships. The intimacy of their friendships appeared to benefit, rather than detract from, their marriages.

Thus, it seems clear that for women, talk with friends has salutary effects on their personal and relational well-being. In the words of Johnson and Aries (1983a), "Through extensive talk about the most routine of daily activities to the most private of personal problems and crises, women friends establish connections with one another that function significantly in their lives" (p. 358).

The conclusion that women reap important benefits from talking with friends raises a number of complex questions about sex differences in this domain: Do men shy away from personal talk with friends because they are unaware of these benefits? Or do men not value these kinds of benefits (and hence have little need for intimate talk)? Unfortunately, there are no easy answers. Reisman (1990, Study 2) wondered whether men might not be aware that they engage in less personal talk than women. However, he found that both women and men believed that women were more likely to talk about personal problems and tender feelings. Reisman also asked the participants how much they would like to discuss personal problems and tender feelings. When he calculated the difference between men's ratings of how often they talk about these issues and how often they would like to, there was evidence that men wanted to discuss personal problems and express tender feelings significantly more often than they did. This result suggests that men may anticipate positive benefits from engaging in intimate talk.

Would it actually be beneficial for men if they talked intimately with their male friends? The evidence suggests that it would. For example, Reisman (1990, Study 1) obtained a significant, positive correlation between self-disclosure and satisfaction in same-sex friendships for both women and men. Similarly, Jones (1991, Study 2) found that although women rated their friendships higher in self-disclosure and enjoyment than did men, these variables predicted friendship satisfaction for both sexes. Finally, the benefits of talk also were apparent in Raffaelli and Duckett's study in that both boys and girls experienced elevated affect when talking with friends.

Gender Differences in Context

The gender differences discussed so far do not tell the whole story of women's and men's interactions with friends. First, the finding that women talk about personal problems and feelings more than men do may create an impression that women talk only about such issues. This does not seem to be the case. Second, most of the research has focused on conversations between same-sex friends. As will be seen, these effects are moderated somewhat in cross-sex interactions.

Not All Talk Is Intimate

Even though women engage in intimate talk more than men, and benefit from doing so, this does not mean that women *only* talk about intimate matters with their friends. Research presented in Chapter 4, for example, showed that in early and even established friendships, for both sexes the bulk of self-disclosure occurred in nonintimate domains (even though women engaged in more intimate self-disclosure than men). The middle-aged women in Johnson and Aries's (1983a) study talked about their work and daily lives and activities, as well as engaging in very personal talk about their deepest feelings and problems. A study by Davidson and Duberman (1982) also sheds light on this issue. They asked college students to provide accounts and examples of their usual conversations with their same-sex best friend. Responses were classified as *topical,* which were nonintimate discussions of topics that were external to the individual and the friendship (e.g., politics, work, movies); *relational,* which were interactive conversations about the friendship; and *personal,* which were intimate disclosures of thoughts and feelings about oneself. Women produced twice as many personal accounts and three times as many relational accounts as men. However, women and men did not differ in the frequency of topical accounts. When asked which level was primary or most important, women's responses were equally distributed across the three levels, whereas the majority of men rated the topical level as most important. Thus, women did not value talk only on the personal or relational levels.

Effects of Gender of Conversation Partner

The gender differences discussed so far are most pronounced when women and men are interacting with same-sex friends. Thus, women are more likely to have intimate, personal conversations with their female, than their male, friends. In contrast, when men talk about personal problems and issues, they are more likely to do so with a female friend (e.g., Aukett et al., 1988; Goodstein & Russell, 1977), although not all studies have found this pattern. In Reis's (1988) program of research in which university students record their interactions for days or even weeks, both women and men consistently self-disclose more to women than to men (Reis, Senchak, & Solomon, 1985; Wheeler, Reis, & Nezlek, 1983). However, men do not self-disclose more to women than women disclose to men.

Reisman (1990, Study 1) used a modified version of Reis's interaction record and found that both adolescent and young adult women reported significantly more self-disclosure with same-sex friends, but there was no gender difference in self-disclosure to cross-sex friends. These effects also varied somewhat with age. Among adolescents, boys reported approximately equal self-disclosure to girls and boys, but girls reported less disclosure to boys than to other girls. Among adults, men reported a higher level of self-disclosure to women than to men; women reported equal disclosure to female and male friends.

In Hacker's (1981) study, the percentage of same-sex dyads classified as high, moderate, and low self-disclosers was similar for women and men. Self-disclosure among cross-gender dyads was generally lower than in same-gender dyads. Thus, in this study, men were not more confiding to women than to other men. However, analyses of the *content* of disclosure painted quite a different picture. Not one man reported revealing only weaknesses in his friendships (same- and other-sex). However, 33% of women reported that they revealed only weaknesses in their friendships with men (18% in same-sex friendships). Conversely, not one woman reported revealing only strengths in her friendships, whereas 9% and 31% of men reported doing so in their same- and other-sex friendships, respectively. Thus, one third of the women revealed only weaknesses in their friendships with men, whereas nearly one third of the men revealed only their strengths in their friendships with women.

Finally, based on a meta-analysis of the self-disclosure literature, Dindia and Allen (1992) concluded that women disclose more than men to same-sex partners. Women also disclose more than men to other-sex partners (friends, parents, spouses). However, women do not disclose more than men to other men. Overall, it appears that women's self-disclosure to other women is generally more intimate than men's disclosure to other men. Findings for cross-sex friendships are less clear, with some studies reporting that men disclose more to women than vice versa, others reporting just the opposite, and still others finding no sex difference.

Developmental Origins

The gender differences in conversation topics observed among adult same-sex friends again appear to be entrenched at a relatively early age. The tendency for girls to engage in more relationship talk has been observed in several studies. Tannen (1990) analyzed videotapes of students in Grades 2, 6, and 10 having a conversation about something serious and/or intimate with their same-sex best friend. In each age group, girls were more likely to explore a few topics in depth, whereas boys would flit from topic to topic. The Grade 6 boys, for instance, touched on an average of 55 topics during their 20-minute conversation! They began with school and homework, then moved to TV, sports, sex, and so on. Remarkably, even the youngest boys chose the same topics discussed by adult males—school (work) and sports. In contrast, the Grade 2 girls told stories about their experiences and made supportive comments to one another. The Grade 6 girls' discussions centered on intimacy and fights with friends and family members. Similarly, girls in Grade 10 talked about problematic relationships, particularly with their boyfriends. Boys in Grade 10 did not shy away from discussions of personal problems altogether. However, unlike the girls, they discussed their problems in parallel, not interactively. Each minimized the other's concerns and responded to self-disclosure of a problem by revealing a problem of his own.

In a longitudinal study of students in Grades 6 to 8, Crockett et al. (1984) found that both boys and girls spent a lot of time talking about the other gender, although at each age, girls reported more of this kind of talk. By Grade 8, roughly one half of the boys and two thirds of the girls mentioned boy-girl relations as a topic of discussion with their friends. The authors note that these boys and girls spent more time talking about each other than with each other!

Finally, Raffaelli and Duckett (1989) found that among students in Grades 5 to 9, there was an intensification of gender-related patterns in talk with friends. By Grade 9, girls discussed personal concerns or other people nearly 75% of the time (peers, 50%; family, 11%; self, 12%). These topics dominated only one third of the Grade 9 boys' conversations (peers, 21%; family, 6%; self, 6%). Boys were more likely than girls to spend time talking about sports (24%) and leisure (games or TV, 15%). Topics also varied somewhat with age. For example, the topic of "self" did not emerge until Grade 9.

Cultural Differences

Reisman (1990, Study 2) investigated cultural differences in conversations with friends. He noted that in Hungary, childhood friendships are maintained through adulthood, in contrast to the United States, which is characterized by greater mobility. Moreover, Hungary's mandatory military service might further strengthen friendships, at least among men. To explore these issues, American and Hungarian college students were given a list of topics, and for each, indicated how frequently they discussed it, how frequently they believed other women and men their age discussed it, and so on. Women and men in both countries believed that men talk about sports and athletics, and politics and current affairs more frequently than women; women were perceived as talking about eating and food, and personal appearance. With regard to self-reports of these behaviors, in both countries women reported discussing personal problems and talking about affectionate and tender feelings significantly more often than men did. Responses in the two countries were more alike than different, although Americans reported discussing school/work more than Hungarians.

Cultural differences may be more apparent when comparisons are made between Western and Eastern countries. In Berman et al.'s (1988) comparison of best friendships in India and the United States, individuals rated four possible reasons why this person was their best friend: status, assistance, gregariousness (socializing), and problem sharing. In the United States, women assigned higher ratings than men to gregariousness and problem sharing. However, in India, no sex differences were found.

﹖ Social Support

Sex differences in social support have been summarized by several writers (e.g., Buhrke & Fuqua, 1987; Fehr & Perlman, 1985). Generally, this literature shows that, compared to men, women have a larger number of supportive relationships, have more family members as supporters, receive more help from supporters, and so on. In his review, Sherrod (1989) concluded that women also perceive more social support, especially emotional support, to be available from friends than do men. Rubin (1986) illustrated this phenomenon rather dramatically by asking women and men: "Who would you turn to if you came home one night and your wife [or husband or lover] announced she [or he] was leaving you?" (p. 170). Almost invariably, women had a ready answer; most of the men did not. Women named female friends and some-times family members—but never to the exclusion of friends. The few men who had a response usually named a family member, not a friend, and this person was generally female (sister, mother). Buhrke and Fuqua (1987) also found that men were much more likely to produce the names of women as supporters. In contrast, women listed significantly more same- than other-sex supporters.

Other research suggests that women's friendships in fact are characterized by greater provision of emotional support than are men's. Hays and Oxley (1986) found that women receive more emotional and informational support from friends (and other network members) than men. Women also provide more emotional support (and report greater willingness to help a friend in emotional distress; Otten, Penner, & Waugh, 1988). In Aukett et al.'s study of New Zealanders, both women and men claimed that they received more therapeutic support from their friendships with women. Finally, in a Canadian study, Wellman (1992) found that women received emotional support from 82% of their female friends compared to 27% of their male friends. For men, the pattern was similar but less pronounced with 73% of female friends and 56% of male friends providing emotional support.

It would be inaccurate to conclude that men do not receive any support from their male friends. When discussing his finding that men received less emotional support from same-sex friends than did women, Wellman (1992) emphasized that " 'less' does not mean 'none' or even 'little' " (p. 98). Nevertheless, the evidence suggests that women generally receive more social support from friends, especially emotional support. This may account for why the young women (ages 17 to 25) in Richey and Richey's (1980) study had such high expectations for support from their female friends. They anticipated much more material and psychological help from their friends than the men did. For example, 50% of the women believed that if they died, they could count on their best friend to raise their children. Even among children, girls (age 11) rate help/support as more important in their friendships than do boys (Bukowski et al., 1987). Thus, it is not surprising that researchers such as Hays (1985) find that adult women are more likely than men to mention emotional support as a benefit of friendship.

Before leaving this issue, it is important to acknowledge that gender differences may vary depending on the kind of support that is provided. In Wellman's study, for example, men relied on a greater number of male than female friends for all other categories of support (companionship, small services, and large services). Although contrary findings were reported by Roberto and Scott (1986), they interviewed elderly adults and found that instrumental exchanges (e.g., financial aid, transportation, help when ill) were less frequent between male than female friends. Affectionate exchanges, which included providing/receiving comfort, sharing personal problems, and physical displays of affection, also were more frequent among women. For men, affectional exchanges took the form of sharing problems or visiting, and usually revolved around a shared activity (e.g., on the golf course).

✖ Quality of Friendship

Some researchers have assessed quality of friendships by measuring relationship satisfaction. Other researchers, such as Sapadin (1988), have asked individuals to make direct ratings of quality. She divided her sample into two age groups: 21 to 34 years and 35 to 55 and over. Older women's same-sex friendships were rated highest in quality (M = 6.2 on a 7-point scale); young unmarried men's were rated the lowest (M = 4.5). In addition, women rated their same-sex friendships higher in quality than their other-sex friendships, whereas men's ratings of these two types of friendship did not differ. Similarly, McCoy, Brody, and Stoneman (1994) reported that girls' best friendships received higher scores than boys' on a composite measure of quality (e.g., intimacy, enhancement of self-worth, approachability, importance).

The findings for satisfaction are somewhat mixed. Buhrke and Fuqua (1987) found that women were more satisfied with their female, than male, friendships in terms of closeness, frequency of contact, and so on. Similarly, the women in Reisman's (1990) sample were significantly more satisfied with their same-sex friendships than were men. However, Jones (1991) found that women were more satisfied with both their female and male friendships. Elkins and Peterson (1993) reported that men were less satisfied with their same- than their opposite-sex friendships, whereas women were equally satisfied with both kinds of friendship.

A consistent finding in Reis's (1988; Reis, Senchak, & Solomon, 1985; Wheeler et al., 1983) research is that men's ratings of meaningfulness (a composite of intimacy, self-disclosure, other-disclosure, pleasantness, and satisfaction) in same-sex interactions are significantly lower than women's. In fact, men's ratings of same-sex interactions are significantly lower than either women's or men's ratings of other-sex interactions. Thus, according to Reis, all that is required for an interaction to become meaningful is the involvement of one woman.

♨ Love and Affection

When children first enter school, it is common for boys and girls to show affection by touching or holding hands with friends. However, by Grades 4 or 5, striking gender differences have surfaced. Girls sit closer than boys, touch more, and stroke or comb each other's hair. Thorne and Luria (1986) noted that the latter gesture is never observed among boys. Once these patterns are set, they persist. For example, Richey and Richey (1980) observed that young adult women were more physically affectionate with one another than were men. Hays (1985) found that female university students were more affectionate with close friends than not-close friends; male students showed very little affection, whether they were close friends or not. In Rands and Levinger's (1979) research, a variety of relationship types were rated along various dimensions, including affective interdependence (e.g., hugging, showing affection). Both university students and elderly adults rated female-female pairs higher on this dimension than male-male pairs. In the same vein, Roberto and Scott (1986) reported that elderly women were more physically affectionate with their friends than were elderly men.

With regard to love, research with children of various ages has found that girls express greater attraction to their best friend than boys do (e.g., Diaz & Berndt, 1982). In Richey and Richey's study, late adolescent women (ages 17 to 25) were more likely to say that they loved their friend. This gender difference also has been reported in young adulthood (e.g., Reisman, 1990; Rubin, 1973; Williams, 1985) as well as in middle and later adulthood. Bell (1981b), for example, found that the adult women in his sample were much more likely than the men to describe their feelings for a friend as love. He quotes a 37-year-old respondent who claimed that she loved her friends as much as her husband. Finally, when

Rubin's (1970) love scale is completed with regard to feelings for a same-sex friend, women's scores are consistently higher than men's.

To be fair, it has been suggested that men simply show love and affection in less direct ways. According to Swain (1989), "Joking relationships provide men with an implicit form of expressing affection, which is an alternative to explicit forms such as hugging and telling people they care about them" (p. 83). However, in terms of the overt expression of love and affection, a variety of kinds of evidence points to the conclusion that women are more affectionate and loving in their friendships than are men.

ɜ Closeness and Intimacy

Gender differences are typically reported in studies that have compared the closeness or intimacy of women's and men's relationships (see, e.g., Perlman & Fehr, 1987; Tognoli, 1980; Winstead, 1986, for reviews). In the friendship literature generally, three kinds of comparisons are made: women's versus men's ratings of their same-sex friendships, women's versus men's ratings of their opposite-sex friendships, and comparisons of same- and other-sex friendships within each gender.

Gender Differences in Same-Sex Friendships

Given the findings for quality, love, and affection just discussed, it is not surprising that women's friendships with other women are regarded as closer than men's friendships with other men (e.g., Buhrke & Fuqua, 1987; Fischer & Narus, 1981; Omoto & Mooney, 1993; Powers & Bultena, 1976; Reisman, 1990). Hacker (1981) reported that 32% of the female-female dyads in her sample considered their friendship to be "very close" compared to 15% of the male-male dyads (and 13% of the female-male dyads). When Sapadin (1988) asked professional women and men to rate their friendships in terms of closeness, enjoyment, and nurturance, women's same-sex friendships received the highest ratings on these items; men's same-sex friendships the lowest.

With regard to intimacy, studies of children and adolescents have shown that girls' same-sex friendships are more intimate than boys' (e.g., Bukowski et al., 1987; Reisman, 1990, Study 1). In Israel, female students in Grades 5, 7, and 11 rated their same-sex friendships higher on Sharabany's Intimacy Scale than did males (Sharabany, Gershon, & Hofman, 1981). When separate analyses were conducted for each of the eight scale items, significant effects were found for only three: girls rated their friendships higher in terms of trust and loyalty, giving and sharing, and attachment. Blyth and Foster-Clark (1987) examined friendship patterns among more than 2,000 junior high and high school students. They found that at each age, girls rated their same-sex friendships as more intimate than did boys. This finding held regardless of whether the friend was younger, the same age, or older than the participant. In fact, girls considered their closest same-sex friendship to be the most intimate relationship in their lives—more intimate than their relationship with their mother, father, or siblings. Boys at each age regarded their relationship with their mother and father as more intimate than their closest same-sex friendship.

Research with adults has produced similar findings. For example, in Williams's (1985) sample of more than 500 university students, men's scores on an emotional intimacy scale were significantly lower for same-sex friendships than were women's. Bell (1981b) interviewed 101 women and 65 men and concluded that "the evidence clearly indicates that female patterns of friendship are much more revealing and intimate than those found among men" (p. 62). For example, 60% of women, compared to 35% of men, reported that they would and did reveal anything at all to at least one close friend.

Gender Differences in Other-Sex Friendships

When rating the closeness or intimacy of opposite-sex friendships, there appears to be an asymmetry: Men regard their friendships with women as closer than their friendships with men, whereas the opposite holds for women (e.g., Buhrke & Fuqua, 1987). Not all studies have obtained this gender difference, however. Women and men assigned similar intimacy and enjoyment ratings to their cross-gender friendships in Sapadin's (1988) study, although men rated their other-sex friendships higher in nurturance than did women. Gender differences typically are not reported in studies of adolescents (e.g., Blyth & Foster-Clark, 1987; Reisman, 1990), although again there are inconsistencies. Among the junior high and high school students in Blyth and Foster-Clark's study, there were no gender differences in rating the intimacy of other-sex friends who were in the same grade as the participant. However, girls reported greater intimacy than did boys when rating an older opposite-sex friend. In the same vein, Sharabany et al. (1981) found that both boys and girls in Grade 5 assigned low intimacy scores to opposite-sex friendships. Intimacy increased in the higher grades, but much more quickly for girls than for boys.

Within-Gender Comparisons of
Same- and Other-Sex Friendships

Generally, men regard their other-sex friendships to be closer and more intimate than their same-sex friendships, whereas the opposite is true for women (e.g., Buhrke & Fuqua, 1987; Fischer & Narus, 1981). Sapadin (1988) found that women rated their same-sex friendships higher than their other-sex friendships in terms of intimacy, enjoyment, and nurturance. Men assigned higher ratings of enjoyment and nurturance to their friendships with women than with men, although they regarded the two kinds of friendships as equally intimate. Blyth and Foster-Clark (1987) found that both male and female adolescents ranked their other-sex friends lower in intimacy than their same-sex friends.

ɜ Are Women's Friendships Really More Intimate Than Men's?

Based on the evidence presented so far, the conclusion that women's friendships generally are closer or more intimate than men's may appear obvious. The usual culprit that is fingered by way of explanation is socialization. Girls in our society are encouraged to be intimate; boys are discouraged (e.g., Berman et al., 1988; Tognoli, 1980; Williams, 1985). However, this conclusion and its explanation are not nearly so straightforward and simple as they may seem. In fact, the issue of whether women's friendships are actually more intimate than men's has generated considerable controversy. In this section, an attempt is made to unravel the complexities of the different perspectives on this issue.

Men Are As Intimate As Women,
but Only in Their Closest Friendships

One point of view is that men may reserve intimacy for their closest friendships (e.g., Rands & Levinger, 1979). Based on a comparison of short-term acquaintances with longstanding friendships, Wright (1982) concluded that "the differences between women's and men's friendships diminish markedly as the strength and duration of the friendship increases" (p. 19). Similarly, Hays (1985) found that early on (after 3 weeks), friendship development was most strongly correlated with affection (expressing feelings) for women and companionship (shared activities) for men. In fact, for men, affection was *least* correlated with closeness. However, as the friendship became closer, the importance of affection increased for men to the point where sex differences disappeared.

In contrast, when Barth and Kinder (1988) compared casual, good, and close friends on measures of relational involvement and depth of conversations, gender differences did not decrease as closeness increased. Caldwell and Peplau (1982) tested this hypothesis using best friend relationships. They, too, failed to find support for it; women were more likely than men to disclose personal information to their same-sex best friend. Similarly, Reis et al. (1985) found that women's interactions were rated as more meaningful than men's even if analyses were conducted only for best friend interactions. On the basis of these data, Reis (1988) concluded that "the tendency for males to engage in relatively less meaningful same-sex interactions is pervasive, extending across close and superficial relationships" (p. 95).

Men Are As Intimate As Women, They Just Don't Like the Word

Another perspective is that women's and men's interactions may be equally intimate but that men resist applying this label when describing same-gender interactions. When Walker (1994) interviewed a small group of men, she found that they defined their friendships in a stereotypic way. For example, one respondent spoke of male friendship as hunting and fishing together, yet further questioning revealed that he actually never had gone hunting or fishing with his friend! When asked to recount their most recent conversation with a male friend, Walker discovered that these men frequently discussed personal and relationship issues.

A study by Reis et al. (1985) paints a different picture. They asked women and men to write out two recent conversations with their same-sex best friend. Content analyses revealed that the two sets of conversations were not equally intimate; women's conversations were rated by coders as more intimate than men's. Thus, they found no support for the notion that men interact as intimately as women, but merely shy away from referring to male interactions as "intimate."

Men Appear Less Intimate Only Because Intimacy Is Defined in a Female Way

Those who maintain that men's friendships are less intimate than women's usually point to research (presented earlier) showing that men engage in activities, whereas women engage in personal self-disclosure. Rawlins (1993), for example, referred to women's greater intimacy competence and remarked that "in contrast, a considerable number of males practice the 'hail-fellow-well-met' and activity-oriented carriage . . . useful for the world of work but not for facilitating intimacy" (p. 54). Recently, this perspective, which has been the dominant one, has come under sharp attack. The critics argue that women's friendships appear to be more intimate only because intimacy has been conceptualized and measured in a female-biased way (e.g., Camarena, Sarigiani, & Peterson, 1990; Cancian, 1986; Sherrod, 1989; Swain, 1989, 1992;

Wellman, 1992; Wood & Inman, 1993). Thus, men will be branded as "intimacy deficient" as long as researchers continue to subscribe to a female definition of intimacy. If, on the other hand, one allows for two routes to intimacy—personal self-disclosure *or* shared activities—then men's friendships are as intimate as women's. Put another way, women's and men's friendships are equally intimate; what differs is their definition of intimacy. For example, based on interviews with university students, Swain (1989) observed that "activities such as fishing, playing guitars, diving, backpacking, drinking, and weightlifting were central to men's meaningful experiences" (p. 76; see also Huyck, 1982). He coined the term *closeness in the doing* to capture the meaning of intimacy in men's friendships.

In the same vein, Camarena et al. (1990) defined intimacy as "the subjective experience of closeness toward another person" (p. 20) that can be achieved either through self-disclosure or shared experiences and adventures. The former is more likely to be the female path; the latter the male path. This hypothesis was tested in a sample of Grade 8 children. Contrary to expectations, self-disclosure was the best predictor of intimacy in close same-sex friendships for both boys and girls. However, for boys, intimacy also was predicted by shared experiences. Thus, even though boys tended to develop intimate friendships through self-disclosure, the authors maintained that an alternative route in the form of shared experiences and activities also was available to them. Camarena et al. also compared boys' and girls' scores on each of their measures. Girls had higher scores on the emotional closeness (intimacy) and self-disclosure scales, but there was no gender difference on the shared experiences scale. The authors comment, "That the greatest mean gender difference was found in self-disclosure highlights the significance of its exclusion or inclusion from definitions of intimacy that consider gender issues" (p. 27).

The results of this study are consistent with those of Helgeson, Shaver, and Dyer (1987), who found that women conceptualized same-sex intimacy in terms of talking more than shared activities. Men reported equal levels of both talking and activities with a same-sex friend.

A final study casts a different light on this issue. In research on the meanings of intimacy, Monsour (1992) found the standard gender difference, namely, that women were likely to conceptualize same-sex intimacy as self-disclosure; men were more likely to mention shared activities. However, an examination of the frequencies of these responses revealed that self-disclosure was at the top of the list for both women and men, whereas shared activities was near the bottom. Specifically, 56% of men (87% of women) specified self-disclosure as the meaning of intimacy in same-sex relationships compared to only 9% of men (0% of women) for whom intimacy meant shared activities.

The argument that men achieve intimacy through shared activities receives its strongest support in the form of anecdotal accounts drawn from interviews with small numbers of men. The results of quantitative studies show that even though men value shared activities, they place equal, if not greater, emphasis on self-disclosure as the route to intimacy.

Men Simply Are Less Intimate, Regardless of the Definition

According to Fischer and Narus (1981), "If women achieve greater intimacy than men, this says more about our society than about our view of intimacy" (p. 446). They developed an intimacy scale based on a very broad definition of intimacy that included mutual sharing of personal concerns and information, acceptance and caring, use of problem-solving skills, exchanging assistance and helpful criticism, and so on. Men's friendships still received lower intimacy scores than women's. However, the college students in their sample did not score as low as a comparison group of men in couples therapy. The authors suggest that it would be unfair, therefore, to characterize the friendships of their male participants as devoid of intimacy. Instead, they concluded that men "fail to develop as fully intimate relationships as do women" (p. 454).

Similarly, Sharabany's Intimacy Scale contains only one item referring to self-disclosure (frankness and spontaneity) along with items assessing common activities, trust and loyalty, and so on

(Sharabany et al., 1981). Nevertheless, in their study, boys' same-sex friendships received lower intimacy scores than girls'. Like Fischer and Narus, they pointed out that these differences were not so large as to warrant a conclusion of "inhibition of friendship among males." Yet, "we do recognize a pattern of lower intimate friendship among boys than among girls" (p. 806).

Rubin (1986) argues that men can be deeply bonded to one another, "without the kind of sharing of thought and feeling that is associated with the word 'intimacy' " (p. 168). She asserts that bonding does not constitute intimacy, noting that in her sample, only 10% of the 150 men described friendships that included the kind of intimacy and sharing of self that she observed in women's friendships.

The Same Definition, but Different Thresholds for Intimacy

Another point of view is that both men and women define intimacy in terms of self-disclosure, but that they have different thresholds for the level of disclosure that is required before a friendship is considered intimate. For example, in Caldwell and Peplau's (1982) study, when individuals were asked whether they would prefer a few intimate friends (defined as "a very close friend with whom one can really communicate and in whom one can confide about feelings and personal problems," p. 725) or a group of good friends, the vast majority of women (82%) and men (73%) favored a few intimate friends. (In the New Zealand replication of this study, the percentages were 75% of women and 53% of men; Aukett et al., 1988.) Thus, women and men were similar in the value they placed on intimate friendships. However, self-disclosure data revealed that men's interactions with a best friend were less intimate and personal than women's. The authors suggest that "men and women may be equally likely to define friends as intimate; however, men and women may have different standards for assessing the intimacy of friendship" (p. 731). Because men have been socialized to be less disclosing than women, a small amount of personal self-disclosure to a male friend may feel very intimate, whereas for women, much higher doses of self-disclosure might be required.

Reis et al. (1985) examined this possibility. They reasoned that if women and men possess different criteria for intimacy, then the same interaction should be evaluated differently by each gender. Participants were asked to rate the degree of intimacy in a set of videotaped conversations that varied in intimacy level. Men and women had very similar perceptions of the level of intimacy portrayed in the conversations.

Men Are Less Intimate, but They Like It That Way

A related position is that men prefer to have less intimate friendships than do women (e.g., Sherrod, 1989). There is some anecdotal support for this view. For example, Rosecrance (1986) reported that the friendships among men at the race track were not very intimate, but nevertheless, were satisfying. Tannen's (1990) impression was that the late adolescent boys in her study were quite satisfied with their style of interaction. Thus, even though each seemed to downplay the other's concerns and problems, these interactions did not seem uncaring. In contrast, when Reid and Fine (1992) interviewed a small group of married and single men, they reported that "many men complain that their friends will not talk about personal or emotional subjects" (p. 139). These men wanted to be more intimate with their male friends, but feared a negative reaction if they attempted more intimate interaction.

Haas and Sherman (1982) asked adults of all ages, "How would you improve conversations with someone of your own sex?" The most frequent response from men (27.2%) was that no improvement was required. The second most frequent answer was "more openness" (mentioned by 19.8%). Reisman (1990, Study 1) tested the hypothesis that male high school students and young adults would feel as satisfied with their same-sex friends as females, despite lower levels of self-disclosure. It was not supported—men reported less satisfaction with friends than did women. Moreover, for both men and women, the greater the self-disclosure, the greater the satisfaction with friendships. Furthermore, as mentioned earlier, in his second study there was evidence that men wished they interacted more intimately with male friends. Thus, although the literature is rather confusing, the evidence overall suggests that men generally are less intimate in their friendships, and do not particularly like it that way.

Men Can Be As Intimate As Women,
but Simply Choose Not to Be

A final point of view is that men are as capable of intimacy as are women but simply choose not to behave that way (e.g., O'Connor, 1992). In a study of self-disclosure in interactions with a friend, Walker and Wright (1976) reported that "male friendships were more strongly affected by intimate than nonintimate self-disclosure *if and when* the partners were willing to interact at a highly intimate level" (p. 740). Apparently, 5 of the 10 male pairs assigned to the intimate disclosure condition refused to cooperate.

Reis's data speak to this issue as well. In his studies of daily interaction, "when males interacted with females, the level of meaningfulness rose to a point where it no longer diverged from females' same-sex interaction. This seems to suggest that men are capable of interacting meaningfully but prefer to do so in the company of women" (Reis, 1988, p. 102). In another test of this hypothesis, Reis et al. (1985) asked women and men to engage in a meaningful conversation with their same-sex best friend. Content analyses of these conversations revealed that men's conversations were just as intimate as women's (see also Winstead, 1986). Thus, it does not appear that men lack the capacity for intimacy, but rather that they prefer not to exercise it in their interactions with other men.

The question of whether women's friendships are really more intimate than men's is certainly complex and not easily answered. Even to summarize the various positions and the evidence for or against them imposes a simplicity that does not exist. In virtually every case, some support was found for both sides of the issue. With these caveats in mind, overall, the evidence seems to suggest that men's friendships are less intimate than women's. It is not the case that men are reserving intimacy only for their closest friends.

It is also not the case that men simply are reluctant to use the word. Nor is it a matter of being evaluated by the wrong (i.e., feminine) metric or having a different threshold. Instead, it appears that men are less intimate than women in their friendships because they choose to be, even though they may not particularly like it.

There is one final issue that should be addressed before leaving this topic. Even though men may have less intimate friendships than women, intimate friendship is not "all there is" to friendship. This point is clear in Wellman's (1992) wry remark that "to define friendship solely as emotionally supportive companionship is to limit one's worldview to a California hot tub" (p. 104). Granted, there is evidence that men would benefit from adopting women's more intimate style (e.g., Reisman, 1990). However, the converse also has been argued, namely, that women would benefit from adopting men's activity-based orientation in which companionship and fun are emphasized (e.g., O'Connor, 1992). Duck and Wright (1993) commented that "the focus on the feminine mode of enacting intimacy fosters and legitimizes an unfortunate stereotype of women's friendships as noninstrumental, or at least less instrumental than those of men" (p. 725). Others favor the status quo, arguing that women's expressive style and men's instrumental style are complementary approaches that work well together (e.g., Huyck, 1982). Still others maintain that the optimal situation is one in which all people, regardless of gender, embrace both affective and activity-oriented modes of relating to friends (e.g., Swain, 1989; Winstead, 1986).

⊱ Gender Role Differences

In a provocative article, Wright (1988) cautions that the extent of similarity between women's and men's friendships should not be overlooked. One of his arguments is that gender effects might be attributable to variables that are correlated with gender, rather than gender per se. One such variable is gender role defined as the extent to which one fulfills societal expectations of masculinity or femininity (or both—androgyny, or neither—undifferentiated). Several studies have explored the relation between gender role and friendship variables such as self-disclosure and intimacy, as well as friendship characteristics, conceptions, and quality. As is evident in Table 5.1, these studies have produced quite a mixture of results. Part of the difficulty stems from the different ways of classifying individuals into various gender roles. In addition, the studies vary in terms of whether analyses are conducted separately for women and men within each gender role category. What can be gleaned from the table is that androgyny generally is positively associated with intimacy, self-disclosure, friendship quality, and various positive attitudes toward friendship, particularly cross-sex friendship. Some studies report parallel findings for femininity, although the results are not consistent. The findings for masculinity are very confusing, with studies reporting both positive and negative correlations with variables such as self-disclosure and intimacy. Individuals in the undifferentiated category usually score lowest on the measures used in these studies.

✒ Issues in Cross-Sex Friendships

"Friendship between a woman and a man? For many people, the idea is charming but improbable" (Rawlins, 1993, p. 51). Certainly, in the popular literature there has been lively debate over whether cross-sex friendships are possible (Ambrose, 1989) or not (Pogrebin, 1989). Recently, relationships scholars have begun to examine the issues involved in the formation and maintenance of cross-sex friendships. In an influential article, O'Meara (1989) delineated four challenges that must be negotiated in cross-sex friendships and has since added a fifth (O'Meara, 1994). Each of these challenges will be presented along with relevant empirical evidence, where available.

Determining the Nature of the Emotional Bond

According to O'Meara, women and men have been socialized to regard one another as potential romantic partners, not friends.

(text continues on page 149)

Table 5.1 Relations Between Gender Role and Friendship Variables

Author(s)	Participants	Measure	Results
Grigsby and Weatherley (1983)	University students	PAQ	No relation between femininity and intimacy of self-disclosure to a stranger
			Negative relation between masculinity and intimacy of self-disclosure to a stranger
			Feminine sex-typed participants self-disclosed more intimately than masculine sex-typed participants but not significantly more than undifferentiated types
			Androgynous participants self-disclosed significantly less than feminine participants but did not differ from masculine or undifferentiated participants
Stokes, Childs, and Fuehrer (1981)	University students	BSRI	No relation between femininity and willingness to self-disclose to best friend
			Positive relation between masculinity and willingness to self-disclose to strangers and acquaintances
			Masculinity × Femininity predicted willingness to self-disclose to best friend
			Willingness to self-disclose highest among androgynous participants

(continued)

143

Table 5.1 (Continued)

Author(s)	Participants	Measure	Results
Lombardo and Lavine (1981)	University students	BSRI	Self-disclosure of *intimate* topics • Androgynous females reported greater self-disclosure to both male and female best friend than sex-typed females but no difference in self-disclosure to mother and father • Androgynous males reported greater self-disclosure to all targets (male and female best friend, parents) than sex-typed males Self-disclosure of *nonintimate* topics • Androgynous females reported greater disclosure to male and female best friend and to father than sex-typed females • Androgynous males reported greater disclosure to all targets than sex-typed males
Lavine and Lombardo (1984)	University students	BSRI	Androgynous males and females reported greater self-disclosure to all targets (male and female best friend, mother, father) than sex-typed and undifferentiated males and females Sex-typed males and females reported greater self-disclosure to all targets than undifferentiated males and females
Narus and Fischer (1982)	Male university students	BSRI	Androgynous men reported greater ease of communication and sharing of confidences to the person they were closest to than sex-typed and undifferentiated men; sex-typed men reported greater ease of communication and sharing confidences than undifferentiated men

			Androgynous men reported equal sharing of confidences in same- and other-sex relationships; masculine men reported greater sharing of confidences in other-sex than in same-sex relationships; undifferentiated men reported equal sharing of confidences in same- and other-sex relationships (but at a lower level than androgynous men)
			The men did not differ in terms of ease of communication in same- vs. other-sex relationships
			Masculinity was positively correlated with sharing of confidences and ease of communication in both same- and other-sex relationships
			Femininity was positively correlated only with sharing of confidences in same-sex relationships
Fischer and Narus (1981)	University students	BSRI	Femininity predicted intimacy for females (regardless of gender of friend) but not for males
			Androgynous participants scored higher on intimacy than undifferentiated but not significantly higher than sex-typed participants
			Sex-typed participants scored higher on intimacy than undifferentiated participants
			Androgynous females scored highest in intimacy, particularly when rating same-sex friendships
			Sex-typed females were higher in intimacy than sex-typed males, especially when rating same-sex friendships

(continued)

145

Table 5.1 (Continued)

Author(s)	Participants	Measure	Results
Williams (1985)	University students	PAQ	Positive relation between femininity and emotional intimacy
			Negative relation between masculinity and emotional intimacy
			Androgynous and cross-sex-typed men scored higher in emotional intimacy than undifferentiated and sex-typed men (no difference between the latter two groups)
			Sex-typed and androgynous women scored higher in emotional intimacy than undifferentiated and cross-sex-typed women (no difference between the latter two groups)
Wheeler, Reis, and Nezlek (1983)	University students	PAQ	Positive relation between femininity and meaningfulness in same- and opposite-sex interactions for males but not females
			Feminine participants spent more time socializing with females than males
			No relation between masculinity and these variables
Conrad and Perlman (1987)	Community residents	BSRI	Androgynous participants had higher-quality friendships than sex-typed or undifferentiated participants (the latter two groups did not differ)
			Androgynous participants had more positive attitudes to friendship, reported more interaction with friends, and were more approving of cross-sex friendships than the other groups

Wright and Scanlon (1991)	Adults from various work settings, business organizations, and service groups	PAQ	When best same- and cross-sex friends were rated on 13 Acquaintance Description Form variables, sex role had an effect on only one variable: feminine and androgynous men rated their cross-sex best friend higher in self-affirmation value than masculine and undifferentiated men
Barth and Kinder (1988)	University students	PAQ	Sex-typed females ($M = 3.38$), androgynous females ($M = 3.40$), and androgynous males ($M = 3.39$) reported higher level of involvement in same-sex friendships than sex-typed males ($M = 3.13$ on a 5-point scale)
			No effects of sex role orientation on depth of conversations, friendship duration, or amount of time spent with same-sex friends
Jones, Bloys, and Wood (1990)	University students	BSRI	No relation between sex role and total number of close friends and number of close female friends; however, androgynous participants had the greatest number of close male friends, followed by sex-typed participants, and then undifferentiated participants
			Androgynous participants reported highest levels of reliable trust in friends, followed by sex-typed participants, and then undifferentiated participants
			Sex-typed females and androgynous females and males reported higher levels of communal orientation than the other groups; no differences in exchange orientation

(continued)

Table 5.1 (Continued)

Author(s)	Participants	Measure	Results
			Androgynous participants rated the affective and arousal-inducing (activity) characteristics of their friends more positively than sex-typed and undifferentiated participants
			Androgynous participants were significantly less lonely and more satisfied with their friendships than undifferentiated participants
Thorbecke and Grotevant (1982)	High school students	PAQ	Positive relation between femininity and exploration of ideas about friendship for males, but not females
			No relation between masculinity and friendship exploration

NOTE: PAQ = Personal Attributes Questionnaire (Spence & Helmreich, 1978); BSRI = Bem Sex Role Inventory (Bem, 1974).

Thus, one of the partners may misinterpret the friendship as a romance. Adams (1985) reported that elderly women assumed that cross-sex friendship entailed romance or courtship. This belief resulted in the elimination of married men from the already shrunken field of eligibles (given men's shorter life span), leaving extremely few friendship candidates. In fact, cross-sex, same-age friendships comprised only about 2% of their friendship network (see Booth & Hess, 1974, for related findings).

Reid and Fine (1992) noted that men in dating or marital relationships felt they should limit the amount of intimacy in their cross-sex friendships. Thus, they shied away from discussing intimate topics (e.g., sexual issues in their marriage) with female friends. Single men reported that they limited intimate self-disclosure if they felt sexually attracted to a female friend but believed a romantic relationship was not a possibility. Emotional closeness in cross-sex friendships also may be regulated by not reciprocating gestures of affection. For example, Gaines (1994) found that in cross-sex friendships, respect was reciprocated, but not affection.

The Sexual Challenge

As Huyck (1982) comments, "There is often an implicit or explicit assumption that adult cross-sex friendships may or will become sexualized" (p. 481; see also Allan, 1989; Bell, 1981a). Because of this assumption, friendships with the other sex are often discouraged, especially for married people (see also Lampe, 1985; Rose, 1985). If a married person does have other-sex friends, certain "precautions" may be taken such as socializing in the presence of a spouse (e.g., Allan, 1989) or limiting cross-sex friends to those met through one's spouse (Booth & Hess, 1974).

In general, men are more likely than women to view cross-sex friendships in a sexual way. For example, there is evidence that men misinterpret women's friendliness as sexual interest (e.g., Abbey, 1982; Shotland & Craig, 1988). In other research, Monsour (1992; see also Helgeson et al., 1987) found that twice as many men as women mentioned sexual contact when describing intimacy in cross-sex friendships, although these percentages were quite low for both sexes (16% vs. 8%). In a subsequent study, both women and men reported that sexual overtones were minimal in their cross-sex friendships (Monsour, Betty, & Kurzweil, 1993).

There is some debate over whether sexual attraction merely adds "spice" to cross-sex friendships or whether it is a source of strain. In Rose's (1985) research, sexual attraction was the most frequently listed strategy for forming cross-sex friendships, although it was rarely mentioned as a maintenance strategy. When Sapadin (1988) asked, "What do you like most about your friendships?" only 6% of women and 7% of men mentioned sexual excitement. However, when asked, "What do you dislike . . ." 20% of women and 28% of men reported "sexual tensions." Cupach and Metts (1991) point out that for some cross-sex friends, "sexual bantering and teasing add a playful component to the relationship that both partners find comfortable and nonthreatening. For other friendship pairs, sexual attraction may be too intense or too threatening to treat indirectly and/or playfully" (p. 95). The authors note that sexual tensions can be difficult to manage because explicit discussion of this topic may be awkward, especially if sexual attraction is one-sided. Moreover, if friends become sexually involved, the confusion about whether the relationship is a friendship or a romantic relationship can be distressing, especially for women. This may explain why women are less likely than men to agree with the statement: "Having a sexual relationship adds deeper feelings and closeness to the friendship" (Sapadin, 1988, p. 396).

Whether sexual attraction is considered a blessing or a curse may depend on other factors such as conventionality. Bell (1981a) found that conventional women and men (in the United States and Australia) tended to believe that the sexual feelings underlying cross-sex friendships served as a constant threat to the friendship (and other relationships). Nonconventional women and men were less likely to comment on the inherent dangers of sexuality. In fact, more than half of the nonconventional women welcomed a sexual dimension in at least some friendships and believed it could have positive effects. The various perspectives on this issue are perhaps best summed up in Swain's (1992) comment that "cross-sex friendships are both enriched and plagued by fluctuating and unclear sexual boundaries" (p. 167).

Relationship Quality in a Societal Context of Gender Inequality

Many social scientists consider equality an essential feature of friendship (see Chapter 1). Thus, as long as men are afforded higher status in our society, true friendship between women and men is not possible (O'Meara, 1989; see also Pogrebin, 1989). Although empirical research cannot address this issue directly, there is evidence that in cross-sex interactions, women conform to men's style more than vice versa (e.g., Bendtschneider & Duck, 1993; Gaines, 1994). However, other research presented earlier (e.g., Reis, 1988) showed that men are more personal and intimate in their interactions with women than with other men. Thus, these studies suggest that men adopt women's (presumably lower status) style of relating in cross-sex interactions. The issue is further complicated by Booth and Hess's (1974) findings. They reported that the greatest amount of confiding occurred in cross-sex friendships where the man had superior educational status. People were less comfortable in nonnormative situations (e.g., equal status, or a higher-status woman). Thus, the issue of equality in cross-sex friendships remains unresolved.

The Challenge of Public Relationships

Because cross-sex friendship is anomalous in our society, a woman and a man who are friends may be called on to "explain" or justify the relationship to family and other friends (e.g., Rawlins, 1993). Allan (1989) maintains that outsiders "attempt to influence and control" cross-sex friendships to a greater extent than same-sex friendships (p. 83). In Adams's (1985) study, the women generally did not condone courtship among the elderly, and given that cross-sex friendships were regarded as romances, friendships with men were discouraged. Thus, those who were interested in developing cross-sex friendships felt inhibited from doing so. After all, what would other people think?

Romantic partners may be particularly likely to demand explanations for cross-sex friendships or seek assurances that the friendship is not a threat. Several writers have pointed out that jealousy over a cross-sex friend can be a contentious issue in marital and dating relationships (e.g., Allan, 1989; Cupach & Metts, 1991; Lampe, 1985).

The Opportunity Challenge

Recently, O'Meara (1994) added another difficulty in becoming friends with members of the other sex; namely, *where* do you meet them? The workplace has been suggested as a particularly important venue for the formation of cross-sex friendships (e.g., Fine, 1986). Indeed, Booth and Hess (1974) found that women in the labor force reported more cross-sex friendships than women who were not employed. However, places of employment are still largely sex-segregated. Even if women and men do work together, typically their statuses are not equal (Fine, 1986; Huyck, 1982; O'Meara, 1994). Moreover, cross-sex friendships in the workplace are frequently misinterpreted as sexual affairs. Based on these considerations, O'Meara concluded that "the world of work is more restraining than facilitating of cross-sex friendship contact opportunities" (p. 6).

Thus, the formation and maintenance of cross-sex friendships requires the management of a set of thorny issues from which same-sex friendships are largely exempt. Given the scarcity of research on these issues, it is difficult to determine just how formidable these obstacles are. In an attempt to answer this question, Monsour, Harris, and Kurzweil (1994) presented participants with O'Meara's (1989) challenges and asked them whether these had been issues in their interactions with an other-sex friend over the past 3 weeks. The emotional bond challenge was most frequently reported, followed by the audience challenge, the sexual challenge, and finally, the equality challenge. The extent to which these issues arose depended to some extent on variables such as the nature of the friendship, gender, and romantic involvement. For close cross-sex friends, the nature of the bond and explaining the friendship to others were more likely to be relevant issues than for casual friends. Women were somewhat less likely to mention difficulties surrounding sexuality than were men. For men who were not romantically involved, the sexual challenge was a greater issue than for men who were in dating or marital relationships. The authors concluded that these four challenges presented a problem for some cross-sex friendships, but not a majority.

ఆ Summary

Women and men appear to experience friendship differently. From childhood on, women like talking with friends, particularly about feelings and relationships, whereas men like to do things together. When men talk, it is frequently about their activities— sports and work. However, these conclusions are not as straight-forward as they appear. Some writers accept the portrayal of men's friendships as activity based and women's as affectively based and argue that each should be regarded as a legitimate path to inti-macy. Others take exception to this depiction, arguing that men's friendships are more affective and women's friendships entail more activities than the literature suggests. Moreover, there are multiple perspectives on the issue of whose friendships are more intimate. Thus, currently, there are a number of contentious issues in this literature. Overall, the evidence suggests that women have more intimate, close, and satisfying friendships with one another than do men. Research aimed at explaining why suggests that it is not the case that men lack the capacity for intimacy but rather that they choose not to exercise it.

It has been suggested that at least some gender differences may be attributable to differences in gender roles. Unfortunately, so far, research on this issue has failed to provide a clear answer, given varied and sometimes contradictory findings. Nevertheless, there was evidence that androgynous women and men generally have open, intimate, and satisfying friendships. Finally, the issues involved in forming cross-sex friendships were discussed. Women and men may have difficulty becoming friends because of inadequate opportunities for contact, particularly in a context of equality. If these barriers are overcome, they still face challenges such as dealing with romantic and sexual attraction and having to explain the friendship to other people.

❧ Note

1. From "The National Snowplow Hockey League," *Miami Herald*. Dave Barry is a syndicated humor columnist with the *Miami Herald*. Reprinted with permission.

6

&

Friendship Maintenance

After it has started one is still faced with having to make the
friendship *work*.

—Harré (1977, p. 341)

In the words of Duck (1994), " 'Relationship maintenance' refers
generally to the vast unstudied void in relational research—that
huge area where relationships continue to exist between the point
of their initial development (which has been intensively studied)
and their possible decline (which has also been studied but somewhat less intensively)" (p. 45). The purpose of this chapter is to
discuss the studies that have begun to fill this vast void in order
to glean what knowledge there is about the process of making
friendships "work." As Eidelson (1980) has shown, early on in a
relationship, satisfaction is high and the future looks bright. However, inevitably one encounters certain costs. Friends make demands for social support (e.g., Rook, 1989; Rook & Pietromonaco,
1987), they take time, and they cost money. Eidelson found that

satisfaction plunges as costs are incurred and only rises again if the benefits are sufficient to offset the costs. Clearly, there is maintenance work involved in ensuring that the benefits outweigh the negative aspects of friendship.

This chapter is organized around two central questions: First, *what* are the issues that must be negotiated to maintain a friendship? To answer this question, the tensions or dialectics that must be managed will be examined. The process of maintaining friendships also involves dealing with anger and resolving conflicts. The other focal question is, *how* do people go about maintaining their friendships? As will be seen, to a large extent, maintenance is a by-product of our mundane, everyday interactions with friends. However, when asked, people also are able to report on the explicit strategies they use to keep their friendships alive and prosperous.

⠶ Dialectics of Friendship Maintenance

There are a number of dilemmas involved in maintaining any relationship, and friendship is no exception. We have to juggle our need for dependence with our need to be independent; wanting to be completely open versus wanting to protect ourselves by not revealing everything; wanting to have a lot in common, but not so much that the relationship feels boring and predictable. Communication researchers in particular have made progress in identifying the major dialectics inherent in close relationships. Unfortunately, to date, little research has been conducted on these dynamics, particularly in friendship relationships. However, management of these issues may be especially important in friendships. Unlike other kinds of relationships, there are few external structures to promote continuance of friendships. Brenton (1974), among others, has noted that kin, romantic, and marital relationships operate within fairly clearly defined bounds. In contrast, friendships are not highly organized, institutionalized relationships. In Brenton's view, this freedom is one of the great attractions of friendship, but it is also a double-edged sword: "It slices us free of restrictions but it also cuts us off from the comfort and security of knowing exactly what is expected of us and how we should behave with our friends" (p. 23).

Similarly, Wiseman (1986) commented that friendship is an anomalous relationship in our society because it is an intimate relationship that operates voluntarily, without societal or contractual regulation. She solicited accounts of problems with friends from women and men (ages 18 to 80). The various problems were interpreted as reflecting a continual tension between intimacy and commitment, on the one hand, and voluntary association and freedom, on the other.

The dynamic of stable intimacy versus freedom identified by Wiseman is related to the dialectics of integration-separation (which entails connection vs. autonomy; Baxter, 1994), closeness versus distance (Brenton, 1974), and dependence-independence. In fact, Rawlins (1983a, 1992) has argued that the successful resolution of the dynamic of independence and dependence is a fundamental requirement for maintaining a friendship. Each person must feel free to pursue his or her own individual interests separate from the other. At the same time, each must feel that the other can be relied on for help and support regardless of the circumstances. In his view, "When negotiated together, these liberties provide a basis for preserving close friendship" (p. 260).

Based on interviews with pairs of close friends, Rawlins (1983a, 1983b) identified several other dynamics, centering on the issue of openness, that come into play when maintaining friendships. For example, for a friendship to be close, it is necessary to reveal personal information. However, there is the risk of being hurt because of the vulnerability that accompanies self-disclosure. Thus, expressiveness and openness must be balanced with self-protectiveness. (In a related conceptualization, Baxter, 1994, identified openness-closedness as part of an expression-privacy dialectic.) Rawlins (1992) posited that the development of trust in a friendship is contingent on the successful management of this dialectic.

Another dilemma pertaining to openness is the dialectic of candor versus restraint (Rawlins, 1983b). This dialectic (candor vs. discretion) is regarded as another exemplar of the expression-privacy dialectic in Baxter's (1994) writings. In order for a friendship to become intimate and close, it is important for friends to be honest with each other. On the other hand, there is the risk of hurting the other if one is too honest ("No, I really don't like your haircut."). This dialectic is similar to the tension between judgment and acceptance—wanting to accept one's friend as he or she is, versus feeling free to offer criticism (Rawlins, 1992).

Other kinds of dilemmas or dialectics that must be managed to maintain a friendship include the tension between constancy and change (Brenton, 1974). We want to believe that our friend will continue to be the same person and that the friendship will endure. However, we are also confronted with the reality that people change. Baxter (1994) focused on a related dialectic of stability-change, which she discussed in terms of wanting both predictability and novelty in the same relationship.

Finally, Rawlins (1992) also spoke of a dialectic of affection versus instrumentality. This is the tension between caring for a friend as an end in itself versus valuing the friendship for the instrumental benefits it provides (i.e., the friendship as a means to an end). Even though we enjoy the benefits our friends shower on us, we believe that this should not be the basis of the friendship.

In summary, as is apparent, there are a number of complex, competing tensions to be managed in friendship relationships. One must strike a balance between independence and dependence, closeness and distance, and openness and self-protection, to name a few. Wiseman (1986) commented that "friendship is a unique and fragile relationship containing the seeds of its own destruction in the cross-pressures of freedom and stable intimacy" (p. 193). These ominous words underline the difficulties inherent in dealing with these kinds of tensions. Dialectics by definition involve change and flux between competing forces. Thus, these issues cannot be settled "for once and for all" but instead must continually be apprehended and negotiated. Moreover, to maintain a friendship, these tensions must be resolved to the satisfaction of each person. If you are wanting independence at a time when your friend is seeking dependence, dealing with these competing forces may require some delicate negotiations. Thus, some writers in this area (e.g., Burleson & Samter, 1994) have suggested that conflict management skills are important for maintaining friendships. As will be seen in the next section, such skills are likely to be beneficial not only for managing dialectics but also for dealing with the anger and conflict that inevitably arises.

❧ Conflict and Anger in Friendships

According to Solano (1986), "Friendship should not be considered as an unmixed blessing . . . but rather as a complex and sometimes problematic relationship" (p. 241). Studies of friendship development have shown that although perceptions of the benefits of the friendship increase as the relationship progresses, reports of anger and conflict also increase (Ginsberg & Gottman, 1986; Hays, 1985; Hays & Oxley, 1986; Shaver et al., 1985). In fact, when people are asked to describe an anger experience, friends are frequently the target or perceived cause (e.g., Averill, 1983; Fehr & Baldwin, in press; Perlman, 1990; Russell & Fehr, 1994). For example, among the young women in Fehr and Baldwin's study, friends were surpassed only by boyfriends as provokers of anger. Even children are faced with conflict and negativity in their friendships. Berndt and Das (1987) found that over a 6-month period, children viewed their best friend less positively. Girls made more negative comments about their friend; boys made fewer positive comments and, in some cases, reported increased aggression. Werebe (1987) found that adolescent girls experienced considerable ambivalence in their friendships. Although stating that they were close, some girls also were highly critical of their friends. Girls also mentioned having quarrels and conflicts more often than boys did. These findings may simply reflect girls' greater willingness to report negative feelings and experiences. However, it is also possible that the intense closeness of these girls' friendships heightened the probability of conflict and disagreements. Conflicts may have been initiated to create distance and thereby strike a balance between intimacy and autonomy. For example, Gottman (1983) found that young children escalate and de-escalate play as a means of managing both the level of amity and conflict. Regardless of the reasons for conflict, the fact is that friends have fights and get angry with one another.

What causes anger and conflict in friendships? Unfortunately, most of the literature on elicitors of anger and conflict has focused on marital or romantic relationships. However, many of the instigators identified in that literature also apply to friendships. These include rebuff or rejection, being mocked or minimized, cumulative annoyances, negligence or lack of consideration, unwarranted criticism, and betrayal of trust (see Fehr & Baldwin, in press). The latter instigator has received the most attention in the friendship literature. Wiseman (1986) observed that "the intimacy and closeness that is an integral part of friendship and creates mutual expectations makes both participants vulnerable to betrayals of trust" (p. 201). In Jones and Burdette's (1994) research on betrayal, women were most likely to have been betrayed by their spouse (28.1%), followed by a same-sex friend (26.5%). These percentages were lower for men (14.3% and 9.7%, respectively), who were more likely to report being betrayed by a coworker (18.8%). Data on committing betrayals revealed parallel findings; the most common target of betrayal for both women and men was their spouse. For women, but not men, a same-sex friend was the next most likely target. Finally, Davis and Todd (1985) asked individuals whether their best or closest friend had ever "engaged in any action or failure to act that seemed to be a violation or betrayal of the relationship" (p. 31). More than one third of the individuals reported having experienced one or more violations. In addition, 37% admitted to having committed friendship violations.

Effects of Conflict and Anger on Friendships

Given the many positive experiences in our friendships, one might think that we would overlook our friends' occasional misdeeds. Not so, according to Rook and Pietromonaco (1987). They argue that the rarity of negative events relative to positive ones makes them more salient, and therefore they have a particularly potent effect on a relationship. Moreover, as Rook (1989) explains, there is an asymmetry such that negative events in a relationship can cancel the effects of positive events, but not vice versa. Thus, "a single heated exchange during the course of an otherwise pleasant dinner party may spoil the experience; in contrast, a single pleasant exchange in the midst of an evening marred with strife has little power to restore tranquility" (p. 187).

In friendships, the negative event that is particularly damaging is anger triggered by the betrayal of trust. This was evident in Fehr and Baldwin's (in press) research on anger accounts. For example, a 24-year-old woman wrote:

> My best friend and I were like sisters. We grew up together, we went to the same school and finished high school together. I was closer to her than anybody in my life. We did everything together. We dated different boys and shared our secrets, everything. I knew her like a book. But two years ago [it] all changed. She started to tell lies about me to my boyfriend, and we broke up. After a few weeks, I found out they were going out behind my back. I did talk to her since and she apologized. But I don't want to talk to her anymore. I am very sad because I love her.

Based on her research on problems in friendships, Wiseman (1986) commented that "betrayal of trust can result in a complete (and sorrowful) recasting of the entire personality of the erring friend" (p. 201). The effects of betrayal also were examined in Jones and Burdette's (1994) research. When the participant was the perpetrator, 51% of men and 38% of women reported that their behavior had either ended the relationship, or at least made it worse. Approximately 40% of women and men claimed that the relationship was not affected and the remaining 20% or so felt that the relationship had actually improved. A very different picture emerged, however, when it was the participant who was the victim of betrayal. In this case, 93% or more of the women and men reported that the betrayal harmed the relationship. Davis and Todd (1985) compared friendships in which violations had or had not occurred, using their Relationship Rating Form. Participants who had experienced violations (i.e., committed by the friend) rated the friendship lower on the Viability (trust, respect, acceptance) and Success scales. Participants who committed violations rated the friendship lower on the Intimacy, Support, Stability, and Success scales than participants who did not self-report violations.

As these studies show, even the extreme action of betraying a friend is not all that rare. Moreover, this event can have devastating consequences for the friendship. The prospect of maintaining friendships when such difficult circumstances can arise seems rather daunting. How do friends deal with anger and conflict? This issue is discussed next.

Dealing With Conflict and Anger

Regardless of how anger is caused, whether by an extreme event such as betrayal or an annoying event such as your friend talking to you incessantly during a movie, it seems reasonable to assume that anger must be dealt with in order for a friendship to remain healthy. Yet, little is known about whether, or how, friends handle conflict and anger. A few studies have explored hypothetical conflicts in friendship or roommate relationships (e.g., Canary & Spitzberg, 1987; Gergen & Gergen, 1988; Miller, 1991; see Fehr & Baldwin, in press, for a review). In Gergen and Gergen's (1988) research, undergraduates were asked to imagine that their roommate had just told them "I am really angry at you" because the participant had allegedly betrayed the roommate's confidence. In Miller's (1991) study, individuals were presented with a description of a conflict between two same-sex friends caused by broken promises. In both cases, the goal was to identify the interaction sequences that comprise a conflict script. These researchers were able to elucidate the kinds of responses that escalate conflict between friends (e.g., responding to accusations with retaliation rather than apology) as well as those that facilitate successful resolution of the conflict (e.g., responding to a friend's apology with compassion rather than anger). Although Gergen and Gergen did not examine gender differences, Miller did not find evidence of many gender differences in her sample.

Even fewer studies have dealt with actual, rather than hypothetical, conflicts between friends. Sillars (1980a, 1980b) conducted a series of studies on conflict among college roommates. Three major categories of conflict strategies were identifiable in these data: The *passive and indirect* (or avoidance) strategy was to avoid directly discussing the problem. The *distributive* strategy involved explicit discussion of conflict in which the partner was evaluated negatively and pressured to make concessions. The third strategy, *integrative,* also involved explicit discussion of conflict, except in this case the partner received a neutral or positive evaluation and concessions were not demanded. When roommates described problems (Sillars, 1980a) or were videotaped discussing a conflict issue (Sillars, 1980b), the most commonly used strategy was avoidance. Integrative tactics were least likely to be adopted in dealing with roommate problems. Ironically, these tactics were the most likely to result in a positive outcome. Specifically, use of integrative strategies was positively correlated with satisfactory resolution of the conflict and satisfaction with the roommate, and negatively correlated with the frequency and duration of conflict. The finding that integrative tactics produced the most effective conflict resolution has been reported in other research as well (e.g., Canary & Spitzberg, 1987, 1990).

Gender Differences

Although Sillars did not examine gender differences, there is evidence that conflict may take different forms in male and female friendships. In particular, conflict in male friendships tends to be more direct or overt than in female friendships. After observing the interactions of children in Grades 4 and 5, Thorne and Luria (1986) commented that "girls *do* engage in conflict, although it tends to take more indirect forms than the direct insults and challenges more often found in interactions among boys" (p. 179). When Tannen (1990) analyzed videotaped conversations of students in Grades 2, 6, and 10, she concluded that girls were much more concerned than boys with avoiding conflict and disagreement in their friendships. This tendency for girls to shy away from conflict extends to late adolescence and adulthood. Richey and Richey (1980), for example, reported that in their sample of 17- to 25-year-olds, males' quarrels were more overt and less controlled than those of females. Finally, based on interviews with adult women (in their 20s to 50s), Oliker (1989) reported that "each of these women felt that suppressing conflict was the way to preserve harmony in the relationship, although for some it nonetheless left troubled feelings" (p. 71).

The usual explanation for this gender difference is that girls and women fear that overt expression of anger or conflict will lead to loss of the friendship. Thus, from childhood on, women may adopt a more indirect approach in the interests of relationship preservation. However, the dynamics become more complex when one considers cross-gender interaction. In research on children's interactions, there is evidence that boys are not very responsive to girls' indirect style (see, e.g., Maccoby, 1990; Phinney, 1979). However, Thorne and Luria (1986) found that conflict in cross-gender friendships more closely resembled the style of boys' than girls' same-sex interactions. Perhaps girls ultimately adopt a more direct approach in the wake of frustration at having their polite suggestions repeatedly ignored.

In the adult literature, there also is evidence that conflict and the expression of negative emotions such as anger are more direct in opposite- than in same-sex relationships (e.g., Allen & Haccoun, 1976; Helgeson et al., 1987). However, the situation is complicated by research showing that men are uncomfortable directly expressing anger to women. For example, Blier and Blier-Wilson (1989) asked women and men to imagine expressing anger to their best friend (male or female). Men reported that they would be more comfortable expressing anger to a male, than a female, best friend. In fact, they were less confident than women that they could express anger to a female friend.

What can be extracted from this rather confusing set of findings is a general reticence on the part of both sexes to directly confront conflict in friendships. (Sillars's findings were particularly clear in this regard.) This avoidant tendency is exacerbated in particular kinds of friendships, depending on the gender composition of the pair.

The fragility of friendships may contribute to the use of avoidance tactics. Unlike marriage, for example, there are few external sources of commitment to help preserve the relationship. Thus, friends may worry more than spouses that a direct confrontation could end the relationship. Fitzpatrick and Winke (1979) found that in casual friendships, individuals reported using tactics of manipulation and nonnegotiation (i.e., avoidance tactics). However, the greater the commitment to the relationship, the more direct and open the conflict strategies. Thus, participants were most likely to use emotional appeals and personal rejection tactics with their spouses. Consistent with these results, Davis and Todd (1982) found that spouses/lovers scored higher on conflict and relationship maintenance scales than friends. Interestingly, their interpretation was that the greater commitment demanded in marriage than in friendship engenders more conflict.

In conclusion, when anger and conflict occur in friendships, it appears that the most common response is to bury one's head in the sand. This is not a particularly adaptive approach given compelling evidence that the use of integrative tactics (i.e., explicit discussion of the conflict) is most likely to lead to satisfaction with the outcome of the conflict and with the relationship itself. The negative correlations between the use of integrative tactics and both frequency and duration of conflict further suggest that the use of this strategy may ultimately reduce the number of conflicts and the amount of time it takes to resolve them. (Given the correlational nature of these data, it is also possible that when conflicts are few and far between, it is easier to use integrative tactics.) Nevertheless, friends generally opt for the path of least resistance and avoid directly dealing with conflict issues. This may account for Davis and Todd's finding that resolution of violations were quite rare. Only 30% of participants who reported violations were completely satisfied with the outcome. There was some evidence that friends who were able to deal satisfactorily with violations had stronger friendships (as assessed by the Relationship Rating Form) than those who had not experienced a violation. Thus, having weathered a storm seemed to create an even closer bond. However, most of these friendships were unable to survive the storm.

❧ Maintenance Strategies

Despite a rather dismal record of dealing with anger and conflict, many friendships seem to carry on, presumably because maintaining friendships entails more than dealing with conflict. In this section, the focus is on the myriad ways in which friends ensure the continuance of their relationship on a normal, day-to-day basis. According to Duck (1994; see also Canary & Stafford, 1994), there are two elements to relationship maintenance: One is strategic planning for the continuation of the relationship; the other is "the breezy allowance of the relationship to continue by means of the routine everyday interactions and conversations that make the relationship what it is" (p. 46).

Implicit Strategies

As noted in Chapter 5, both women and men spend time with friends either engaging in activities, talking, or both. Presumably, when friends choose to engage in an activity or have a conversation, they are motivated by the intrinsic rewards of such interactions, rather than planning them with purposive maintenance in mind. Such interactions nevertheless serve to maintain the relationship.

In fact, Duck (1994) argues that everyday talk is the essence of relationship maintenance. Talk provides a vision or image of what the relationship is and will be; talk is the vehicle for sharing one another's worlds of experience, and talk serves to sustain or reinforce reality for the partners. Moreover, the mere occurrence of talk, regardless of its content, signifies to the partners that the relationship exists and is important. As support for this view, he cites Duck et al.'s (1991) finding that simply having a conversation with a friend was more important than the actual topics discussed. Thus, it appears that friendships are sustained through ordinary, everyday interaction.

Explicit Strategies

Research has focused mainly on the *explicit* strategies people use to maintain relationships. These studies generally deal with marriage (e.g., Dindia & Baxter, 1987; Stafford & Canary, 1991). Fortunately, the maintenance of friendships has not been neglected completely.

Scenario Studies

In the earliest studies, participants were not asked directly how they maintained their friendships, but rather responded to hypothetical relationship scenarios. Ayres's (1983) study serves as the prototype of this kind of research. Individuals were presented with scenarios that varied in relationship type (acquaintance, friend, teacher-student, and coworker), gender, and whether relationship stability, development, or deterioration was desired. The scenarios were rated in terms of 38 possible maintenance strategies, which were reduced to three factors: avoidance (ignoring or avoiding events or issues that might change the relationship); balance (maintaining equity by keeping number of favors the same, maintaining emotional support levels); and directness (directly telling the other that one prefers to keep the relationship as it is). Ratings of these factors did not differ as a function of relationship type or gender of the protagonist. However, participants endorsed different strategies depending on whether the protagonist and his or her partner desired relationship maintenance or change. For example, individuals endorsed the use of balance for the protagonist if his or her partner wanted the relationship to deteriorate rather than remain stable or develop. If the partner wanted to develop the relationship and the protagonist did not, avoidance or directness were chosen.

A follow-up study was conducted by Shea and Pearson (1986) who varied not only whether the protagonist was male or female but whether his or her partner was male or female. Only acquaintances and friends were compared. As in Ayres's study, no effect for relationship type was found. However, there was an interaction between gender and relationship intent. Generally, women were more likely than men to report that they would use directness strategies to keep their relationships with men stable. (Women's purported use of directness strategies was greater for relationships with men than with women.) No effects were found for avoidance and balance strategies, even though both women and men reported greater use of these strategies than directness. The authors attribute their failure to replicate Ayres's findings to inadequacies in his measure. This measure was also criticized by

Dindia and Baxter (1987), who investigated the strategies that married couples employ to maintain and repair their relationship. None of the strategies these couples reported appeared on the list of 38 strategies that Ayres (1983) generated.

Self-Report Studies

According to Canary and Stafford (1994), the kinds of maintenance activities that are engaged in may differ depending on the type of relationship and its stage of development. Fortunately, both of these factors have been examined in the handful of studies on this topic. For example, Canary, Stafford, Hause, and Wallace (1993) asked nearly 600 students in communication classes to delineate strategies they used to maintain different kinds of relationships and to provide behavioral examples of each. The most frequently mentioned strategy (by 52.7% of respondents) was "direct discussions and listening to one another" (p. 9), labeled *openness*. The behavior that was regarded as most representative of this strategy was self-disclosure. The second most frequent strategy (45.8%) was communicating that the relationship was important. The behavior that was seen to exemplify this *assurance* strategy was supportiveness. Nearly the same number of participants (44.6%) also mentioned spending time together as a way of maintaining friendships, termed *joint activities*. Strategies listed by 30% to 35% of the participants included *positivity* (trying to make interactions pleasant), *cards/letters/calls*, and *avoidance* (evasion of partner or relationship issues). Responses such as using humor, sharing tasks, and relying on one's social network to help maintain the relationship were generated by fewer than 10% of the sample.

Interestingly, the more direct strategies of openness, assurances, and positivity were likely to be used to maintain romantic, rather than friendship, relationships. The strategies of assurances, cards/letters/calls, and sharing tasks were reported more frequently when describing a familial relationship, rather than a friendship. In discussing these results, Canary et al. (1993) speculate that people may be more concerned about maintaining their romantic and familial relationships than their friendships. If so, they should generate and endorse categories such as "self-maintaining" or "no maintenance" when describing friendships. However, research by Rose (1985; Rose & Serafica, 1986) shows that these are very infrequent responses, especially for same-sex friendships. The fact that Canary et al.'s participants opted for more direct maintenance strategies in their romantic relationships is parallel to the finding (reported earlier) that people use more direct conflict tactics in their romantic than in their friendship relationships.

The remaining studies to be discussed focused exclusively on friendships. Some studies compared the strategies used to maintain different types of friendships (e.g., high vs. low in commitment; same- vs. opposite-sex), whereas others examined friendships at different stages of development (e.g., casual, close, best friend).

Matthews (1986) found that commitment to a friendship was associated with different approaches to maintenance. She obtained detailed life stories from elderly women and men ($M = 74$ years), using friendships as the core theme. Participants were highly committed to some friendships and made extensive efforts to ensure their continuance (e.g., taking long trips to visit the person). In other cases, long-term friendships were maintained through letters and telephone calls. For less committed friendships, circumstantial factors determined whether they kept in contact. For example, living in the same place throughout one's life contributed to the continuation of these friendships. Individuals who had moved away frequently maintained such ties to friends from their hometown. In these cases, visits to friends were a by-product of visits to family members. If family ties ceased to exist (e.g., through death, moving away), as a rule, so did the friendship. Less committed friendships also were maintained by formalizing the relationship (e.g., forming a club). This kind of structural commitment then supplanted personal commitment as the impetus for continuing the relationship. A related approach was involvement in established formal groups such as alumni associations. Apparently, one respondent's friendship with a college friend continued primarily because of what each read about the other in their fraternity's newsletter.

In Richey and Richey's (1980) sample of late adolescents, best friend relationships were extremely stable. When asked about the maintenance strategies that contributed to the longevity of these friendships, both males and females responded that the most important factor was allowing friends to be themselves. Female participants also were likely to report that they became closer when they and their friend had a similar problem, or when one of them was experiencing a crisis.

A less open-ended approach was taken by Peretti and Venton (1984, 1986), who asked students (ages 18 to 25) about the role of intimacy, acceptance, attachment, emotional satisfaction, and caring in maintaining closest friendships. Emotional satisfaction, defined as reciprocal expression of positive and negative feelings, received the highest endorsement from both women and men. Women in particular believed that the more feelings and emotions were expressed, the greater the mutual understanding, trust, and commitment in a friendship. The remaining four components also were regarded as important by both women and men, although more so by women. Intimacy was considered instrumental in creating a bond that fostered and maintained a long-term friendship. Attachment served to stabilize and sustain the relationship even when friends were apart. Finally, caring facilitated the maintenance of friendships by making the other feel wanted. Women conceptualized caring in terms of interacting at a deep level, whereas for men, caring meant that they could rely on their friends for help in times of need.

The category of close friendship targeted by Peretti and Venton can be further differentiated into same- and other-sex close friendships. In an extensive analysis, Rose (1985) asked single undergraduate, single graduate, and married graduate students to describe how they maintained same- and other-sex close friendships. Responses were coded using nine categories that emerged from the data (including "no maintenance"—not willing or interested in maintaining the friendship). Communication, affection, time together, acceptance, and effort were mentioned most frequently. Longitudinal research on friendship formation suggests that these strategies are probably quite effective. For example, in Shaver et al.'s (1985) study, increases in affection, support, and intimacy were associated with longevity of closest friendships. Similarly, in Hays's (1984, 1985) research, consideration, affection, companionship, and communication were all correlated with the development of friendship.

When Rose compared same- and other-sex friendships, interestingly, "no maintenance" was the most frequent response for cross-gender friendships (31.6% vs. 3.7% for same-sex friendships). Affection was also mentioned more often for other-sex friends. In contrast, acceptance, effort, time, communication, and common interests were listed with significantly greater frequency for same-sex friendships. For both friendship types, the maintenance strategies of proximity and sexual attraction were listed very infrequently.

Maintenance strategies also varied as a function of friendship type, gender, and life stage (marital status, student status). For example, women were more likely than men to report "no strategy" for maintaining opposite-sex friendships. Unmarried participants were more likely to mention spending time together as a way of maintaining a same-sex friendship than were married participants, and so on.

Finally, Rose and Serafica (1986) compared same-sex friendships at different stages of development. Responses to the question "How do two people stay friends?" resulted in the development of four coding categories: proximity, affection, interaction, and self-maintaining (statements that no active maintenance was required; this category applied mainly to hypothetical, not actual, friendships). Casual friendships were perceived as requiring significantly more proximity and less affection than close or best friends. The three groups did not differ in terms of amount of interaction. Close and best friends did not differ on any category: "Both required little proximity, some affection, and considerable interaction to maintain" (Rose & Serafica, 1986, p. 280).

Importance of Self-Disclosure,
Supportiveness, and Rewards

In research on the maintenance of same- and other-sex friendships, Afifi, Guerrero, and Egland (1994) found that for both women and men, the use of self-disclosure, supportiveness, and positivity as maintenance strategies was positively correlated with friendship closeness. The importance of these variables has also been highlighted in the research presented so far. Data from additional sources underscore the role that each plays in the maintenance of friendships.

Self-Disclosure

The most frequently mentioned maintenance strategy listed in Canary et al.'s (1993) study was *openness* as exemplified by self-disclosure. In Rose's (1985; Rose & Serafica, 1986) research, the importance of communication was emphasized. Moreover, self-disclosure in the form of everyday talk was considered the primary form of implicit friendship maintenance. These findings are bolstered by other research on self-disclosure. Rosenfeld and Kendrick (1984), for example, found evidence that self-disclosure, especially intimate self-disclosure, is a vehicle for maintaining friendships. Participants received scenarios depicting intimate or nonintimate disclosure between a friend or a stranger. They indicated how much they would be willing to disclose in each situation as well as their reasons for disclosing. For stranger scenarios, reciprocity (disclosing in order to elicit self-disclosure from the other) and impression formation were the reasons for disclosing endorsed most often. For friendship scenarios, the reason that received the highest ratings was relationship maintenance and enhancement, followed by reciprocity, and then self-clarification. In a regression analysis, relationship maintenance and enhancement also emerged as the best predictor of the amount individuals were willing to disclose, but only for intimate disclosure scenarios. The authors concluded that "the primary motivation to engage in self-disclosure with a friend is to help the relationship solidify and grow" (p. 337).

Data gathered on actual friendships corroborate Rosenfeld and Kendrick's finding that self-disclosure can serve a relationship maintenance and enhancement function. Schmidt and Cornelius (1987) asked women and men about a recent situation in which they had self-disclosed to their best friend. "Attempt to strengthen and improve the relationship" was one of the reasons given for having self-disclosed. Thus, in addition to the implicit benefits of talking, people may also quite consciously use self-disclosure, particularly intimate self-disclosure, as a means of maintaining and improving their friendships.

Supportiveness

The second most frequently mentioned maintenance strategy in Canary et al.'s study was *assurance* that the relationship was important. The behavior most representative of this strategy was supportiveness. Supportiveness has also been emphasized in other friendship maintenance research (e.g., Afifi et al., 1994). Once again, there is additional literature that verifies its importance for the maintenance of friendships. According to Burleson and Samter (1994), most young adults regard close friends as their primary source of social support, which has implications for the maintenance of friendships. In their words, "To maintain a close friendship, partners are thus obligated to provide comfort, help solve problems, work through uncertainties, celebrate victories, offer encouragement . . . and so on" (p. 74). The authors suggest that in times of distress, support is given simply because "that's what friends do," rather than as a conscious, deliberate maintenance strategy. This tacit understanding "drives the enactment of various behaviors, and these behaviors, in turn, have the effect of sustaining the relationship" (p. 67). Thus, in Burleson and Samter's conceptualization, friendship maintenance is a by-product of the provision of social support.

Rewards

Several writers have suggested that to maintain a friendship, it is necessary to keep up levels of rewards. Wright (1984), for example, argues that friendships are formed and maintained because they are rewarding—not in the exchange sense of the word, but rather in communal terms where each is deeply concerned about the other's well-being. Although research participants may not use this terminology, many of the maintenance strategies listed could be classified as reward strategies. For instance, *positivity* (trying to make interactions pleasant) was listed in Canary et al.'s study. In Newcomb and Brady's (1982) study of children's relationships, friends' interactions were characterized by greater mutuality and reciprocated affect than were acquaintances'. In discussing this result, the authors suggest that such behaviors have very high social reinforcement value and ultimately serve to maintain the relationship.

Argyle and Henderson's (1984) research on rules of friendship also is relevant to maintenance. They comment that "rules are needed to keep up the rewards, and to minimize the conflicts" (p. 213). They found that friends subscribed to rules that presumably bolstered the level of rewards in the relationship. For example, rules such as "show emotional support," "volunteer help in time of need," and "strive to make him or her happy while in each other's company" were seen as important. To maintain a friendship, it also was necessary to develop rules to avoid jealousy in the relationship, particularly pertaining to outsiders who could be a potential threat to the relationship. In addition, following rules about keeping confidences and respecting privacy was regarded as important in sustaining friendships. As evidence for the importance of these rules, Argyle and Henderson (1984, 1985) found that reward rules were applied less frequently in lapsed than ongoing friendships. Based on an extensive program of research, they concluded that the following of reward rules distinguishes intimate from nonintimate friendships.

The findings of longitudinal research also highlight the importance of rewards. In Berg's (1984) study of college roommates, the strongest predictor of satisfaction and liking was a general index of rewards. Moreover, roommates who decided to continue living together (or were undecided) reported increases in rewards over time, whereas roommates who decided not to live together showed a pattern of diminished rewards. Similarly, Hays (1985) found that rewards (ratings of benefits) were higher, and in fact increased, among friendships that progressed. Friendships that did not become close were characterized by fewer benefits, and these decreased over time.

Importance of Spending Time Together

In Chapter 3, it was pointed out that people are less likely to form new friendships if their social calendar is already filled. It was acknowledged that friends require time, energy, and resources and if these are committed to existing friends, it is less likely that new friendships will be sought out. Conversely, if time usually spent with established friends is channeled into new friendships (or other pursuits), existing friendships can suffer. Spending time together, like supportiveness, is a maintenance strategy that can be conceptualized as both explicit and implicit.

Research supports the importance of spending time together in order to maintain a friendship. In a study of children's conceptions of friendship (Berndt, 1986), the most frequent response by boys and girls in kindergarten, Grade 3, and Grade 6 was play or association. "Friends were expected to play together or spend lots of time with each other. If they stopped spending time together, their friendship was expected to end" (Berndt, 1986, p. 192). The importance of playing together does not end in childhood. Harré (1977), for example, discussed friendship maintenance in terms of shared mundane activities such as friendly eating, drinking, giving rides, and so on. A study of the social interaction patterns of British adults was conducted by Argyle and Furnham (1982). Friends' interactions were least likely of all relationships to be task oriented and most likely to revolve around leisure activities such as eating, drinking, and intimate talking. In the same vein, Larson, Mannell, and Zuzanek (1986) found that time with friends was spent socializing and in active leisure activities, whereas time with family members revolved around household maintenance and passive leisure (watching television). Moreover, research presented earlier showed that having fun together is a significant predictor of both friendship development and satisfaction (see Chapter 4).

The children in Berndt's (1986) research emphasized the importance of not only playing together but also simply spending time with friends. Berndt et al. (1986) found that over a 6-month period, children who remained friends were more likely to comment on their frequent interactions (and liking) than children whose friendships ended. The importance of time is a theme that also appears in the adult literature. For example, Rawlins (1994) interviewed middle-aged adults and reported that "the primary culprit cited for problems with friends and losing friends was a lack of time. Consequently, keeping friendships alive and rekindling them involved 'taking,' 'making,' or 'finding the time' " (p. 290). A closely related theme was the importance of "making the effort" to keep in touch, particularly with friends who no longer lived nearby. Thus, individuals mentioned the importance of phone calls, cards, letters, and visits for sustaining these friendships.

There seems to be some disagreement over just how much interaction is required to maintain a friendship. According to Adams (1985-1986), frequent interaction is important with new friends but not once a friendship is established. In fact, she obtained a small, *positive* correlation between physical distance and emotional closeness in a sample of elderly women (which diminished to zero when duration of the friendship was taken into account). However, others have argued that frequent interaction remains important, even in established friendships. Hays (1988) maintains that "To continue to exist, a friendship requires ongoing interaction between the partners" (p. 402). Similarly, Allan (1989) notes that lasting friendships between people who rarely see one another are rare. He maintains that the majority of friendships require active input if they are to continue. It is difficult to resolve this issue, in part because it is unclear what these writers count as interaction—is it only face-to-face interaction or do letters and phone calls also qualify as spending time together? The elderly women in Adams's study may not have had the resources or mobility for frequent face-to-face interaction with friends but could have maintained these relationships through letters or phone calls. Regardless of the mode of interaction, as Wilmot and Shellen (1990) commented, "Some tending of the friendship garden appears to be necessary even if it is merely the yearly Christmas card sent to 'milestone' friends with whom we no longer share much in common except memories" (p. 415).

⚘ Summary

Literature on the maintenance of friendship is scarce, but what there is contributes substantially to our understanding. It is apparent that the maintenance of friendship can be a difficult and challenging task. Friends have to strike a delicate balance between each person's constantly changing needs for independence and dependence, intimacy and distance, and so on. These dialectics may contribute, in part, to the relatively frequent experience of anger and conflict in friendship relationships. The research on how such issues are resolved paints a rather bleak picture of friends passively doing nothing when there is evidence that constructive discussion of contentious issues has salutary effects. This passivity was again apparent in the literature on maintenance strategies in that some people responded with "no strategy" or "no maintenance" when asked how they sustained their friendships.

However, the majority of responses revealed that friends have a diverse repertoire of strategies that they use to maintain the relationship. Moreover, there is a differentiation such that strategies are selectively applied depending on the nature of the friendship. Some of the key strategies identified were engaging in self-disclosure, providing support and assurance, and more generally, keeping up the level of rewards and spending time together. Furthermore, the kinds of activities and conversations that friends naturally engage in serve to maintain the friendship, even though the activities may not have been initiated with strategic maintenance in mind. Thus, even though friends do not appear to be particularly adept at handling anger and conflict, many friendships survive. This may be the result of greater proficiency in strategic maintenance than conflict management, or perhaps because friendship maintenance happens to be a by-product of simply spending time together.

7

Deterioration and Dissolution

One has risked rebuff, got over the initial awkwardness, and
found the pleasure in the other's company to be a nice balance
for whatever effort or trouble is involved in obtaining it. Still,
most friendships prove impermanent.

—Rodin (1982, p. 42)

Sooner or later, virtually every friend will disappoint us in
some way. As was discussed in the last chapter, conflicts,
tensions, and feelings of anger are a part of friendship. Sometimes
conflicts and disagreements are resolved to the mutual satisfaction
of each partner. Other times, issues are not dealt with and the
relationship begins to decline. Although a decline does not invariably lead to dissolution, the loss of a friendship is not uncommon—whether it "fades away," as is generally the case, or comes
to an abrupt end. This chapter acknowledges the dark side of
friendship, examines the process of deterioration, and considers

the factors contributing to the dissolution of friendships. The chapter concludes with a discussion of how people go about ending a friendship.

ੈ The Dark Side of Friendship

Social scientists have only recently begun to study the darker side of close relationships (e.g., Cupach & Spitzberg, 1994; Miller, Mongeau, & Sleight, 1986). Friendships are not exempt. As Rook and Pietromonaco (1987) comment:

> Whether intentionally or unintentionally, our friends occasionally criticize us, reject us, ignore our needs, mock our beliefs, and violate our privacy. Most of us can remember times when we felt sharply stung by the actions of a close friend. (p. 14)

The last chapter dealt with anger and conflict in friendships. Unfortunately, these are not the only difficulties that can beset this relationship. When participants in Helgeson et al.'s (1987) study described a distance experience in a same-sex friendship, they listed negative feelings such as feeling hurt, angry, sad, confused, lonely, and guilty, and behaviors such as lack of communication, disapproval of the other's behavior, arguing, confronting the situation, acting cold or cruel, and breaking up. There were few gender differences in the experience of distance in a same-sex friendship. Gender differences did surface, however, when Sapadin (1988) asked professional women and men: "What do you dislike about your friendships?" A minority (16% of women and 25% of men) reported that nothing was disliked about their same-sex friendships. However, the majority produced complaints. Both women (22%) and men (25%) were most likely to dislike competition, followed by superficiality (21% women; 11% men), feeling misunderstood (9% women; 14% men), lack of time (11% women; 11% men), lack of commitment (10% women; 0% men), and overpossessiveness (9% women; 0% men). Sex differences in these percentages were significant for superficiality, lack of commitment, and overpossessiveness.

It is interesting that competition was the most common complaint for both women and men, given that competitiveness is generally associated with male rather than female friendships (e.g., Reid & Fine, 1992; Richey & Richey, 1980; see Chapter 3 for evidence of competition in boys' friendships). Thorbecke and Grotevant (1982) found that for adolescent males, but not females, there was a positive correlation between competitiveness and friendship commitment. Similarly, in a study involving pairs of male friends and strangers, Tesser and Smith (1980) found that if performance on a task mattered, the men were more likely to help a stranger than a friend.

It is possible that competitiveness exists in both male and female friendships, but simply takes a different form. Parallel to the conflict findings discussed in the last chapter, there is some evidence that competition is more indirect in women's friendships, whereas men simply may compete more overtly (e.g., Rubin, 1986). Davidson and Duberman (1982) found that women provided more examples of *covert* competition for power in their friendships than did men. The authors' interpretation was that women have to resort to covert strategies because they have been socialized not to openly compete for power. Sapadin (1988) found that despite similarity in frequency of listing, the term *competition* was imbued with different meanings for each sex. For women, competitiveness involved feelings of jealousy and competing for men; for men, competitiveness entailed one-upmanship and competing in sports.

Participants in Sapadin's study also described what they disliked about their opposite-sex friendships. Again, a substantial proportion of participants reported "nothing" (22% of women; 22% of men). The next most frequent response was sexual tensions (20% women; 28% men), followed by superficiality (20% women; 8% men), feeling misunderstood (10% women; 16% men), having fewer interactions (9% women; 9% men), and patronizing or sexist behavior (9% women; 0% men). Women and men's responses differed significantly for the superficiality and patronizing/sexist categories. The particular challenges that are faced in cross-gender friendships were discussed in Chapter 5.

These studies suggest that friends can encounter a number of difficulties, including misunderstandings, competition, not having enough time to devote to the relationship, and as discussed in the last chapter, perhaps worst of all—betrayal. These kinds of events can be responsible for the deterioration, if not the dissolution, of the relationship.

❧ Deterioration

Altman and Taylor's (1973) and Knapp's (1978) models of relationship development have already been described. According to Altman and Taylor's social penetration theory, the development of a relationship is characterized by increases in breadth and depth of self-disclosure. Knapp refined this model by specifying eight communication dimensions that characterize developing relationships. These theorists conceptualized the deterioration of relationships as a reversal of these self-disclosure dimensions, a position known as the "reversal hypothesis." A study by Wilmot and Baxter (1983) suggests that people's perceptions of relational decline may be consistent with the reversal hypothesis. They presented participants with a hypothetical conversation between friends. Some participants were told that the friendship was growing closer, whereas others were told that the friendship was growing apart. The same conversation was regarded as less personal and less honest if participants believed the friendship was growing apart rather than closer. (Glueck and Ayres, 1988, however, did not find that communication was rated as less personalized in deteriorating relationships.)

Baxter has conducted a number of studies to test whether the reversal hypothesis actually captures the process of deterioration in friendships (see Baxter, 1985, for a review). In one study, Baxter (1979) constructed friendship scenarios that varied in terms of whether maintenance or disengagement from the friendship was desired. The dependent variable was willingness to self-disclose. Consistent with the reversal hypothesis, participants were less willing to disclose—especially on high intimacy and openness

topics—when the intent was disengagement rather than maintenance of the friendship.

Baxter (1983) pointed out that some of Knapp's communication
dimensions depict increases in closeness, whereas others refer to
increased knowledge of the other. She reasoned that when a
friendship deteriorates, feelings of closeness may wane, but
knowledge of a friend would not necessarily diminish. Thus, she
predicted that the reversal hypothesis would hold only for those
communication dimensions related to closeness. Participants in
this study rated whether each of Knapp's communication dimensions had remained the same, or was less or more characteristic of
a same-sex friendship during its deterioration. Consistent with
predictions, there was greater reversal on dimensions that referred
to closeness (e.g., personalized communication) than on knowledge or familiarity dimensions (e.g., flexibility, uniqueness of
communication).

Finally, Baxter and Wilmot (1986) conducted a study in which
participants maintained diaries of their interactions with a same-
and other-sex friend over a 2-week period. These relationships
were classified as growing, stable, or disengaging (based on
whether the participant perceived each interaction as serving to
increase closeness or distance). Disengaging relationships were
characterized by less effective and less personal communication
than were growing relationships. However, contrary to predictions based on Knapp's model, they were not characterized by
reduced topic breadth or less frequent encounters.

Based on the results of these and other studies (see, e.g., Ayres,
1982; Bigelow & La Gaipa, 1980; Duck, 1982; Rose, 1984), the
reversal hypothesis has fallen out of favor. However, the research
conducted to test this hypothesis has been important in elucidat-
ing the process of decline in friendships. For example, Ayres found
that people in deteriorating friendships reported a decrease in
evaluative communication such as offering one's opinion on issues. Baxter's program of research reveals that when a friendship
is deteriorating, the partners are likely to avoid intimate, open
self-disclosure as well as shy away from communication that
indicates closeness.

❧ Rejuvenation

One theme that has surfaced previously is the voluntariness of friendships. This theme also is relevant to the deterioration and dissolution of friendships. According to Wiseman (1986), no other social bond is as fragile. Unlike institutionalized relationships such as marriage, there are no societal mechanisms to ensure or encourage reconciliation when a friendship is on the brink of dissolution. A similar point was made by Rose (1984). A number of the participants in her research regretted that they had allowed a friendship to deteriorate past the point where it could be saved.

On a more positive note, there are some indications that even when left to their own devices, people do sometimes manage to resuscitate a flagging friendship. Studies on repair and rejuvenation are quite recent (see Wilmot, 1994; Wilmot & Shellen, 1990; Wilmot & Stevens, 1994), but so far the results are encouraging. Wilmot and Stevens analyzed interview data in which participants described the decline of a relationship (friendship, romantic, marital, or familial) and the turning points that resulted in its rejuvenation. Six rejuvenation events were identified in these accounts. A change in the behavior of one or both partners was most commonly reported (by 33% of participants) as responsible for arresting the decline and heading the relationship in a positive direction. These behaviors included giving the other more "space," spending more time together, talking more, being more independent, and so on. Generally, these behaviors were linked to the perceived cause of the decline. Thus, if the decline was attributed to one partner smothering the other, behavior change might take the form of giving that person more space.

The second most frequent rejuvenation event (mentioned by 31%) was labeled *have big relationship talk*. Big relationship talks took the form of apologizing, acknowledging the importance of the relationship, arguing, setting ground rules, and the like. Talking also appeared in some of the other categories, but the difference was that in this case, the "big talk" was explicitly credited as having restored the relationship. The third rejuvenation event involved gestures of reconciliation (19%), usually after a period of physical or emotional separation. These gestures took the form of participating in a joint activity (e.g., going for lunch) or directly communicating one's desire to reconcile. Next, reassessment of the importance of the relationship was reported as contributing to rejuvenation (8%), followed by accepting or forgiving the other person (8%). Finally, a mere 2% of respondents referred to seeking third-party help (e.g., seeing a counselor, talking to friends, family).

The patterning of these responses differed, depending on the relationship that was being described. For example, friends were least likely to seek third-party help, reinforcing the notion that external structures for the restoration and repair of friendships are lacking (or at least are perceived as lacking). Big relationship talks were more common among friends than family members. Family relationships were more likely to be restored by simply deciding to accept and forgive. The authors suggest that the voluntariness of the relationship may determine the particular rejuvenation strategy that is employed. For example, state-of-the-relationship talks may be more permissible and necessary in friendships (and romantic relationships) because there is no guarantee that a relationship in decline will continue. In contrast, in family relationships, continuation of the relationship may be assumed.

Wilmot and Stevens (1994) also were interested in the kinds of strategies that people who had successfully rejuvenated a relationship would recommend to others. Thus, respondents were asked, "If someone wanted to improve a relationship that was declining, what advice would you give?" The authors were particularly curious "whether people who had experienced a rejuvenation would come forth with the typical advice that communication is the 'elixir' for improvement" (p. 106). In fact, nearly three quarters of the respondents did just that! By far the most common advice offered was "communicate." The remaining responses largely mirrored the rejuvenation strategies reported earlier (e.g., accept other, seek help from third party), along with a few folk remedies such as persistence and effort (e.g., "One has to work at a relationship") and leaving it to fate or destiny (e.g., "If it's meant to be, it'll happen").

Given the importance assigned to communication, Wilmot and Stevens conducted supplementary analyses to see whether individuals who recommended communication had actually engaged in big talks when rejuvenating their own relationship. The results of these analyses led them to conclude that "one thing we know for sure: If you ask people what should be done to improve a relationship, they will tell you to communicate, whether or not they did it in their own relationships" (p. 123).

❧ Dissolution

Imagine the following scenario:

> Lately Kim had been feeling unhappy in her friendship with Jill. Some of Kim's friends had begun to notice signs of deterioration in the friendship and had offered their support through this difficult time. "I'll be there for you no matter what you decide" one friend said. Kim's family was very upset when they heard that she was considering ending the relationship. Her father solemnly reminded her of the permanence of friendship and pointed out that the family's reputation was at stake here as well. Kim's mother began to cry and asked if there wasn't some way they could work things out—had they seen a counselor? Despite pressure from friends and family, Kim eventually decided to end the friendship, even though she felt like a failure for not making it work. It took all of her courage to tell Jill that she no longer wished to continue the friendship. Jill begged her to reconsider the decision. Kim was torn, but eventually called a lawyer and began the lengthy, costly process of formally dissolving the friendship.

This scenario probably sounds quite absurd. However, that would not be the case if the word *friendship* were replaced with *marriage*. As has already been noted, the societal structures that are in place to hold marital and familial relationships together are curiously absent when it comes to friendships. It is for this reason that many writers in the friendship literature regard friendship as such a fragile bond.

The Rate of Dissolution

Does Rodin's (1982) proclamation, with which this chapter opened, that "most friendships prove impermanent" accurately portray the fate of friendships? We know that many friendships end. We also know that many friendships last. In this section, a sampling of studies that have charted the longevity of friendships will be presented to help establish a baseline regarding the permanence (or impermanence) of friendships. In reviewing the literature on children's friendships, Berndt (1988) concluded that children's friendships were more stable than had been supposed. For example, among children in Grades 1 to 4, the majority of friendships that were close in the fall were still close 6 months later (Berndt & Hoyle, 1985, Study 1). In the second study, participants were students in Grades 4 and 8. More than two thirds of the friendships in each grade remained stable from fall to spring. Berndt and Hawkins (1987; see Berndt, 1988) assessed friendship choices of Grade 6 students in the spring and again in the fall when they had made the transition to junior high school. About half of these friendships were stable. When assessed again the following spring, approximately the same proportion remained intact. Finally, Crockett et al. (1984) found that among students in Grades 6 to 8, the majority of best friend relationships had lasted for at least 1 and up to 5 years.

Continuing across the life span, Richey and Richey (1980) reported that in their sample of 17- to 25-year-olds, best friend relationships were extremely stable. Only a few friendships had terminated; 94% continued at some level of intimacy. In a study of single and married undergraduate and graduate students (Rose & Serafica, 1986), every student reported the loss of a close friendship, although only 27% had experienced the dissolution of a best friendship. More than two thirds of the elderly men and women in Roberto and Kimboko's (1989) study reported having a lifetime close friend; 17% reported having a close friend established in their adolescence, and 11% reported a close friend from midlife. Only 4% claimed not to have had a close friend until later life. Babchuk and Anderson (1989) similarly found high degrees of stability in the friendships of married and widowed elderly women (ages 65 to 98, $M = 73.5$). For example, 76% of the widows reported that their close friendships had been established when they were in their 40s or younger. More than 25% of these women had at least one intimate friendship from their childhood or adolescence. Even friendships formed after the age of 40 often had been maintained for a very long time. The pattern for married women was virtually identical. Nearly 80% of the respondents had known all of their close friends for more than 5 years. The authors attributed the longevity of these friendships to the high degree of residential stability that characterized this sample. As will be seen, friendships remain quite stable unless they are threatened by events such as the loss of proximity or a life transition. Thus, it may not be the case that *most* friendships prove impermanent. Nevertheless, the loss of friendships appears to be a ubiquitous experience. Reasons why friendships end are considered next.

Reasons for the Dissolution of Friendships

In Chapter 3, the formation of friendships was conceptualized as a convergence of environmental, individual, situational, and dyadic factors. Each of these factors also is implicated in the dissolution of friendships. For example, Chapter 3 identified proximity as an important predictor of friendship formation. As will be seen, if a friend moves away, the loss of proximity frequently contributes to the dissolution of the friendship. Perhaps the most important predictor of friendship formation presented in Chapter 3 was similarity. Conversely, the discovery of dissimilarities can contribute to the termination of a friendship. This is not to imply that the dissolution of friendships is simply the reverse of the formation process. (Evidence to the contrary was presented earlier.) Nevertheless, if some of the factors that initially contributed to the formation of a friendship no longer hold, the probability of termination is increased.

Environmental Factors: Proximity

When asked why a particular friendship ended, a common answer is that one of the partners moved away (e.g., Rawlins, 1994; Rose & Serafica, 1986). Children's friendships frequently end for this reason (e.g., Rubin, 1980). Loss of proximity also occurs when people attend different schools, move within the same city, change jobs, or retire (e.g., Matthews, 1986; Richey & Richey, 1980; Rose &

Serafica, 1986), with negative effects on friendships. For example, the lowest rate of stability in Berndt's research was found in the study where participants experienced the transition to junior high school (Berndt & Hawkins, 1987). In Rose's (1984) study of college students ages 17 to 22, more than half of the students (57.4%) reported having lost at least one close friend in the past 5 years. For the majority (35.5%), the loss had occurred since they entered college. (This is probably a conservative estimate of friendship loss associated with the transition to university life given that students in her sample tended to be local residents.) Only 13.5% of the respondents had experienced the dissolution of a friendship during high school (8.4% lost a friend in both college and high school).

When Rawlins (1994) interviewed middle-aged adults about their friendships, he was struck by the fact that

> the interviews were riddled with accounts of how vulnerable friendships were to altered circumstances—. . . shifting schedules, changing jobs, moving away, developing new interests. It felt like valued friendships were continually slipping away from these adults, in most cases due to events that transcended the friendships. (p. 287)

Allan (1989) also observed that the majority of friendships do not survive significant changes in either person's circumstances (e.g., geographic mobility). Unfortunately, to date there is no research on whether access to electronic mail mitigates such effects. A friend relayed that for years she worried that a close friend and colleague would take a position at another university and that the loss of proximity might undermine the friendship. However, these fears have subsided because she now anticipates that they would remain in close contact via E-mail.

Finally, in the literature on the termination of friendships, it is assumed that changes in circumstances are responsible for causing the dissolution of friendships. However, Kurth (1970) offers an intriguing alternative interpretation. She suggests that many friendships are maintained even though one or both partners would like to end it. Changes in circumstances such as moving or getting a new job simply provide an opportunity to make a graceful exit. If Kurth is correct, this implies that the effects of life transitions may not be quite as devastating as it would appear. Rather than life changes ruining a perfectly good friendship, they may allow us at long last to bow out of a situation from which we were wanting to escape.

Individual Factors: Dislike Criteria

Rodin's (1982) notion of "dislike criteria" was introduced in Chapter 3. In her view, we eliminate possible friendship candidates who possess qualities that we dislike. However, some disliked qualities by their very nature do not manifest themselves until a friendship has formed. For example, characteristics such as being demanding, jealous, or possessive may not be apparent in the early stages of a friendship. The subsequent revelation of such qualities can contribute to the dissolution of the friendship. Based on her investigation of serious problems in friendships, Wiseman (1986) commented that "the presentation of just one undesirable trait can cause the recasting of the character of a friend" (p. 199). Consistent with this observation, in La Gaipa's (1987; Bigelow & La Gaipa, 1980) research, the second most frequent reason given for the termination of adolescents' friendships was low morals or character flaws that undermined the admiration that had been felt. (The primary reason was disloyalty or lack of commitment.) Similarly, the elderly adults in Matthews's (1986) research reported that friendships sometimes ended because a friend behaved in a way that changed the participant's evaluation of him or her. Betrayal of trust was a behavior that was especially likely to lead to a negative evaluation of the friend's character. The results of these studies are consistent with Duck's (1982) statement that "new, surprising, and significantly negatively charged information about the other can hasten the relationship's death" (p. 7). He suggests that the discovery of betrayal or deception is so damaging that it is likely to result in the "sudden death" of the relationship (see also Wilmot & Stevens, 1994). As was documented in the previous chapter, it is rare for friendships to survive a betrayal of trust.

Situational Factors

Availability

Friendships sometimes end because one or both partners is no longer as available. Rawlins (1994) interviewed middle-aged adults and concluded that "friendship discontinuities are shaped by other social circumstances, like marital and family status, occupation, emerging interests, and friendship circles" (p. 285). It has already been noted that the resources required by friendships, such as time and energy, are limited. Thus, the formation of new friendships frequently requires a culling of the old (e.g., Rodin, 1982). In fact, several writers have suggested that the intrusion of a new partner is a major reason why relationships end (e.g., Davis, 1973; Wilmot & Stevens, 1994).

Young adults are particularly vulnerable to friendship attrition because of the unavailability that accompanies romantic involvement. Probably most of us have been happy for a friend who has fallen in love, only later to discover that he or she now no longer has time for us. This phenomenon is known as the dyadic withdrawal hypothesis—the greater the involvement with a romantic partner, the lower the involvement with one's larger network of relationships, particularly friendships. Johnson and Leslie (1982) found that number of friends decreased from an average of 4.13 for occasional daters to 1.06 for married respondents. Moreover, romantic involvement was associated with reduced quantity and quality of interaction with the friends who were retained. Similarly, Bendtschneider and Duck (1993) found that 71% of women and 65% of men in romantic relationships reported that one or more of their friendships had become less close as a result.

In a study by Milardo, Johnson, and Huston (1983), individuals in dating relationships kept records of their interactions for two 10-day periods (separated by a few months). Surprisingly, the number of close and intermediate friends did not vary with the degree of romantic involvement. However, casual daters had more frequent and longer interactions with close friends than engaged individuals. In addition, people in the early stages of a romantic relationship interacted nearly twice as often (and for longer periods) with intermediate friends. For example, casual daters spent nearly 2 hours per day interacting with intermediate friends compared to less than 30 minutes for engaged participants.

Thus, there is evidence that development of a romantic relationship reduces the number of friends and truncates interactions with retained friends. This phenomenon apparently is not limited to college-age students (Oliker, 1989; Rawlins, 1994). Women's same-sex friendships are particularly vulnerable given that couple-based socializing tends to occur with the male partner's friends (e.g., Bendtschneider & Duck, 1993; Johnson & Leslie, 1982; Milardo, 1982; Oliker, 1989; Rose & Serafica, 1986).

Frequency of Exposure

If, as was discussed in Chapter 3, repeated exposure to someone leads to greater attraction, then one might also expect the opposite, namely, that insufficient exposure would produce decreased attraction. The deleterious effects of changing circumstances (e.g., loss of proximity) that reduce or eliminate interaction between friends have already been documented. In addition, in the chapter on friendship maintenance, the importance of spending time together in order to preserve a friendship was emphasized. In fact, Wilmot and Stevens (1994) found that the relational issue that was listed most frequently as responsible for the decline of a relationship was a reduction of interaction or involvement (e.g., spending less time together, sharing fewer activities). Thus, it seems clear that people who do not spend at least some time with their friends tend to lose them. (As will be seen in the next section, too much togetherness also can have negative dyadic effects.)

Dyadic Factors

Similarity

As mentioned earlier, one of the best predictors of friendship formation is similarity. Thus, it is perhaps not surprising that if friends become dissimilar, the relationship itself may be threatened. When people are asked to provide an account of why a friendship ended, responses such as "we no longer had anything in common" reflect a loss of similarity that once held the relationship together (e.g., Matthews, 1986). Similarity also can erode when friends experience differences in physical and psychological growth and development (see, e.g., Berndt, 1986). Rubin (1980) noted that the differential rates of development as children approach adolescence make these friendships vulnerable to disruption. As one of the older girls in his sample observed, "Sometimes a kid grows up and sometimes the friend doesn't. . . . So then all of a sudden you find out you don't have anything in common. You like boys and she's interested in dolls" (p. 83).

Adults also report losing friendships because of dissimilar developmental paths (e.g., Matthews, 1986; Rawlins, 1994; Wiseman, 1986). One example is the strain and disruption to friendships experienced by women who decide to attend a university in midlife (e.g., Levy, 1981; Suitor, 1987). This research contains poignant accounts of women who lost friendships that had been formed on the basis of similarity in their roles as homemakers and parents. As was already reported, even students who attend a university immediately after high school experience the dissolution of former friendships (e.g., Rose, 1984). This may be especially true if dissimilarities in career ambitions are made salient by the transition.

The validity of these self-report studies is corroborated by longitudinal research (e.g., Griffin & Sparks, 1990). In a study of adolescents' best friendships, Kandel (1978b) found that over the course of the school year, pairs whose relationship remained intact were more similar (particularly in terms of attitudes and behaviors pertaining to deviant activities such as drug use) than pairs whose friendship ended. Duck and Allison (1978) also explored the role of similarity in predicting friendship dissolution. Participants were students in England who had chosen to live as roommates after spending a year together in residence. The researchers compared the amount and type of similarity between the three pairs of roommates who remained friends (i.e., were still rooming together 8 months later) and the three pairs who did not. The two groups were found to differ in type, but not amount, of similarity.

Specifically, roommates whose friendship remained intact were more similar in terms of psychological (the most intimate) constructs than those whose friendship ended.

Familiarity

In Chapter 3, it was argued that repeated exposure to a stimulus leads to increased liking. Recently, Bornstein, Kale, and Cornell (1990) reported that positive feelings do increase as exposure to a stimulus increases but only to a point—once the stimulus becomes too familiar, boredom sets in. At that point, positive feelings begin to decrease. The same may be true of friendship. Even though familiarity leads to liking, too much familiarity may not be a good thing. As American composer Ned Rorem quipped, "Sooner or later you've heard about all your best friends have to say. Then comes the tolerance of real love."

Social scientists have been reluctant to suggest that we might end friendships out of sheer boredom. Nor do research participants mention boredom when generating reasons for the dissolution of a friendship. However, if La Gaipa (1982) is correct, this is not because people do not end friendships for this reason, but rather because they do not want to admit it. Put another way, in our culture it is not acceptable to terminate a friendship because we are bored. Thus, if asked why a friendship ended, we are more likely to report that the person committed a violation of one of the fundamental tenets of friendship such as loyalty or trust.

Rodin (1982) is among the few who have implicated boredom as a major reason that relationships end (see also Scott & Powers, 1978), although boredom has been identified as one of the costs of friendship (e.g., Hays, 1989). In Wilmot and Stevens's (1994) study, unequal investment or involvement was the second most frequent reason given for the decline of relationships. Boredom was included in this category.

McCarthy and Duck (1976) proposed that in forming friendships, people first seek out similarity. Once a relationship is established, dissimilarity may provide stimulation and stave off boredom. However, ultimately, one would want to return to the comforts of similarity. These hypotheses were tested by having individuals participate in a study alone, with an established friend, or with a tentative friend (up to 6 months' duration). Each person filled out an attitude scale and then received a copy of the scale ostensibly completed by a stranger (for individuals who participated alone) or their friend. The questionnaires were constructed to appear totally similar, mildly dissimilar, or totally dissimilar to the individual's own responses. When the partner was a stranger or an established friend, similarity led to the greatest attraction. However, as predicted, among tentative friends, dissimilarity was preferred.

Research by Baxter and Wilmot (1986) suggests that the return to the comforts of similarity may come at a price, however. In their study, stable same- and opposite-sex relationships were rated lower in satisfaction, interaction effectiveness, and personalness than growing relationships. In fact, stable relationships did not differ from ratings of disengaging relationships on these variables. In discussing these findings, the authors comment that "a relationship can withstand only so much stability before the parties experience boredom and stagnation" (p. 158).

Intimacy/Liking

In the friendship formation chapter, the role of reciprocity of liking was discussed. The importance of intimacy was emphasized in Chapter 4 on achieving closeness. Moreover, when discussing the deterioration of friendships, it was noted that willingness to disclose intimate information distinguishes maintained from deteriorating relationships (e.g., Baxter, 1979). Thus, one would expect that a reduction in positive qualities such as intimacy and liking would be associated with the dissolution of friendships. Research on children's friendships confirms this view (Berndt et al., 1986). Similarly, adolescents are likely to cite a lack of intimacy as the reason for friendship termination (see Berndt, 1986, for a review).

Davis and Todd (1985) administered their Relationship Rating Form to 150 adults who completed the scale with reference to their best friend, closest same- and opposite-sex friend, a social acquaintance, and a former friend. Former friends had the lowest scores on all seven subscales of the Relationship Rating Form: Viability, Support, Intimacy, Spontaneity, Stability, Success, and Enjoyment. Similarly, in Argyle and Henderson's (1984) research on the rules of friendship, violation of intimacy rules differentiated intact from terminated friendships.

Convergence of Environmental, Individual, Situational, and Dyadic Factors

The role of an environmental factor, proximity, and a dyadic factor, attitude similarity, in the dissolution of friendship was explored by Shapiro (1977). Participants were children, ages 8 to 15, who spent 4 weeks at a summer camp. In the second week, the children were asked to list their "very best," "second best," and "third best" friend at camp. They were then assigned to teams and spent the next 4 days interacting primarily with team members. Contrary to expectations, friends who were separated for 4 days were no more likely to experience dissolution than friends who were not separated. However, when analyses were conducted by level of attraction, low attraction ("third best") friendships were more likely to have ended than high attraction ("very best") friendships. In fact, there was some evidence that for high-attraction friends, the 4-day absence had made the heart grow even fonder.

With regard to similarity, the friendships of children who had similar attitudes were more likely to endure than those of dissimilar children, although these effects were rather weak. Interestingly, for dissimilar friends who had been assigned to the same team, the increased proximity heightened the probability of dissolution.

A variety of dyadic factors was examined in another study of children's friendships (Berndt et al., 1986). Students in Grades 4 and 8 were interviewed in the fall and spring of the school year. At both times, children with unstable friendships gave lower intimacy ratings and commented on the lack of intimacy more frequently than children in stable friendships. Children whose friendships ended also made fewer comments about liking and similarity and reported a lower frequency of interaction. Finally, children whose friendship ended made a greater number of negative comments (especially about disloyalty and unfaithfulness) and rated their (former) friend lower in terms of similarity and social behavior in the spring than in the fall.

The role of environmental, individual, situational, and dyadic factors in the dissolution of friendships is apparent in Rose's (1984) research. Participants were asked to write an essay describing the decline of a closest, same-sex friendship. Four patterns of friendship termination were identified in these reports:

1. Physical separation (mentioned by 47% of participants): moving to another city, to another area in the same city, or going to different schools. (Men's friendships were significantly more likely than women's to end for this reason.)
2. New friends (18%): old friends were replaced by new ones.
3. Dislike (22%): a friend demonstrated a behavior or revealed information that met the participant's dislike criteria (e.g., hostility, drug abuse, violence, betrayal, criticism, religious differences).
4. Dating or marriage (12%): involvement in a romantic relationship contributed to the cessation of friendships, especially for women.

These findings were largely replicated in a subsequent study (Rose & Serafica, 1986) in which dissolution accounts were gathered for different types of friendship. Participants' responses were classified using five categories: less proximity (e.g., friend moves); less affection (decrease in liking, commitment, acceptance); less interaction (decrease in quality or quantity of interaction); interference (dating/marriage caused the friendship to end); and finally, statements about the termination process (e.g., "friendships just fade away"). Interestingly, casual, close, and best friendships were perceived as ending for different reasons. For example, casual friendships were more likely to end because of reduced proximity, whereas close and best friendships were more likely to end because of decreased interaction or interference. These findings are evocative because they suggest that environmental, individual, and dyadic factors may have a differential impact at different stages of friendship.

Summary

The kinds of responses that people provide to account for the termination of friendships highlights how vulnerable friendships are to dissolution. As Matthews (1986) has commented:

> Changes in geographical proximity, marital status, and occupation are all given as reasons for the termination of friendships. None of these, of course, could be used as reasons for the termination of family membership. Sisters who marry do not cease to be sisters. That these kinds of reasons are seen as legitimate ones points to the fragility of friendships. Because there are no institutional supports to sustain them, changes in circumstances work against their continuation. (p. 74)

The results of Rose and Serafica's study suggest that casual friendships may be particularly susceptible to dissolution as a result of changes in circumstances (e.g., proximity). Close friendships may be better able to withstand these sorts of pressures; some combination of environmental, individual, situational, and dyadic factors may have to conspire against them. In Rose's (1984) study, for example, more than 40% of the participants conceptualized termination as a multistage process, rather than as a single, discrete event. A friendship might be weakened by a loss of proximity, for example. If that friend then also gets married, or behaves in an unacceptable way, the convergence of these events could ultimately result in dissolution of the relationship (see Davis, 1973, for a similar argument). Bell (1981b) remarked that "friendships can be ended by external forces that drive friends apart. But whatever the causal origins, friendships are ultimately broken from inside the relationship, not from outside it" (p. 24). This statement may be most applicable to close friendships.

❧ Strategies for Ending Friendships

It is generally assumed that friendships gradually drift apart rather than coming to a cataclysmic end. This may account for why the dissolution of friendships has not received much attention in the literature. The focus instead has been on the termination of dating and marital relationships where one or both partners usually takes active steps to end the relationship—a process referred to as "breaking up." People are much less likely to speak of breaking up when referring to the termination of a friendship. Yet, as we have seen, friendships do end. Moreover, termination is frequently desired by only one, not both, partners. This implies that the person who wants to disengage from the friendship must take certain actions to achieve that goal. In fact, the termination of a friendship has been conceptualized as a persuasion attempt in which one person tries to induce the other to accept a different definition of the relationship (Baxter & Philpott, 1982; Miller & Parks, 1982). Miller and Parks suggest that the strategy that is chosen depends on the degree of motivation to end the relationship, whether the termination is desired by only one, rather than both, partners, and so on. They speculate that people generally begin with reward-oriented strategies, promising rewards for compliance. However, if unsuccessful, they are likely to move toward punishment-oriented strategies (e.g., threats), particularly in situations in which the dissolution is not mutually desired and the dissatisfied partner is highly motivated to end the relationship.

An extensive study of persuasion strategies for ending friendships was conducted by Baxter and Philpott (1982). Students in Grades 5 and 10, as well as undergraduate and graduate students, were presented with a scenario, titled "Letting Someone Know That the Friendship Is Over":

> Sometimes we decide that a person we used to like is no longer our friend. Imagine that you no longer wish to continue the friendship with a *boy/girl from your school* (person from your school or work whose sex is the same as yours).

Participants were asked to list ways in which termination of the friendship could be accomplished. Their responses were coded according to six categories of persuasion attempts: other negation (give cues that show that the other is no longer liked), difference (demonstrate areas of dissimilarity), self-presentation (behave less personally or present self in a negative way), cost-rendering (increase costs to the other while decreasing benefits), disinterest (stop seeking out information about the other), and exclusion (avoid spending time with other). The most common termination strategies across age groups were other negation (e.g., "I'd tell him that I really didn't like him anymore") and exclusion (e.g., "I'd go sit at the other end of the lunchroom and be busy whenever she called").

Baxter (1982) explored whether disengagement strategies might differ depending on the closeness of the friendship. Students were presented with scenarios in which disengagement was sought either from a friend or a close friend and rated the likelihood of using various strategies classified as withdrawal/avoidance, manipulatory, positive tone (concern for the other's feelings), and open confrontation. Overall, participants were most likely to endorse positive tone and withdrawal/avoidance strategies. However, strategy type also varied with the closeness of the friendship. Specifically, close friendships were less likely to be terminated through the use of indirect (withdrawal/avoidance) or manipulative strategies.

In the previous chapter, we saw that friends are most likely to adopt a strategy of avoidance when faced with conflict. Not surprisingly, they do not suddenly engage in open and active confrontation when attempting to end a friendship. The preferred strategy for dealing with conflict also appears to be the strategy of choice for ending a friendship (e.g., Baxter, 1979). In fact, in one data set (reported in Baxter, 1979), 72% of the termination strategies that participants reported having used to end a friendship were indirect. This reliance on indirect strategies may account for the perception that friendships just "fade away." If one gradually reduces the number of phone calls and invitations to socialize, and generally avoids contact, the friendship may simply wither on the vine.

The image of friendships dying a slow death is not particularly pleasant. However, it may be that hibernation is actually a more appropriate image. Rawlins's (1994) respondents used terms such as "fading away" and "drifting apart" to describe previous friendships. They also avoided assigning blame for the situation. In his view, this left the door open for resumption of the friendship. Similarly, some of Matthews's (1986) elderly respondents construed faded friendships as relationships that could be revived. In contrast, it was thought that friendships that had been explicitly terminated would be much more difficult to rekindle. Findings by Davis and Todd (1985) suggest that this perception is accurate. They compared friendships that drifted apart with those that ended by a violation. Participants who had experienced a violation rated their former friendship lower on all seven Relationship Rating Form subscales. Thus, death by violation appeared to be a more negative experience than drifting apart.

ᴥ Ending on a Happy Note

The termination of a friendship is generally regarded as a negative event. However, as Duck (1982) points out:

> We should not assume that all relationship dissolution is necessarily a bad thing. . . . For one thing some relationships stifle the individuals' growth and their dissolution can be a creative act of rejuvenation, full of promise and freedom. For another thing not all relationships "matter" in deep psychological or personal ways such that, for instance, the dissolution of a temporary working relationship is not usually a powerful psychological experience. (p. 3)

This is not to deny that the ending of a close friendship can be a source of trauma and intense grief, particularly in cases where the termination was not desired. However, people seem to recover from these losses and establish new and satisfying friendships. Rubin (1980) observed that for children, the loss of a friendship sometimes triggered extreme sadness and grief. Parents' assurances that "Don't worry, you'll make another friend soon" only seemed to minimize the child's pain. Nevertheless, in most cases, these children went on to develop very close and satisfying new friendships. The same appears to be true for adults. Duck and Miell (1986) found that university students' ratings of new friends plummeted at the winter break as students anticipated a joyous reunion with their old friends. However, it seems they discovered that they no longer had as much in common with those friends. When they returned from their holiday, ratings of interaction quality, especially intimacy, with new friends soared. Finally, in Rose's (1984) study reported earlier, 35% of the participants experienced the dissolution of a friendship since they began college. What should not be overlooked is that 37% of the participants also reported that they had established one or more new friendships in their new environment. Thus, the processes of friendship are a continuing theme as friendships weave in and out of our lives.

References

Abbey, A. (1982). Sex differences in attributions for friendly behavior: Do males misperceive females' friendliness? *Journal of Personality and Social Psychology, 42*, 830-838.

Adams, R. G. (1985). People would talk: Normative barriers to cross-sex friendships for elderly women. *The Gerontologist, 25*, 605-611.

Adams, R. G. (1985-1986). Emotional closeness and physical distance between friends: Implications for elderly women living in age-segregated and age-integrated settings. *International Journal of Aging and Human Development, 22*, 55-76.

Afifi, W. A., Guerrero, L. K., & Egland, K. L. (1994, May). *Maintenance behaviors in same- and opposite-sex friendships: Connections to gender, relational closeness, and equity issues.* Paper presented at the 1994 International Network on Personal Relationships Conference, Iowa City, IA.

Allan, G. (1989). *Friendship: Developing a sociological perspective.* London: Harvester Wheatsheaf.

Allen, J. G., & Haccoun, D. M. (1976). Sex differences in emotionality: A multidimensional approach. *Human Relations, 29*, 711-722.

Altman, I. (1973). Reciprocity of interpersonal exchange. *Journal for the Theory of Social Behaviour, 3,* 249-261.

Altman, I., & Haythorn, W. W. (1965). Interpersonal exchange in isolation. *Sociometry, 28,* 411-426.

Altman, I., & Taylor, D. A. (1973). *Social penetration: The development of interpersonal relationships.* New York: Holt, Rinehart & Winston.

Ambrose, S. F. (1989). Men and women can be friends. In N. Bernards & T. O'Neill (Eds.), *Male/female roles* (pp. 207-212). San Diego, CA: Greenhaven.

Archer, R. L., & Berg, J. H. (1978). Disclosure reciprocity and its limits: A reactance analysis. *Journal of Experimental Social Psychology, 14,* 527-540.

Archer, R. L., & Burelson, J. A. (1980). The effects of timing of self-disclosure on attraction and reciprocity. *Journal of Personality and Social Psychology, 38,* 120-130.

Argyle, M. (1987). *The psychology of happiness.* London: Methuen.

Argyle, M., & Furnham, A. (1982). The ecology of relationships: Choice of situations as a function of relationship. *British Journal of Social Psychology, 21,* 259-262.

Argyle, M., & Henderson, M. (1984). The rules of friendship. *Journal of Social and Personal Relationships, 1,* 211-237.

Argyle, M., & Henderson, M. (1985). The rules of relationships. In S. Duck & D. Perlman (Eds.), *Understanding personal relationships: An interdisciplinary approach* (pp. 63-84). London: Sage.

Argyle, M., Lefebvre, L., & Cook, M. (1974). The meaning of five patterns of gaze. *European Journal of Social Psychology, 4,* 125-136.

Aries, E. J., & Johnson, F. L. (1983). Close friendship in adulthood: Conversational content between same-sex friends. *Sex Roles, 9,* 1183-1196.

Aristotle. (1931). *Ethica nicomachea* (W. D. Ross, Trans.). London: Oxford University Press.

Aristotle. (1984). Rhetoric. In J. Barnes (Ed.), *The complete works of Aristotle: The revised Oxford translation* (Vol. 2, pp. 2152-2269). Princeton, NJ: Princeton University Press.

Aron, A., Dutton, D. G., Aron, E. N., & Iverson, A. (1989). Experiences of falling in love. *Journal of Social and Personal Relationships, 6,* 243-257.

Asher, S. R., Renshaw, P. D., & Geraci, R. L. (1980). Children's friendships and social competence. *International Journal of Psycholinguistics, 7,* 27-39.

Atkins, C. J., Kaplan, R. M., & Toshima, M. T. (1991). Close relationships in the epidemiology of cardiovascular disease. In W. H. Jones & D. Perlman (Eds.), *Advances in personal relationships: A research annual* (Vol. 3, pp. 207-231). London: Jessica Kingsley.

Aukett, R., Ritchie, J., & Mill, K. (1988). Gender differences in friendship patterns. *Sex Roles, 19,* 57-66.

Averill, J. R. (1983). Studies on anger and aggression: Implications for theories of emotion. *American Psychologist, 38,* 1145-1160.

Ayres, J. (1982). Perceived use of evaluative statements in developing, stable, and deteriorating relationships with a person of the same or opposite sex. *Western Journal of Speech Communication, 46*, 20-31.

Ayres, J. (1983). Strategies to maintain relationships: Their identification and perceived usage. *Communication Quarterly, 31*, 62-67.

Babchuk, N., & Anderson, T. B. (1989). Older widows and married women: Their intimates and confidants. *International Journal of Aging and Human Development, 28*, 21-35.

Backman, C. W., & Secord, P. F. (1959). The effect of perceived liking on interpersonal attraction. *Human Relations, 12*, 379-383.

Banikiotes, P. G., Neimeyer, G. J., & Lepkowsky, C. (1981). Gender and sex-role orientation effects on friendship choice. *Personality and Social Psychology Bulletin, 7*, 605-610.

Barry, D. (1995, January 9). Hockey like you've never seen. *Winnipeg Free Press* (reprinted from *Miami Herald*), p. C4.

Barth, R. J., & Kinder, B. N. (1988). A theoretical analysis of sex differences in same-sex friendships. *Sex Roles, 19*, 349-363.

Basu, J., & Mukhopadhyay, P. K. (1986). Perception of friendship qualities. *Psychological Research Journal, 10*, 33-41.

Baxter, L. A. (1979). Self-disclosure as a relationship disengagement strategy: An exploratory investigation. *Human Communication Research, 5*, 215-222.

Baxter, L. A. (1982). Strategies for ending relationships: Two studies. *Western Journal of Speech Communication, 46*, 223-241.

Baxter, L. A. (1983). Relationship disengagement: An examination of the reversal hypothesis. *Western Journal of Speech Communication, 47*, 85-98.

Baxter, L. A. (1985). Accomplishing relationship disengagement. In S. Duck & D. Perlman (Eds.), *Understanding personal relationships* (pp. 243-265). London: Sage.

Baxter, L. A. (1994). A dialogic approach to relationship maintenance. In D. J. Canary & L. Stafford (Eds.), *Communication and relational maintenance* (pp. 233-254). New York: Academic Press.

Baxter, L. A., & Philpott, J. (1982). Attribution-based strategies for initiating and terminating friendships. *Communication Quarterly, 30*, 217-224.

Baxter, L. A., & Wilmot, W. (1986). Interaction characteristics of disengaging, stable, and growing relationships. In R. Gilmour & S. W. Duck (Eds.), *The emerging field of personal relationships* (pp. 145-159). Hillsdale, NJ: Lawrence Erlbaum.

Becker, C. S. (1987). Friendship between women: A phenomenological study of best friends. *Journal of Phenomenological Psychology, 18*, 59-72.

Bell, R. R. (1981a). Friendships of women and of men. *Psychology of Women Quarterly, 5*, 402-417.

Bell, R. R. (1981b). *Worlds of friendship.* Beverly Hills, CA: Sage.

Bem, S. (1974). The measurement of psychological androgyny. *Journal of Consulting and Clinical Psychology, 42,* 155-162.

Bendtschneider, L., & Duck, S. (1993). What's yours is mine and what's mine is yours: Couple friends. In P. Kalbfleisch (Ed.), *Interpersonal communication: Evolving interpersonal relationships* (pp. 169-186). Hillsdale, NJ: Lawrence Erlbaum.

Berg, J. H. (1984). Development of friendship between roommates. *Journal of Personality and Social Psychology, 46,* 346-356.

Berg, J. H. (1987). Responsiveness and self-disclosure. In V. J. Derlega & J. H. Berg (Eds.), *Self-disclosure: Theory, research, and therapy* (pp. 101-130). New York: Plenum.

Berg, J. H., & Archer, R. L. (1980). Disclosure or concern: A second look at liking for the norm breaker. *Journal of Personality, 48,* 245-257.

Berg, J. H., & Clark, M. S. (1986). Differences in social exchange between intimate and other relationships: Gradually evolving or quickly apparent? In V. J. Derlega & B. A. Winstead (Eds.), *Friendship and social interaction* (pp. 101-128). New York: Springer-Verlag.

Berman, J. J., Murphy-Berman, V., & Pachauri, A. (1988). Sex differences in friendship patterns in India and in the United States. *Basic and Applied Social Psychology, 9,* 61-71.

Berndt, T. J. (1981). Effects of friendship on prosocial intentions and behavior. *Child Development, 52,* 636-643.

Berndt, T. J. (1982). The features and effects of friendship in early adolescence. *Child Development, 53,* 1447-1460.

Berndt, T. J. (1986). Children's comments about their friendships. In M. Perlmutter (Ed.), *Cognitive perspectives on children's social and behavioral development* (pp. 189-212). Hillsdale, NJ: Lawrence Erlbaum.

Berndt, T. J. (1988). The nature and significance of children's friendships. In R. Varta (Ed.), *Annals of child development* (Vol. 5, pp. 155-186). Greenwich, CT: JAI.

Berndt, T. J., & Das, R. (1987). Effects of popularity and friendship on perceptions of the personality and social behavior of peers. *Journal of Early Adolescence, 7,* 429-439.

Berndt, T. J., & Hawkins, J. A. (1987). *The contribution of supportive friendships to adjustment after the transition to junior high school.* Unpublished manuscript, Purdue University.

Berndt, T. J., Hawkins, J. A., & Hoyle, S. G. (1986). Changes in friendship during a school year: Effects on children's and adolescents' impressions of friendship and sharing with friends. *Child Development, 57,* 1284-1297.

Berndt, T. J., & Hoyle, S. G. (1985). Stability and change in childhood and adolescent friendships. *Developmental Psychology, 21,* 1007-1015.

Berndt, T. J., & Perry, T. B. (1986). Children's perceptions of friendships as supportive relationships. *Developmental Psychology, 22,* 640-648.

Berscheid, E. (1977). Interpersonal attraction. In B. B. Wolman (Ed.), *International encyclopedia of psychiatry, psychology, psychoanalysis, and neurology* (Vol. 2, pp. 201-204). New York: Van Nostrand Reinhold.

Berscheid, E., & Graziano, W. (1979). The initiation of interpersonal relationships and social attraction. In R. L. Burgess & T. L. Huston (Eds.), *Social exchange in developing relationships* (pp. 31-60). New York: Academic Press.

Berscheid, E., Graziano, W., Monson, T., & Dermer, M. (1976). Outcome dependency: Attention, attribution, and attraction. *Journal of Personality and Social Psychology, 34,* 978-989.

Berscheid, E., & Peplau, L. A. (1983). The emerging science of relationships. In H. H. Kelley, E. Berscheid, A. Christensen, J. H. Harvey, T. L. Huston, G. Levinger, E. McClintock, L. A. Peplau, & D. R. Peterson (Eds.), *Close relationships* (pp. 1-19). New York: W. H. Freeman.

Berscheid, E., Snyder, M., & Omoto, A. M. (1989). Issues in studying close relationships: Conceptualizing and measuring closeness. In C. Hendrick (Ed.), *Review of personality and social psychology: Vol. 10. Close relationships* (pp. 63-91). Newbury Park, CA: Sage.

Berscheid, E., & Walster, E. H. (1978). *Interpersonal attraction* (2nd ed.). Reading, MA: Addison-Wesley.

Bigelow, B. J., & La Gaipa, J. J. (1975). Children's written descriptions of friendship: A multidimensional analysis. *Developmental Psychology, 11,* 857-858.

Bigelow, B. J., & La Gaipa, J. J. (1980). The development of friendship values and choice. In H. C. Foot, A. J. Chapman, & J. R. Smith (Eds.), *Friendship and social relations in children* (pp. 15-44). Chichester, UK: John Wiley.

Birch, L. L., & Billman, J. (1986). Preschool children's food sharing with friends and acquaintances. *Child Development, 57,* 387-395.

Blier, M. J., & Blier-Wilson, L. A. (1989). Gender differences in self-rated emotional expressiveness. *Sex Roles, 21,* 287-295.

Blieszner, R., & Adams, R. G. (1992). *Adult friendship.* Newbury Park, CA: Sage.

Blyth, D., & Foster-Clark, F. (1987). Gender differences in perceived intimacy with different members of adolescents' social networks. *Sex Roles, 17,* 689-718.

Booth, A. (1972). Sex and social participation. *American Sociological Review, 37,* 183-192.

Booth, A., & Hess, E. (1974). Cross-sex friendship. *Journal of Marriage and the Family, 36,* 38-47.

Bornstein, R. F. (1989). Exposure and affect: Overview and meta-analysis of research, 1968-1987. *Psychological Bulletin, 106,* 265-289.

Bornstein, R. F., Kale, A. R., & Cornell, K. R. (1990). Boredom as a limiting condition on the mere exposure effect. *Journal of Personality and Social Psychology, 58,* 791-800.

Bradac, J. J. (1983). The language of lovers, flovers, and friends: Communicating in social and personal relationships. *Journal of Language and Social Psychology, 2,* 141-162.

Brehm, S. S. (1985). *Intimate relationships.* New York: McGraw-Hill.

Brenton, M. (1974). *Friendship.* New York: Stein & Day.

Buhrke, R., & Fuqua, D. (1987). Sex differences in same- and cross-sex supportive relationships. *Sex Roles, 17,* 339-352.

Buhrmester, D., Furman, W., Wittenberg, M. T., & Reis, H. T. (1988). Five domains of interpersonal competence in peer relationships. *Journal of Personality and Social Psychology, 55,* 991-1008.

Bukowski, W. M., Newcomb, A. F., & Hoza, B. (1987). Friendship conceptions among early adolescents: A longitudinal study of stability and change. *Journal of Early Adolescence, 7,* 143-152.

Burleson, B. R. (1994). Friendship and similarities in social-cognitive and communication abilities: Social skill bases of interpersonal attraction in childhood. *Personal Relationships, 1,* 371-389.

Burleson, B. R., Kunkel, A. W., & Birch, J. D. (1994, July). *How similarities in cognitive complexity influence attraction to friends and lovers: Experimental and correlational studies.* Paper presented at the Seventh International Conference on Personal Relationships, Groningen, Netherlands.

Burleson, B. R., & Samter, W. (1994). A social skills approach to relationship maintenance: How individual differences in communication skills affect the achievement of relationship functions. In D. J. Canary & L. Stafford (Eds.), *Communication and relational maintenance* (pp. 61-90). New York: Academic Press.

Burleson, B. R., Samter, W., & Lucchetti, A. E. (1992). Similarity in communication values as a predictor of friendship choices: Studies of friends and best friends. *Southern Communication Journal, 57,* 260-276.

Byrne, D. (1971). *The attraction paradigm.* New York: Academic Press.

Byrne, D., & Clore, G. L. (1970). A reinforcement model of evaluative responses. *Personality, 1,* 103-128.

Caldwell, M., & Peplau, L. (1982). Sex differences in same-sex friendship. *Sex Roles, 8,* 721-732.

Camarena, P., Sarigiani, P., & Peterson, A. (1990). Gender-specific pathways to intimacy in early adolescence. *Journal of Youth and Adolescence, 19,* 19-32.

Canary, D. J., & Spitzberg, B. H. (1987). Appropriateness and effectiveness perceptions of conflict strategies. *Human Communication Research, 14,* 93-118.

Canary, D. J., & Spitzberg, B. H. (1990). Attribution biases and associations between conflict strategies and competence outcomes. *Communication Monographs, 57,* 139-151.

Canary, D. J., & Stafford, L. (1994). Maintaining relationships through strategic and routine interaction. In D. J. Canary & L. Stafford (Eds.),

Communication and relational maintenance (pp. 3-22). New York: Academic Press.

Canary, D. J., Stafford, L., Hause, K. S., & Wallace, L. A. (1993). An inductive analysis of relational maintenance strategies: Comparisons among lovers, relatives, friends, and others. *Communication Research Reports, 10,* 5-14.

Cancian, F. M. (1986). The feminization of love. *Signs: Journal of Women in Culture and Society, 11,* 692-709.

Candy, S. G., Troll, L. E., & Levy, S. G. (1981). A developmental exploration of friendship functions in women. *Psychology of Women Quarterly, 5,* 456-472.

Caplow, T., & Forman, R. (1950). Neighborhood interaction in a homogeneous community. *American Sociological Review, 15,* 357-366.

Carnegie, D. (1936). *How to win friends and influence people.* New York: Simon & Schuster.

Cash, T. F., & Derlega, V. J. (1978). The matching hypothesis: Physical attractiveness among same-sexed friends. *Personality and Social Psychology Bulletin, 4,* 240-243.

Cheek, J. M., & Busch, C. M. (1981). The influence of shyness on loneliness in a new situation. *Personality and Social Psychology Bulletin, 7,* 572-577.

Clark, M. S. (1981). Noncomparability of benefits given and received: A cue to the existence of friendship. *Social Psychology Quarterly, 44,* 375-381.

Clark, M. S., & Mills, J. (1979). Interpersonal attraction in exchange and communal relationships. *Journal of Personality and Social Psychology, 37,* 12-24.

Clore, G. L., & Byrne, D. (1974). A reinforcement-affect model of attraction. In T. L. Huston (Ed.), *Foundations of interpersonal attraction* (pp. 143-170). New York: Academic Press.

Collins, N. L., & Miller, L. C. (1994). Self-disclosure and liking: A meta-analytic review. *Psychological Bulletin, 116,* 457-475.

Conrad, L. M., & Perlman, D. (1987, August). *Sex role orientation and personal relationships.* Paper presented at the American Psychological Association Conference, New York.

Cook, M. (1977). The social skill model and interpersonal attraction. In S. Duck (Ed.), *Theory and practice in interpersonal attraction* (pp. 319-338). London: Academic Press.

Cozby, P. (1972). Self-disclosure, reciprocity and liking. *Sociometry, 35,* 151-160.

Crawford, M. (1977). What is a friend? *New Society, 20,* 116-117.

Creekmore, C. R. (1985, January). Cities won't drive you crazy. *Psychology Today,* pp. 46-53.

Crockett, L., Losoff, M., & Peterson, A. C. (1984). Perceptions of the peer group and friendship in early adolescence. *Journal of Early Adolescence, 4,* 155-181.

Csikszentmihalyi, M., & Larson, R. (1984). *Being adolescent: Conflict and growth in the teenage years.* New York: Basic Books.

Cupach, W. R., & Metts, S. (1991). Sexuality and communication in close relationships. In K. McKinney & S. Sprecher (Eds.), *Sexuality in close relationships* (pp. 93-110). Hillsdale, NJ: Lawrence Erlbaum.

Cupach, W. R., & Spitzberg, B. H. (Eds.). (1994). *The dark side of interpersonal communication.* Hillsdale, NJ: Lawrence Erlbaum.

Curry, T. J., & Kenny, D. A. (1974). The effects of perceived and actual similarity in values and personality in the process of interpersonal attraction. *Quality and Quantity, 8,* 27-44.

Curtis, R. C., & Miller, K. (1986). Believing another likes or dislikes you: Behaviors making the beliefs come true. *Journal of Personality and Social Psychology, 51,* 284-290.

Darley, J. M., & Berscheid, E. (1967). Increased liking as a result of the anticipation of personal contact. *Human Relations, 20,* 29-40.

Davidson, L., & Duberman, L. (1982). Friendship: Communication and interactional patterns in same-sex dyads. *Sex Roles, 8,* 809-822.

Davidson, S., & Packard, T. (1981). The therapeutic value of friendship between women. *Psychology of Women Quarterly, 5,* 495-510.

Davis, D. (1981). Implications for interaction versus effectance as mediators of the similarity-attraction relationship. *Journal of Experimental Social Psychology, 17,* 96-116.

Davis, D., & Perkowitz, W. T. (1979). Consequences of responsiveness in dyadic interaction: Effects of probability of response and proportion of content-related responses on interpersonal attraction. *Journal of Personality and Social Psychology, 37,* 534-550.

Davis, J. D. (1976). Self-disclosure in an acquaintance exercise: Responsibility for level of intimacy. *Journal of Personality and Social Psychology, 33,* 787-792.

Davis, K. E., & Todd, M. J. (1982). Friendship and love relationships. In K. E. Davis & T. Mitchell (Eds.), *Advances in descriptive psychology* (Vol. 2, pp. 79-122). Greenwich, CT: JAI.

Davis, K. E., & Todd, M. J. (1985). Assessing friendships: Prototypes, paradigm cases and relationship description. In S. Duck & D. Perlman (Eds.), *Understanding personal relationships: An interdisciplinary approach* (pp. 17-38). London: Sage.

Davis, M. S. (1973). *Intimate relations.* New York: Free Press.

Derlega, V. J., Wilson, M., & Chaikin, A. L. (1976). Friendship and disclosure reciprocity. *Journal of Personality and Social Psychology, 34,* 578-582.

Deutsch, F. M., & Mackesy, M. E. (1985). Friendship and the development of self-schemas: The effects of talking about others. *Personality and Social Psychology Bulletin, 11,* 399-408.

Deutsch, F. M., Sullivan, L., Sage, C., & Basile, N. (1991). The relations among talking, liking, and similarity between friends. *Personality and Social Psychology Bulletin, 17,* 406-411.

Diaz, R. M., & Berndt, T. J. (1982). Children's knowledge of a best friend: Fact or fancy? *Developmental Psychology, 18,* 787-794.

Dickens, W. J., & Perlman, D. (1981). Friendship over the life cycle. In S. Duck & R. Gilmour (Eds.), *Personal relationships: Vol. 2. Developing personal relationships* (pp. 91-122). London: Academic Press.

Dindia, K., & Allen, M. (1992). Sex differences in self-disclosure: A meta-analysis. *Psychological Bulletin, 112,* 106-124.

Dindia, K., & Baxter, L. A. (1987). Strategies for maintaining and repairing marital relationships. *Journal of Social and Personal Relationships, 4,* 143-158.

Donelson, E., & Gullahorn, J. E. (1977). Friendship. In E. Donelson & J. E. Gullahorn, *Women: A psychological perspective* (pp. 154-167). New York: John Wiley.

Duck, S. (1982). A topography of relationship disengagement and dissolution. In S. Duck (Ed.), *Personal relationships: Vol. 4. Dissolving personal relationships* (pp. 1-30). London: Academic Press.

Duck, S. (1994). Steady as (s)he goes: Relational maintenance as a shared meaning system. In D. J. Canary & L. Stafford (Eds.), *Communication and relational maintenance* (pp. 45-60). New York: Academic Press.

Duck, S., & Allison, D. (1978). I liked you but I can't live with you: A study of lapsed friendships. *Social Behavior and Personality, 6,* 43-47.

Duck, S., & Craig, G. (1978). Personality similarity and the development of friendship: A longitudinal study. *British Journal of Social and Clinical Psychology, 17,* 237-242.

Duck, S., & Miell, D. (1986). Charting the development of personal relationships. In R. Gilmour & S. Duck (Eds.), *The emerging field of personal relationships* (pp. 133-143). Hillsdale, NJ: Lawrence Erlbaum.

Duck, S., Rutt, D. J., Hurst, M. H., & Strejc, H. (1991). Some evident truths about conversations in everyday relationships: All communications are not created equal. *Human Communication Research, 18,* 228-267.

Duck, S., & Wright, P. H. (1993). Reexamining gender differences in same-gender friendships: A close look at two kinds of data. *Sex Roles, 28,* 709-727.

Duck, S. W. (1973a). Personality similarity and friendship choice: Similarity of what, when? *Journal of Personality, 41,* 543-558.

Duck, S. W. (1973b). Similarity and perceived similarity of personal constructs as influences in friendship choice. *British Journal of Social and Clinical Psychology, 12,* 1-6.

Ebbesen, E. B., Kjos, G. L., & Konecni, V. J. (1976). Spatial ecology: Its effects on the choice of friends and enemies. *Journal of Experimental Social Psychology, 12,* 505-518.

Eidelson, R. J. (1980). Interpersonal satisfaction and level of involvement: A curvilinear relationship. *Journal of Personality and Social Psychology, 39,* 460-470.

Elkins, L. E., & Peterson, C. (1993). Gender differences in best friendship. *Sex Roles, 29,* 497-508.

Emerson, R. W. (1868). Friendship. In R. W. Emerson, *The complete works of Ralph Waldo Emerson* (Vol. 1, pp. 80-92). London: Bell & Daldy.

Epstein, J. L. (1986). Friendship selection: Developmental and environmental influences. In E. C. Mueller & C. R. Cooper (Eds.), *Process and outcome in peer relationships* (pp. 129-160). New York: Academic Press.

Erwin, P. G. (1985). Similarity of attitudes and constructs in children's friendships. *Journal of Experimental Child Psychology, 40,* 470-485.

Farrell, M. P. (1985-1986). Friendship between men. *Marriage and Family Review, 9,* 163-197.

Fehr, B. (1988). Prototype analysis of the concepts of love and commitment. *Journal of Personality and Social Psychology, 55,* 557-579.

Fehr, B. (1993). How do I love thee . . .? Let me consult my prototype. In S. Duck (Ed.), *Understanding personal relationships: Vol. 1. Individuals in relationships.* (pp. 87-120). Newbury Park, CA: Sage.

Fehr, B. (1994). Prototype-based assessment of laypeople's views of love. *Personal Relationships, 1,* 309-331.

Fehr, B., & Baldwin, M. (in press). Prototype and script analyses of laypeople's knowledge of anger. In G. J. O. Fletcher & J. Fitness (Eds.), *Knowledge structures and interaction in close relations: A social psychological approach.* Hillsdale, NJ: Lawrence Erlbaum.

Fehr, B., & Perlman, D. (1985). The family as a social network and support system. In L. L'Abate (Ed.), *Handbook of family psychology and therapy* (Vol. 1, pp. 323-356). Homewood, IL: Dorsey.

Fehr, B., & Russell, J. A. (1991). The concept of love viewed from a prototype perspective. *Journal of Personality and Social Psychology, 60,* 425-438.

Feinberg, R. A., Miller, F. G., & Ross, G. A. (1981). Perceived and actual locus of control similarity among friends. *Personality and Social Psychology Bulletin, 7,* 85-89.

Festinger, L., Schachter, S., & Back, K. (1950). *Social pressures in informal groups: A study of human factors in housing.* New York: Harper.

Fine, G. A. (1986). Friendships in the work place. In V. J. Derlega & B. A. Winstead (Eds.), *Friendship and social interaction* (pp. 185-206). New York: Springer-Verlag.

Fischer, C. S. (1982a). *To dwell among friends: Personal networks in town and city.* Chicago: University of Chicago Press.

Fischer, C. S. (1982b). What do we mean by "friend"? An inductive study. *Social Network, 3,* 287-306.

Fischer, C. S., Jackson, R. M., Stueve, C. A., Gerson, K., Jones, L. M., & Baldassare, M. (1977). *Network and places: Social relations in the urban setting.* New York: Free Press.

Fischer, C. S., & Phillips, S. L. (1982). Who is alone? Social characteristics of people with small networks. In L. A. Peplau & D. Perlman (Eds.), *Loneliness: A sourcebook of current theory, research and therapy* (pp. 21-39). New York: Wiley Interscience.

Fischer, J., & Narus, L. (1981). Sex roles and intimacy in same sex and other sex relationships. *Psychology of Women Quarterly, 5,* 444-455.

Fitzpatrick, M. A., & Winke, J. (1979). You always hurt the one you love: Strategies and tactics in interpersonal conflict. *Communication Quarterly, 27,* 3-11.

Foot, H. C., Chapman, A. J., & Smith, J. R. (1977). Friendship and social responsiveness in boys and girls. *Journal of Personality and Social Psychology, 35,* 401-411.

Franck, K. A. (1980). Friends and strangers: The social experience of living in urban and non-urban settings. *Journal of Social Issues, 36,* 52-71.

Friedman, H. S., Riggio, R. E., & Casella, D. F. (1988). Nonverbal skill, personal charisma, and initial attraction. *Personality and Social Psychology Bulletin, 14,* 203-211.

Furman, W. (1982). Children's friendships. In T. M. Field, A. Huston, H. C. Quay, L. Troll, & G. E. Finley (Eds.), *Review of human development* (pp. 327-339). New York: John Wiley.

Furman, W., & Bierman, K. L. (1983). Developmental changes in young children's conceptions of friendship. *Child Development, 54,* 549-556.

Furman, W., & Bierman, K. L. (1984). Children's conceptions of friendship: A multimethod study of developmental changes. *Developmental Psychology, 20,* 925-931.

Gaines, S. O. (1994). Exchange of respect-denying behaviors among male-female friendships. *Journal of Social and Personal Relationships, 11,* 5-24.

Gergen, K. J., & Gergen, M. M. (1988). Narrative and the self as relationship. *Advances in Experimental Social Psychology, 21,* 17-56.

Gershman, E. S., & Hayes, D. S. (1983). Differential stability of reciprocal friendships and unilateral relationships among preschool children. *Merrill-Palmer Quarterly, 29,* 169-177.

Ginsberg, D., & Gottman, J. (1986). Conversations of college roommates: Similarities and differences in male and female friendship. In J. M. Gottman & J. G. Parker (Eds.), *Conversations of friends: Speculations on affective development* (pp. 241-291). New York: Cambridge University Press.

Glueck, L., & Ayres, J. (1988). Personalization patterns in developing, stable, and deteriorating relationships. *The Communicator, 16,* 61-81.

Godfrey, D. K., Jones, E. E., & Lord, C. G. (1986). Self-promotion is not ingratiating. *Journal of Personality and Social Psychology, 50,* 106-115.

Goldman, J. A., Cooper, P. E., Ahern, K., & Corsini, D. (1981). Continuities and discontinuities in the friendship descriptions of women at six stages in the life cycle. *Genetic Psychology Monographs, 103,* 153-167.

Goodstein, L., & Russell, S. (1977). Self-disclosure: A comparative study of reports by self and others. *Journal of Counseling Psychology, 24,* 365-369.

Gottman, J., Gonso, J., & Rasmussen, B. (1975). Social interaction, social competence, and friendship in children. *Child Development, 46,* 709-718.

Gottman, J. M. (1983). How children become friends. *Monographs of the Society for Research in Child Development, 48*(3, Serial No. 201).

Gouldner, H., & Strong, M. S. (1987). *Speaking of friendship: Middle-class women and their friends.* New York: Greenwood.

Greenberg, J. (1983). Equity and equality as clues to the relationship between exchange participants. *European Journal of Social Psychology, 13,* 195-196.

Griffin, E., & Sparks, G. G. (1990). Friends forever: A longitudinal exploration of intimacy in same-sex pairs and platonic pairs. *Journal of Social and Personal Relationships, 7,* 29-46.

Grigsby, J. P., & Weatherley, D. (1983). Gender and sex-role differences in intimacy of self-disclosure. *Psychological Reports, 53,* 891-897.

Haas, A., & Sherman, M. A. (1982). Reported topics of conversation among same-sex adults. *Communication Quarterly, 30,* 332-342.

Hacker, H. (1981). Blabbermouths and clams: Sex differences in self-disclosure in same-sex and cross-sex friendship dyads. *Psychology of Women Quarterly, 5,* 385-401.

Hallinan, M. T., & Tuma, N. B. (1978). Classroom effects on change in children's friendships. *Sociology of Education, 51,* 270-282.

Hardy, C. L., Doyle, A. B., & Markiewicz, D. (1991, June). *Friendship status and friendship quality.* Paper presented at the annual meeting of the Canadian Psychological Association, Calgary, Alberta, Canada.

Harré, R. (1977). Friendship as an accomplishment: An ethogenic approach to social relationships. In S. Duck (Ed.), *Theory and practice in interpersonal attraction* (pp. 339-354). New York: Academic Press.

Hartup, W. W. (1975). The origins of friendships. In M. Lewis & L. A. Rosenblum (Eds.), *Friendship and peer relations* (pp. 11-26). New York: John Wiley.

Hartup, W. W., Laursen, B., Stewart, M. I., & Eastenson, A. (1988). Conflict and the friendship relations of young children. *Child Development, 59,* 1590-1600.

Hatfield, E., & Traupmann, J. (1981). Intimate relationships: A perspective from equity theory. In S. W. Duck & R. Gilmour (Eds.), *Personal relationships: Vol. 1. Studying personal relationships* (pp. 165-178). London: Academic Press.

Hatfield, E., Traupmann, J., Sprecher, S., Utne, M., & Hay, J. (1985). Equity and intimate relations: Recent research. In W. Ickes (Ed.), *Compatible and incompatible relationships* (pp. 91-117). New York: Springer-Verlag.

Hatfield, E., Utne, M. K., & Traupmann, J. (1979). Equity theory and intimate relationships. In R. L. Burgess & T. L. Huston (Eds.), *Social exchange in developing relationships* (pp. 99-133). New York: Academic Press.

Hayes, D. S., Gershman, E., & Bolin, L. J. (1980). Friends and enemies: Cognitive bases for preschool children's unilateral and reciprocal relationships. *Child Development, 51,* 1276-1279.

Hays, R. B. (1984). The development and maintenance of friendship. *Journal of Social and Personal Relationships, 1,* 75-98.

Hays, R. B. (1985). A longitudinal study of friendship development. *Journal of Personality and Social Psychology, 48,* 909-924.

Hays, R. B. (1988). Friendship. In S. W. Duck (Ed.), *Handbook of personal relationships: Theory, research, and interventions* (pp. 391-408). New York: John Wiley.

Hays, R. B. (1989). The day-to-day functioning of close versus casual friendships. *Journal of Social and Personal Relationships, 6,* 21-37.

Hays, R. B., & Oxley, D. (1986). Social network development and functioning during a life transition. *Journal of Personality and Social Psychology, 50,* 305-313.

Heider, F. (1958). *The psychology of interpersonal relations.* New York: John Wiley.

Helgeson, V. S., Shaver, P., & Dyer, M. (1987). Prototypes of intimacy and distance in same-sex and opposite-sex relationships. *Journal of Social and Personal Relationships, 4,* 195-233.

Hill, C. T., & Stull, D. E. (1981). Sex differences in effects of social and value similarity in same-sex friendship. *Journal of Personality and Social Psychology, 41,* 488-502.

Hinde, R. A. (1979). *Towards understanding relationships.* London: Academic Press.

Hindy, C. G. (1980). Children's friendship concepts and the perceived cohesiveness of same-sex friendship dyads. *Psychological Reports, 47,* 191-203.

Holahan, C. J., & Wilcox, B. L. (1978). Residential satisfaction and friendship formation in high- and low-rise student housing: An interactional analysis. *Journal of Educational Psychology, 70,* 237-241.

Holahan, C. J., Wilcox, B. L., Burnam, M. A., & Culler, R. E. (1978). Social satisfaction and friendship formation as a function of floor level in high-rise student housing. *Journal of Applied Psychology, 63,* 527-529.

Hornstein, G. A. (1985). Intimacy in conversational style as a function of the degree of closeness between members of a dyad. *Journal of Personality and Social Psychology, 49,* 671-681.

Hornstein, G. A., & Truesdell, S. E. (1988). Development of intimate conversation in close relationships. *Journal of Social and Clinical Psychology, 7,* 49-64.

Howes, C. (1983). Patterns of friendship. *Child Development, 54,* 1041-1053.

Huyck, M. H. (1982). From gregariousness to intimacy: Marriage and friendship over the adult years. In T. M. Field, A. Huston, H. C. Quay,

L. Troll, & G. E. Finley (Eds.), *Review of human development* (pp. 471-484). New York: John Wiley.

Jerrome, D. (1984). Good company: The sociological implications of friendship. *Sociological Review, 32,* 696-715.

Johnson, F. L., & Aries, E. J. (1983a). The talk of women friends. *Women's Studies International Forum, 6,* 353-361.

Johnson, F. L., & Aries, E. J. (1983b). Conversational patterns among same-sex pairs of late-adolescent close friends. *Journal of Genetic Psychology, 142,* 225-238.

Johnson, M. A. (1989). Variables associated with friendship in an adult population. *Journal of Social Psychology, 129,* 379-390.

Johnson, M. P., & Leslie, L. (1982). Couple involvement and network structure: A test of the dyadic withdrawal hypothesis. *Social Psychology Quarterly, 45,* 34-43.

Jones, D. C. (1985). Persuasive appeals and responses to appeals among friends and acquaintances. *Child Development, 56,* 757-763.

Jones, D. C. (1991). Friendship satisfaction and gender: An examination of sex differences in contributors to friendship satisfaction. *Journal of Social and Personal Relationships, 8,* 167-185.

Jones, D. C., Bloys, N., & Wood, M. (1990). Sex roles and friendship patterns. *Sex Roles, 23,* 133-145.

Jones, W. H., & Burdette, M. P. (1994). Betrayal in relationships. In A. L. Weber & J. H. Harvey (Eds.), *Perspectives on close relationships* (pp. 243-262). Needham Heights, MA: Allyn & Bacon.

Jones, W. H., & Carpenter, B. N. (1986). Shyness, social behavior, and relationships. In W. H. Jones, J. M. Cheek, & S. R. Briggs (Eds.), *Shyness: Perspectives on research and treatment* (pp. 227-238). New York: Plenum.

Jormakka, L. (1976). The behaviour of children during a first encounter. *Scandinavian Journal of Psychology, 17,* 15-22.

Kandel, D. B. (1978a). Homophily, selection, and socialization in adolescent friendships. *American Journal of Sociology, 84,* 427-436.

Kandel, D. B. (1978b). Similarity in real-life adolescent friendship pairs. *Journal of Personality and Social Psychology, 36,* 306-312.

Kaplan, M. F., & Anderson, N. H. (1973). Information integration theory and reinforcement theory as approaches to interpersonal attraction. *Journal of Personality and Social Psychology, 28,* 301-312.

Kelley, H. H., & Thibaut, J. W. (1978). *Interpersonal relations: A theory of interdependence.* New York: John Wiley.

Kerckhoff, A. C., & Davis, K. E. (1962). Value consensus and need complementarity in mate selection. *American Sociological Review, 27,* 295-303.

Kleck, R. E., Richardson, S. A., & Ronald, L. (1974). Physical appearance cues and interpersonal attraction in children. *Child Development, 43,* 305-310.

Klinger, E. (1977). *Meaning and void: Inner experience and the incentives in people's lives.* Minneapolis: University of Minnesota Press.

Knapp, C. W., & Harwood, B. T. (1977). Factors in the determination of intimate same-sex friendship. *Journal of Genetic Psychology, 131,* 83-90.

Knapp, M. L. (Ed.). (1978). *Social intercourse: From greeting to goodbye.* Boston: Allyn & Bacon.

Knapp, M. L. (1984). *Interpersonal communication and human relationships.* Newton, MA: Allyn & Bacon.

Knapp, M. L., Ellis, D. G., & Williams, B. A. (1980). Perceptions of communication behavior associated with relationship terms. *Communication Monographs, 47,* 262-278.

Knight, J. A., & Vallacher, R. R. (1981). Interpersonal engagement in social perception: The consequences of getting into the action. *Journal of Personality and Social Psychology, 40,* 990-999.

Kon, I. S., & Losenkov, V. A. (1978). Friendship in adolescence: Value and behavior. *Journal of Marriage and the Family, 40,* 143-155.

Kurth, S. B. (1970). Friendships and friendly relations. In G. J. McCall, M. M. McCall, N. K. Denzin, G. D. Suttles, & S. B. Kurth (Eds.), *Social relationships* (pp. 136-170). Chicago: Aldine.

La Gaipa, J. J. (1977). Testing a multidimensional approach to friendship. In S. Duck (Ed.), *Theory and practice in interpersonal attraction* (pp. 249-270). London: Academic Press.

La Gaipa, J. J. (1979). A developmental study of the meaning of friendship in adolescence. *Journal of Adolescence, 2,* 201-213.

La Gaipa, J. J. (1982). Rules and rituals in disengaging from relationships. In S. Duck (Ed.), *Personal relationships: Vol. 4. Dissolving personal relationships* (pp. 189-210). London: Academic Press.

La Gaipa, J. J. (1987). Friendship expectations. In R. Burnett, P. McChee, & D. D. Clarke (Eds.), *Accounting for relationships: Explanation, representation and knowledge* (pp. 134-157). London: Methuen.

Lampe, P. E. (1985). Friendship and adultery. *Social Inquiry, 55,* 310-324.

Larson, R., Mannell, R., & Zuzanek, J. (1986). Daily well-being of older adults with friends and family. *Psychology and Aging, 1,* 117-126.

Larson, R. W., & Bradney, N. (1988). Precious moments with family members and friends. In R. M. Milardo (Ed.), *Families and social networks* (pp. 107-126). Newbury Park, CA: Sage.

Lassiter, G. D., & Briggs, M. A. (1990). Effect of anticipated interaction on liking: An individual difference analysis. *Journal of Social Behavior and Personality, 5,* 357-367.

Lavine, L. O., & Lombardo, J. P. (1984). Self-disclosure: Intimate and nonintimate disclosures to parents and best friends as a function of Bem sex-role category. *Sex Roles, 11,* 735-744.

Lea, M. (1994). *From social attraction to relationship: Similarity, commonality, and self-referent support in friendships.* Unpublished manuscript, University of Manchester, Department of Psychology, Manchester, UK.

Lea, M., & Duck, S. (1982). A model for the role of similarity of values in friendship development. *British Journal of Social Psychology, 21,* 301-310.

Lea, M., & Spears, R. (1995). Love at first byte: Building personal relationships over computer networks. In J. T. Wood & S. Duck (Eds.), *Understudied relationships: Off the beaten track* (pp. 197-233). Thousand Oaks, CA: Sage.

Lederberg, A. R., Rosenblatt, V., Vandell, D. L., & Chapin, S. L. (1987). Temporary and long-term friendships in hearing and deaf preschoolers. *Merrill-Palmer Quarterly, 33,* 515-533.

Leslie, L. A., & Grady, K. (1985). Changes in mothers' social networks and social support following divorce. *Journal of Marriage and the Family, 47,* 663-673.

Levinger, G. (1974). A three-level approach to attraction: Toward an understanding of pair relatedness. In T. L. Huston (Ed.), *Foundations of interpersonal attraction* (pp. 99-120). New York: Academic Press.

Levinger, G. (1979). A social psychological perspective on marital dissolution. In G. Levinger & O. C. Moles (Eds.), *Divorce and separation: Context, causes and consequences* (pp. 37-63). New York: Basic Books.

Levinger, G. (1980). Toward the analysis of close relationships. *Journal of Experimental Social Psychology, 16,* 510-544.

Levinger, G. (1983). Development and change. In H. H. Kelley, E. Berscheid, A. Christensen, J. H. Harvey, T. L. Huston, G. Levinger, E. McClintock, L. A. Peplau, & D. R. Peterson (Eds.), *Close relationships* (pp. 315-359). New York: W. H. Freeman.

Levinger, G., & Snoek, J. D. (1972). *Attraction in relationship: A new look at interpersonal attraction.* Morristown, NJ: General Learning Press.

Levy, J. A. (1981). Friendship dilemmas and the intersection of social worlds: Re-entry women on the college campus. *Research in the Interweave of Social Roles: Friendship, 2,* 143-170.

Lewis, M., Young, G., Brooks, J., & Michalson, L. (1975). The beginning of friendship. In M. Lewis & L. A. Rosenblum (Eds.), *Friendship and peer relations* (pp. 27-66). New York: John Wiley.

Lewis, R. A. (1972). A developmental framework for the analysis of premarital dyadic formation. *Family Process, 11,* 17-48.

Lewittes, H. (1989). Just being friendly means a lot—Women, friendship, and aging. In L. Grau & I. Susser (Eds.), *Women in the later years: Health, social, and cultural perspectives* (pp. 139-159). New York: Harrington Park.

Lombardo, J. P., & Lavine, L. O. (1981). Sex-role stereotyping and patterns of self-disclosure. *Sex Roles, 7,* 403-411.

Lott, A. J., & Lott, B. E. (1961). Group cohesiveness, communication level, and conformity. *Journal of Abnormal and Social Psychology, 62,* 408-412.

Lott, A. J., & Lott, B. E. (1974). The role of reward in the formation of positive interpersonal attitudes. In T. L. Huston (Ed.), *Foundations of interpersonal attraction* (pp. 171-192). New York: Academic Press.

Lott, B. E., & Lott, A. J. (1960). The formation of positive attitudes toward group members. *Journal of Abnormal and Social Psychology, 61,* 297-300.

Maccoby, E. E. (1990). Gender and relationships: A developmental account. *American Psychologist, 45,* 513-520.

Matthews, S. (1986). *Friendships through the life course: Oral biographies in old age.* Beverly Hills, CA: Sage.

McCarthy, B., & Duck, S. W. (1976). Friendship duration and responses to attitudinal agreement-disagreement. *British Journal of Social and Clinical Psychology, 15,* 377-386.

McCoy, J. K., Brody, G. H., & Stoneman, Z. (1994). A longitudinal analysis of sibling relationships as mediators of the link between family processes and youths' best friendships. *Family Relations, 43,* 400-408.

Menne, J. M. C., & Sinnett, E. R. (1971). Proximity and social interaction in residence halls. *Journal of College Student Personnel, 12,* 26-31.

Mervis, C. B., & Rosch, E. (1981). Categorization of natural objects. *Annual Review of Psychology, 32,* 89-115.

Miell, D., & Duck, S. (1986). Strategies in developing friendships. In V. J. Derlega & B. A. Winstead (Eds.), *Friendship and social interaction* (pp. 129-143). New York: Springer-Verlag.

Milardo, R. M. (1982). Friendship networks in developing relationships: Converging and diverging social environments. *Social Psychology Quarterly, 45,* 162-172.

Milardo, R. M., Johnson, M. P., & Huston, T. L. (1983). Developing close relationships: Changing patterns of interaction between pair members and social networks. *Journal of Personality and Social Psychology, 44,* 964-976.

Miller, G. R., Mongeau, P. A., & Sleight, C. (1986). Fudging with friends and lying to lovers: Deceptive communication in personal relationships. *Journal of Social and Personal Relationships, 3,* 495-512.

Miller, G. R., & Parks, M. R. (1982). Communication in dissolving relationships. In S. Duck (Ed.), *Personal relationships: Vol. 4. Dissolving personal relationships* (pp. 127-154). London: Academic Press.

Miller, J. B. (1991). Women's and men's scripts for interpersonal conflict. *Psychology of Women Quarterly, 15,* 15-29.

Miller, L. C., Berg, J. H., & Archer, R. L. (1983). Openers: Individuals who elicit intimate self-disclosure. *Journal of Personality and Social Psychology, 44,* 1234-1244.

Miller, N., & Marks, G. (1982). Assumed similarity between self and other: Effect of expectation of future interaction with that other. *Social Psychology Quarterly, 45,* 100-105.

Miller, S. (1983). *Men and friendship.* Boston: Houghton Mifflin.

Mills, J., & Clark, M. S. (1982). Communal and exchange relationships. In L. Wheeler (Ed.), *Review of personality and social psychology* (pp. 121-144). Beverly Hills, CA: Sage.

Monsour, M. (1992). Meanings of intimacy in cross- and same-sex friendships. *Journal of Social and Personal Relationships, 9,* 277-295.

Monsour, M., Betty, S., & Kurzweil, N. (1993). Levels of perspectives and the perception of intimacy in cross-sex friendships: A balance theory explanation of shared perceptual reality. *Journal of Social and Personal Relationships, 10,* 529-550.

Monsour, M., Harris, B., & Kurzweil, N. (1994). Challenges confronting cross-sex friendships: "Much ado about nothing?" *Sex Roles, 31,* 55-77.

Moreland, R. L., & Zajonc, R. B. (1982). Exposure effects in person perception: Familiarity, similarity, and attraction. *Journal of Experimental Social Psychology, 18,* 395-415.

Morse, S. J., & Marks, A. (1985). " 'Cause Duncan's me mate": A comparison of reported relations with mates and with friends in Australia. *British Journal of Social Psychology, 24,* 283-292.

Murstein, B. I. (1971). A theory of marital choice and its applicability to marriage adjustment. In B. I. Murstein (Ed.), *Theories of attraction and love* (pp. 100-151). New York: Springer.

Murstein, B. I., & Azar, J. A. (1986). The relationship of exchange-orientation to friendship intensity, roommate compatibility, anxiety, and friendship. *Small Group Behavior, 17,* 3-17.

Murstein, B. I., & Spitz, L. T. (1973-1974). Aristotle and friendship: A factor-analytic study. *Interpersonal Development, 4,* 21-34.

Nahemow, L., & Lawton, M. P. (1975). Similarity and propinquity in friendship formation. *Journal of Personality and Social Psychology, 32,* 205-213.

Narus, L. R., & Fischer, J. L. (1982). Strong but not silent: A reexamination of expressivity in the relationships of men. *Sex Roles, 8,* 159-168.

Neimeyer, G. J., & Neimeyer, R. A. (1981). Functional similarity and interpersonal attraction. *Journal of Research in Personality, 15,* 427-435.

Neimeyer, R. A., & Neimeyer, G. J. (1983). Structural similarity in the acquaintance process. *Journal of Social and Clinical Psychology, 1,* 146-154.

Newcomb, A. F., & Brady, J. E. (1982). Mutuality in boys' friendship relations. *Child Development, 53,* 392-395.

Newcomb, T. M. (1959). Individual systems of orientation. In S. Koch (Ed.), *Psychology: A study of a science* (Vol. 3, pp. 384-422). New York: McGraw-Hill.

Newcomb, T. M. (1961). *The acquaintance process.* New York: Holt, Rinehart & Winston.

Newcomb, T. M. (1971). Dyadic balance as a source of clues about interpersonal attraction. In B. I. Murstein (Ed.), *Theories of attraction and love* (pp. 31-45). New York: Springer.

O'Connor, P. (1992). *Friendships between women: A critical review.* New York: Guilford.

Oliker, S. J. (1989). *Best friends and marriage: Exchange among women.* Berkeley: University of California Press.

O'Meara, J. D. (1989). Cross-sex friendship: Four basic challenges of an ignored relationship. *Sex Roles, 21,* 525-543.

O'Meara, J. D. (1994). Cross-sex friendship's opportunity challenge: Uncharted terrain for exploration. *Personal Relationship Issues, 2,* 4-7.

Omoto, A., & Mooney, J. (1993, June). *Gender differences and correspondence between members of same-sex friendships.* Paper presented at the International Network on Personal Relationships Conference, Milwaukee, WI.

Otten, C. A., Penner, L. A., & Waugh, G. (1988). That's what friends are for: The determinants of psychological helping. *Journal of Social and Clinical Psychology, 7,* 34-41.

Parker, J. (1986). Becoming friends: Conversational skills for friendship formation in young children. In J. M. Gottman & J. G. Parker (Eds.), *Conversations of friends: Speculations on affective development* (pp. 103-138). Cambridge: Cambridge University Press.

Parker, S. R. (1964). Type of work, friendship patterns, and leisure. *Human Relations, 17,* 215-219.

Parks, M. R., & Eggert, L. L. (1991). The role of social context in the dynamics of personal relationships. In W. H. Jones & D. Perlman (Eds.), *Advances in personal relationships* (Vol. 2, pp. 1-34). London: Jessica Kingsley.

Patzer, G. L. (1985). *The physical attractiveness phenomena.* New York: Plenum.

Peretti, P. O., & Venton, W. C. (1984). Functional components of reciprocity and their influences on maintaining and sustaining closest friendships. *Acta Psychiatrica Belgica, 84,* 505-510.

Peretti, P. O., & Venton, W. C. (1986). The influence of functional components of reciprocity of maintaining and sustaining closest friendships. *Journal of Psychological Researches, 30,* 83-87.

Perlman, D. (1990, June). *You bug me: A preliminary report on hassles in three types of relationships.* Paper presented at the Canadian Psychological Association Convention, Ottawa, Ontario, Canada.

Perlman, D., & Fehr, B. (1986). Theories of friendship: The analysis of interpersonal attraction. In V. J. Derlega & B. A. Winstead (Eds.), *Friendship and social interaction* (pp. 9-40). New York: Springer-Verlag.

Perlman, D., & Fehr, B. (1987). The development of intimate relationships. In D. Perlman & S. Duck (Eds.), *Intimate relationships: Development, dynamics, and deterioration* (pp. 13-42). Newbury Park, CA: Sage.

Perlman, D., & Oskamp, S. (1971). The effects of picture content and exposure frequency on evaluations of Negroes and Whites. *Journal of Experimental Social Psychology, 7,* 503-514.

Phinney, J. S. (1979). Social interaction in young children: Initiation of peer contact. *Psychological Reports, 45,* 489-490.

Planalp, S. (1993). Friends' and acquaintances' conversations II: Coded differences. *Journal of Social and Personal Relationships, 10,* 339-354.

Planalp, S., & Benson, A. (1992). Friends' and acquaintances' conversations I: Perceived differences. *Journal of Social and Personal Relationships, 9,* 483-506.

Pogrebin, L. C. (1989). Men and women cannot be friends. In N. Bernardo & T. O'Neill (Eds.), *Male/female roles* (pp. 213-217). San Diego, CA: Greenhaven.

Powers, E. A., & Bultena, G. L. (1976). Sex differences in intimate friendships of old age. *Journal of Marriage and the Family, 38,* 739-747.

Price, J. M., & Ladd, G. W. (1986). Assessment of children's friendships: Implications for social competence and social adjustment. *Advances in Behavioral Assessment of Children and Families, 2,* 121-149.

Pulakos, J. (1989). Young adult relationships: Siblings and friends. *Journal of Psychology, 123,* 237-244.

Raffaelli, M., & Duckett, E. (1989). "We were just talking . . .": Conversations in early adolescence. *Journal of Youth and Adolescence, 18,* 567-582.

Rands, M., & Levinger, G. (1979). Implicit theories of relationship: An intergenerational study. *Journal of Personality and Social Psychology, 37,* 645-661.

Rawlins, W. K. (1983a). Negotiating close friendship: The dialectic of conjunctive freedoms. *Human Communication Research, 9,* 255-266.

Rawlins, W. K. (1983b). Openness as problematic in ongoing friendships: Two conversational dilemmas. *Communication Monographs, 50,* 1-13.

Rawlins, W. K. (1992). *Friendship matters.* Hawthorne, NY: Aldine de Gruyter.

Rawlins, W. K. (1993). Communication in cross-sex friendships. In A. Arliss & D. Borisoff (Eds.), *Women and men communicating: Challenges and changes* (pp. 51-70). Fort Worth, TX: Harcourt Brace Jovanovitch.

Rawlins, W. K. (1994). Being there and growing apart: Sustaining friendships through adulthood. In D. J. Canary & L. Stafford (Eds.), *Communication and relational maintenance* (pp. 275-294). New York: Academic Press.

Reid, H. M., & Fine, G. A. (1992). Self-disclosure in men's friendships: Variations associated with intimate relations. In P. M. Nardi (Ed.), *Men's friendships* (pp. 132-152). Newbury Park, CA: Sage.

Reis, H. T. (1988). Gender effects in social participation: Intimacy, loneliness, and the conduct of social interaction. In R. Gilmour & S. Duck (Eds.), *The emerging field of personal relationships* (pp. 91-105). Hillsdale, NJ: Lawrence Erlbaum.

Reis, H. T., Senchak, M., & Solomon, B. (1985). Sex differences in the intimacy of social interaction: Further examination of potential explanations. *Journal of Personality and Social Psychology, 48,* 1204-1217.

Reis, H. T., Wheeler, L., Spiegel, N., Kernis, M. H., Nezlek, J., & Perri, M. (1982). Physical attractiveness in social interaction: II. Why does appearance affect social experience? *Journal of Personality and Social Psychology, 43,* 979-996.

Reisman, J. M. (1979). *Anatomy of friendship.* New York: Irvington.

Reisman, J. M. (1990). Intimacy in same-sex friendships. *Sex Roles, 23,* 65-82.

Richey, M. H., & Richey, H. W. (1980). The significance of best-friend relationships in adolescence. *Psychology in the Schools, 17,* 536-540.

Riggio, R. E. (1986). Assessment of basic social skills. *Journal of Personality and Social Psychology, 51,* 649-660.

Roberto, K. A., & Kimboko, P. J. (1989). Friendships in later life: Definitions and maintenance patterns. *International Journal of Aging and Human Development, 28,* 9-19.

Roberto, K. A., & Scott, J. P. (1986). Friendships of older men and women: Exchange patterns and satisfaction. *Psychology and Aging, 1,* 103-109.

Roberto, K. A., & Scott, J. P. (1987). Friendships in late life: A rural-urban comparison. *Lifestyles, 8,* 146-156.

Rodin, M. J. (1982). Non-engagement, failure to engage, and disengagement. In S. Duck (Ed.), *Personal relationships: Vol. 4. Dissolving personal relationships* (pp. 31-49). London: Academic Press.

Rook, K. S. (1989). Strains in older adults' friendships. In R. G. Adams & R. Blieszner (Eds.), *Older adult friendship* (pp. 166-194). Newbury Park, CA: Sage.

Rook, K., & Pietromonaco, P. (1987). Close relationships: Ties that heal or ties that bind? In W. H. Jones & D. Perlman (Eds.), *Advances in personal relationships: A research annual* (Vol. 1, pp. 1-35). Greenwich, CT: JAI.

Rose, S. M. (1984). How friendships end: Patterns among young adults. *Journal of Social and Personal Relationships, 1,* 267-277.

Rose, S. M. (1985). Same- and cross-sex friendships and the psychology of homosociality. *Sex Roles, 12,* 63-74.

Rose, S. M., & Serafica, F. C. (1986). Keeping and ending casual, close and best friendships. *Journal of Social and Personal Relationships, 3,* 275-288.

Rosecrance, J. (1986). Racetrack buddy relations: Compartmentalized and satisfying. *Journal of Social and Personal Relationships, 3,* 441-456.

Rosenbaum, M. E. (1986). The repulsion hypothesis: On the nondevelopment of relationships. *Journal of Personality and Social Psychology, 51,* 1156-1166.

Rosenfeld, L. B., & Kendrick, W. L. (1984). Choosing to be open: An empirical investigation of subjective reasons for self-disclosing. *Western Journal of Speech Communication, 48,* 326-343.

Rotenberg, K. J. (1986). Same-sex patterns and sex differences in the trust-value basis of children's friendship. *Sex Roles, 15,* 613-626.

Rotenberg, K. J., & Mann, L. (1986). The development of the norm of the reciprocity of self-disclosure and its function in children's attraction to peers. *Child Development, 57,* 1349-1357.

Rotenberg, K. J., & Sliz, D. (1988). Children's restrictive disclosure to friends. *Merrill-Palmer Quarterly, 34,* 203-215.

Rubin, L. B. (1985). *Just friends.* New York: Harper & Row.

Rubin, L. B. (1986). On men and friendship. *Psychoanalytic Review, 73,* 165-181.

Rubin, Z. (1970). Measurement of romantic love. *Journal of Personality and Social Psychology, 16,* 265-273.

Rubin, Z. (1973). *Liking and loving.* New York: Holt, Rinehart & Winston.

Rubin, Z. (1975). Disclosing oneself to a stranger: Reciprocity and its limits. *Journal of Experimental Social Psychology, 11,* 233-260.

Rubin, Z. (1980). *Children's friendships.* Cambridge, MA: Harvard University Press.

Rubin, Z., & Shenker, S. (1978). Friendship, proximity, and self-disclosure. *Journal of Personality, 46,* 1-22.

Rusbult, C. E. (1980a). Commitment and satisfaction in romantic associations: A test of the investment model. *Journal of Experimental Social Psychology, 16,* 172-186.

Rusbult, C. E. (1980b). Satisfaction and commitment in friendships. *Representative Research in Social Psychology, 11,* 96-105.

Russell, J. A., & Fehr, B. (1994). Fuzzy concepts in a fuzzy hierarchy: The varieties of anger. *Journal of Personality and Social Psychology, 67,* 186-205.

Salzinger, L. L. (1982). The ties that bind: The effect of clustering on dyadic relationships. *Social Networks, 4,* 117-145.

Sapadin, L. A. (1988). Friendship and gender: Perspectives of professional men and women. *Journal of Social and Personal Relationships, 5,* 387-403.

Schmidt, T. O., & Cornelius, R. R. (1987). Self-disclosure in everyday life. *Journal of Social and Personal Relationships, 4,* 365-373.

Scott, M. D., & Powers, W. G. (1978). The deterioration of interpersonal relationships: Contributive and preventive communication. In *Interpersonal communication: A question of needs* (pp. 270-293). New York: H. M. Rogers.

Segal, M. W. (1974). Alphabet and attraction: An unobtrusive measure of the effect of propinquity in a field setting. *Journal of Personality and Social Psychology, 30,* 654-657.

Selman, R. L. (1980). *The growth of interpersonal understanding: Developmental and clinical analyses.* New York: Academic Press.

Serafica, F. C. (1982). Conceptions of friendship and interaction between friends: An organismic-developmental perspective. In F. C. Serafica (Ed.), *Social-cognitive development in context* (pp. 100-132). London: Methuen.

Shapiro, B. Z. (1977). Friends and helpers: When ties dissolve. *Small Group Behavior, 8,* 469-478.

Sharabany, R., Gershon, R., & Hofman, J. E. (1981). Girlfriend, boyfriend: Age and sex differences in intimate friendship. *Developmental Psychology, 17*, 800-808.

Sharabany, R., & Hertz-Lazarowitz, R. (1981). Do friends share and communicate more than non-friends? *International Journal of Behavioral Development, 4*, 45-59.

Shaver, P., Furman, W., & Buhrmester, D. (1985). Transition to college: Network changes, social skills, and loneliness. In S. Duck & D. Perlman (Eds.), *Understanding personal relationships: An interdisciplinary approach* (pp. 193-219). London: Sage.

Shea, B. C., & Pearson, J. C. (1986). The effects of relationship type, partner intent, and gender on the selection of relationship maintenance strategies. *Communication Monographs, 53*, 352-364.

Sherrod, D. (1989). The influence of gender on same-sex friendships. In C. Hendrick (Ed.), *Review of personality and social psychology: Vol. 10. Close relationships* (pp. 164-186). Newbury Park, CA: Sage.

Shotland, R. L., & Craig, J. M. (1988). Can men and women differentiate between friendly and sexually interested behavior? *Social Psychology Quarterly, 51*, 66-73.

Shulman, N. (1975). Life-cycle variations in patterns of close relationships. *Journal of Marriage and the Family, 37*, 813-821.

Sillars, A. L. (1980a). Attributions and communication in roommate conflicts. *Communication Monographs, 47*, 180-200.

Sillars, A. L. (1980b). The sequential and distributional structure of conflict interactions as a function of attributions concerning the locus of responsibility and stability of conflicts. In D. Nimmo (Ed.), *Communication yearbook 4* (pp. 217-235). Edison, NJ: Transaction.

Sinha, A. K., & Kumar, P. (1984). Similarity and complementarity of attributes in friendship formation. *Indian Psychologist, 3*, 93-103.

Solano, C. H. (1986). People without friends: Loneliness and its alternatives. In V. J. Derlega & B. A. Winstead (Eds.), *Friendship and social interaction* (pp. 227-246). New York: Springer-Verlag.

Spence, J. T., & Helmreich, R. L. (1978). *Masculinity and femininity: Their psychological dimensions, correlates, and antecedents.* Austin: University of Texas Press.

Spitzberg, B. H., & Cupach, W. R. (1989). *Handbook of interpersonal competence research.* New York: Springer-Verlag.

Sprecher, S., & Duck, S. (1994). Sweet talk: The importance of perceived communication for romantic and friendship attraction experienced during a get-acquainted date. *Personality and Social Psychology Bulletin, 20*, 391-400.

Stafford, L., & Canary, D. J. (1991). Maintenance strategies and romantic relationship type, gender and relational characteristics. *Journal of Social and Personal Relationships, 8*, 217-242.

Staub, E., & Noerenberg, H. (1981). Property rights, deservingness, reciprocity, friendship: The transactional character of children's sharing behavior. *Journal of Personality and Social Psychology, 40*, 271-289.

Stokes, J., Childs, L., & Fuehrer, A. (1981). Gender and sex roles as predictors of self-disclosure. *Journal of Counseling Psychology, 28*, 510-514.

Suitor, J. J. (1987). Friendship networks in transitions: Married mothers return to school. *Journal of Social and Personal Relationships, 4*, 445-461.

Swain, S. (1989). Covert intimacy: Closeness in men's friendships. In B. J. Risman & P. Schwartz (Eds.), *Gender in intimate relationships* (pp. 71-86). Belmont, CA: Wadsworth.

Swain, S. O. (1992). Men's friendships with women: Intimacy, sexual boundaries, and the informant role. In P. M. Nardi (Ed.), *Men's friendships* (pp. 153-171). Newbury Park, CA: Sage.

Sykes, R. E. (1983). Initial interaction between strangers and acquaintances: A multivariate analysis of factors affecting choice of communication partners. *Human Communication Research, 10*, 27-53.

Tannen, D. (1990). Gender differences in topical coherence: Creating involvement in best friends' talk. *Discourse Processes, 13*, 73-90.

Tedesco, L. A., & Gaier, E. L. (1988). Friendship bonds in adolescence. *Adolescence, 23*, 127-136.

Tesch, S. A. (1983). Review of friendship development across the life span. *Human Development, 26*, 266-276.

Tesch, S. A., & Martin, R. R. (1983). Friendship concepts of young adults in two age groups. *Journal of Psychology, 115*, 7-12.

Tesser, A., & Smith, J. (1980). Some effects of task relevance and friendship on helping: You don't always help the one you like. *Journal of Experimental Social Psychology, 16*, 582-590.

Thibaut, J. W., & Kelley, H. H. (1959). *The social psychology of groups.* New York: John Wiley.

Thorbecke, W., & Grotevant, H. D. (1982). Gender differences in adolescent interpersonal identity formation. *Journal of Youth and Adolescence, 11*, 479-492.

Thorne, B., & Luria, Z. (1986). Sexuality and gender in children's daily worlds. *Social Problems, 33*, 176-190.

Tognoli, J. (1980). Male friendship and intimacy across the life span. *Family Relations, 29*, 273-279.

Tyler, T. R., & Sears, D. O. (1977). Coming to like obnoxious people when we must live with them. *Journal of Personality and Social Psychology, 35*, 200-211.

van Vliet, W. (1981). The environmental context of children's friendships: An empirical and conceptual examination of the role of child density. In A. E. Osterberg, C. P. Tiernan, & R. A. Findlay (Eds.), *Proceedings of the Twelfth International Conference of the Environmental Design Research Association* (pp. 216-224). Ames, IA: Environmental Design Research Association.

Verbrugge, L. M. (1977). The structure of adult friendship choices. *Social Forces, 56,* 576-597.

Walker, K. (1994). Men, women, and friendship: What they say, what they do. *Gender & Society, 8,* 246-265.

Walker, L. S., & Wright, P. H. (1976). Self-disclosure in friendship. *Perceptual and Motor Skills, 42,* 735-742.

Wall, S. M., Pickert, S. M., & Paradise, L. V. (1984). American men's friendships: Self-reports on meaning and changes. *Journal of Psychology, 116,* 179-186.

Walster, E., Walster, G. W., & Berscheid, E. (1978). *Equity: Theory and research.* Boston: Allyn & Bacon.

Walster, E., Walster, G. W., & Traupmann, J. (1978). Equity and premarital sex. *Journal of Personality and Social Psychology, 36,* 82-92.

Weiss, L., & Lowenthal, M. F. (1975). Life course perspectives on friendship. In M. F. Lowenthal, M. Turner, D. Chiriboga & Associates (Eds.), *Four stages of life* (pp. 48-61). San Francisco: Jossey-Bass.

Weiss, R. S. (1969). The fund of sociability. *Transaction, 6,* 36-43.

Weiss, R. S. (1974). The provisions of social relationships. In Z. Rubin (Ed.), *Doing unto others: Joining, molding, conforming, helping, loving* (pp. 17-26). Englewood Cliffs, NJ: Prentice Hall.

Wellman, B. (1985). Domestic work, paid work and net work. In S. Duck & D. Perlman (Eds.), *Understanding personal relationships* (pp. 159-191). London: Sage.

Wellman, B. (1992). Men in networks: Private communities, domestic friendships. In P. M. Nardi (Ed.), *Men's friendships* (pp. 74-114). Newbury Park, CA: Sage.

Werebe, M. J. G. (1987). Friendship and dating relationships among French adolescents. *Journal of Adolescence, 10,* 269-289.

Werner, C., & Parmelee, P. (1979). Similarity of activity preferences among friends: Those who play together stay together. *Social Psychology Quarterly, 42,* 62-66.

Wheeler, L., Reis, H. T., & Bond, M. H. (1989). Collectivism-individualism in everyday social life: The middle kingdom and the melting pot. *Journal of Personality and Social Psychology, 57,* 79-86.

Wheeler, L., Reis, H. T., & Nezlek, J. (1983). Loneliness, social interaction, and sex roles. *Journal of Personality and Social Psychology, 45,* 943-953.

Wilkins, H. (1991). Computer talk: Long-distance conversations by computer. *Written Communication, 8,* 56-78.

Williams, D. G. (1985). Gender, masculinity-femininity, and emotional intimacy in same-sex friendship. *Sex Roles, 12,* 587-600.

Wilmot, W. W. (1994). Relationship rejuvenation. In D. J. Canary & L. Stafford (Eds.), *Communication and relational maintenance* (pp. 255-273). New York: Academic Press.

Wilmot, W. W., & Baxter, L. A. (1983). Reciprocal framing of relationship definitions and episodic interaction. *Western Journal of Speech Communication, 47,* 205-217.

Wilmot, W. W., & Shellen, W. W. (1990). Language in friendships. In H. Giles & W. P. Robinson (Eds.), *Handbook of language and social psychology* (pp. 413-431). New York: John Wiley.

Wilmot, W. W., & Stevens, D. C. (1994). Relationship rejuvenation: Arresting decline in personal relationships. In D. Conville (Ed.), *Uses of structure in communication studies* (pp. 103-124). Westport, CT: Praeger.

Winstead, B. A. (1986). Sex differences in same-sex friendships. In V. J. Derlega & B. A. Winstead (Eds.), *Friendship and social interaction* (pp. 81-99). New York: Springer-Verlag.

Wiseman, J. P. (1986). Friendship: Bonds and binds in a voluntary relationship. *Journal of Social and Personal Relationships, 3,* 191-211.

Wish, M., Deutsch, M., & Kaplan, S. J. (1976). Perceived dimensions of interpersonal relations. *Journal of Personality and Social Psychology, 33,* 409-420.

Won-Doornink, M. J. (1985). Self-disclosure and reciprocity in conversation: A cross-national study. *Social Psychology Quarterly, 48,* 97-107.

Wood, J. T., & Inman, C. C. (1993). In a different mode: Masculine styles of communicating closeness. *Journal of Applied Communication Research, 21,* 279-295.

Woolsey, L. K., & McBain, L. L. (1987). Women's networks: Strengthening the bonds of friendships between women. In K. Storrie (Ed.), *Women: Isolation and bonding* (pp. 59-76). Toronto, Ontario: Methuen.

Wortman, C. B., Adesman, P., Herman, E., & Greenberg, R. (1976). Self-disclosure: An attributional perspective. *Journal of Personality and Social Psychology, 33,* 184-191.

Wright, P. H. (1982). Men's friendships, women's friendships and the alleged inferiority of the latter. *Sex Roles, 8,* 1-20.

Wright, P. H. (1984). Self-referent motivation and the intrinsic quality of friendship. *Journal of Social and Personal Relationships, 1,* 115-130.

Wright, P. H. (1985). The Acquaintance Description Form. In S. Duck & D. Perlman (Eds.), *Understanding personal relationships: An interdisciplinary approach* (pp. 39-62). London: Sage.

Wright, P. H. (1988). Interpreting research on gender differences in friendship: A case for moderation and a plea for caution. *Journal of Social and Personal Relationships, 5,* 367-373.

Wright, P. H., & Scanlon, M. B. (1991). Gender role orientations and friendship: Some attenuation, but gender differences abound. *Sex Roles, 24,* 551-566.

Zajonc, R. B. (1968). Attitudinal effects of mere exposure. *Journal of Personality and Social Psychology, 9*(Monograph Suppl. No. 2, Pt. 2).

Author Index

Subject Index

About the Author

Beverley Fehr is Associate Professor of Psychology at the University of Winnipeg. Her research has focused on lay conceptions of emotion, with an emphasis on the relationship-relevant emotions of love and anger. She also has published articles and book chapters on intimacy, social support, and commitment. Her current research on interaction patterns in close relationships is funded by the Social Sciences and Humanities Research Council of Canada. She serves as Associate Editor for the *Journal of Social and Personal Relationships*, is on the editorial board of *Personal Relationships*, and is organizing the 1996 *International Society for the Study of Relationships* conference.